VULNERABILITY
AND EXPOSURE

VULNERABILITY AND EXPOSURE

FOOTBALLER SCANDALS, MASCULINE IDENTITY AND ETHICS

ROB COVER

UWA PUBLISHING

First published in 2015 by
UWA Publishing
Crawley, Western Australia 6009
www.uwap.uwa.edu.au

THE UNIVERSITY OF
WESTERN AUSTRALIA

UWAP is an imprint of UWA Publishing
A division of The University of Western Australia

National Library of Australia
Cataloguing-in-Publication entry:

Cover, Rob, author.
Vulnerability and exposure: footballer scandals, masculine identity and ethics / Rob Cover.
ISBN: 9781742586496 (paperback)
Includes bibliographical references and index.
Football players—Australia—Attitudes.
Football players—Australia—Conduct of life.
Football players—Australia—Public opinion.
Australian football—Social aspects.
Sports—Moral and ethical aspects—Australia.
Men—Identity.
Masculinity in sports.
306.4830994

Typeset in Bembo by Lasertype
Printed by Lightning Source

CONTENTS

ACKNOWLEDGMENTS

Many people deserve thanks for their contributions – both social and intellectual – towards this research, particularly Rosslyn Prosser, Veronika Petroff, Mandy Treagus, Barbara Baird, Daniel Marshall, Michael Flood, Mary Lou Rasmussen, Katrina Jaworski, Janet Carter, Duc Dau and Melissa Burkett.

Carolyn Lake and Djuna Hallsworth undertook very helpful research-assistant work for which I am grateful.

The University of Western Australia's *Mobility and Belonging* research initiative has provided a fertile intellectual environment for addressing the various intersections of identity, culture and belonging; the support of Farida Fozdar, Loretta Baldassar, Jo Elfving-Hwang, Darren Jorgensen and Chantal Bourgault du Coudray among many others is very much appreciated.

Students in UWA's Communication and Media Studies honours program in 2012 and 2013 deserve much gratitude for stimulating discussion on sports, sexuality and scandal.

I would like to acknowledge the support of the *Fay Gale Centre for Research on Gender* at The University of Adelaide which provided funding for research which contributed to the third and sixth chapters.

ACKNOWLEDGMENTS

The contributions of *Fay Gale Centre* members Christine Beasley, Carol Johnson, Margaret Allen and Anna Szorenyi have been invaluable.

I also owe many thanks to Vera and Ian, Barb and Roger and, as always, Jeff Williams.

Introduction:
Football Scandal, Identity and Ethics

The Field of Scandal

'Heath Shaw suspended for betting on football'[1]

'Nixon should be kicked out, not handballed'[2]

'Saints ban four for six weeks'[3]

'Details emerge of girl at centre of AFL nude pic scandal'[4]

'Stay in the closet, Jason Akermanis tells homosexuals'[5]

'Will Cousins' final confession lead to redemption?'[6]

'Stephen Milne case should have gone on – ex-cop'[7]

Sports scandals are a fact of contemporary media life, with regular, ongoing narratives that draw on allegations of wrongdoing, questionable ethical behaviours, public outrage, commentary on reputation loss and public relations responsiveness. The past decade has seen masculine sport, particularly elite-level team codes, increasingly associated with scandal. Frequently these scandals relate to players or sports officials and stakeholders, and often involve behaviours or attitudes which are sometimes described as antisocial and/or unsavoury.[8] There is nothing particularly new about scandal reporting in news and entertainment media of sports in general and football in particular. As early as 1910, a scandal occurred when players from the Victorian Football League team Carlton were involved in accepting a bribe to lose a match deliberately.[9] Throughout much of the twentieth century, football scandals typically involved reports and sometimes extended narratives around drink driving, career-ending car crashes, on-field violence, the occasional pub brawl, and very occasionally fraud and armed robbery. Sports scandals involving Australian football players, stakeholders and officials since the early 2000s have, however, been markedly different in both the nature of events revealed in scandal reporting, the ways in which scandal issues are debated in the media and public sphere, and the responses and containment strategies of players, managers, agents, clubs and leagues. As news and entertainment coverage of elite-level footballers shifted to encompass an increasing reportage of personal, private and off-field aspects of their lives, so too does the content of scandal reports as dozens of Australian Rules football examples demonstrate: Brendan Fevola and his affair with model Lara Bingle; Ben Cousins and his self-confessed heavy use of recreational drugs; regular sex scandals involving groups of players, partner-sharing and significantly alarming issues around non-consensual sex with women; Jason Akermanis' homophobic remarks insisting that gay players coming out of the closet would upset football culture.

Footballers, like other team sports players, have traditionally been perceived as local, community and national 'heroes', lauded for their skills, fitness and team successes as much as for their masculine on-field abilities and sometimes 'larrikin' off-field behaviours – hence some of the public interest in the lives of players. However, more recently, footballer masculinity and hero status have been commodified and packaged as elements in a marketable form of celebrity. Such celebrity fosters increasing media interest in the off-field lives of footballers in the same way as royalty, singers, actors and other entertainment celebrities have events from their non-professional lives recorded, framed and disseminated through media scandal narratives. This is one of the significant changes in the mediatised culture of Australian Rules football that allows scandal to emerge as a significant part of public sphere discourse. At the same time, increasingly sophisticated public relations strategies deployed by clubs and the AFL to contain scandals have arisen, just as often exacerbating the scandal and increasing media coverage as mitigating or containing the damaging stories. In addition to the ways in which the celebrity status of individual football players make off-field activities available for scandal reporting and both the marketing and public relations management of football governance organisations generating new ways in which scandals play out publicly, changes in media relations themselves have increased the likelihood of scandal reporting. This is particularly the result of a move away from the 'buddy' system in which reporters remained silent on embarrassing off-field issues in order to maintain ongoing access for reporting about the game itself to a media relationality which has been described as a culture of reporting that deliberately 'seeks out scandal to sell copy'.[10] Finally, scandals are also at least partly driven by the market force of audiencehood, whereby viewers and readers engage with scandal stories out of a sometimes prurient interest, positioned through a form of media reception to perform 'moral outrage' over events which, if about anyone other than a high-profile footballer or celebrity, would ordinarily be considered banal, boring and tame.

Without just yet theorising why scandal attracts readership, it is pertinent to bear in mind here that while scandal narratives are part of the media process, on the one hand they rightly air ethical, legal and social issues that are of concern to a broader public yet, on the other hand, are consumed by audiences within a framework of pleasure which can include certain 'cultivated' pleasures in seeing a figure once held up as heroic, successful or just famous being revealed as having the same flaws, failings and poor decision-making capabilities as anyone else.

Scandals emerge more frequently and regularly today as a result of ever greater scrutiny of high-profile persons, whether footballers, politicians, entertainers or corporate chief executives. New digital communication forms have increased the capacity of media organisations as well as the public to capture and disseminate stories and evidence of the sorts of events that, previously, remained relatively unknown or limited to a closed, private circle of people.[11] The concept of 'scandal' itself typically refers today to news or trivial events about a well-known person or personality which may be discreditable, may have a negative impact on a positive public profile or may reveal activities which are criminal or unethical. More importantly, however, scandals are often excuses for social scapegoating,[12] whereby a public and its media institutions become morally outraged about the behaviour of a noted person who takes the place of society itself. In participating in the reputational 'fall' of a person of fame or note, contemporary society expunges itself of its own inherent flaws. However, sometimes the outrage directed at public figures through scandal is well-justified – for example, when a group of footballers are reported to have sexually assaulted a young woman, or when fraud or illegal betting take place. At other times, that outrage – or at least the *representation* of that outrage – in media stories is wholly invalid in terms of news routines and journalism processes. Examples include the formation of scandal reports through complaints over binge drinking by a football team or an extra-marital affair by a footballer, neither of which is necessarily beyond the ordinary behaviour of everyday persons in contemporary Western societies and neither of which necessarily has an impact on the game. In other words, in some cases it is clear why a scandal is generated and why it becomes a topic for public debate, such as rape accusations; at other times, the public discourse around an event that has been deemed scandalous is much more a matter of asking questions and debating contemporary social factors such as the place of hypermasculine binge drinking behaviour among footballers in the context of, say, emerging newer ways of performing masculinities or increasing social concerns around drinking culture more broadly. Thus the discussion of football scandals in this book is undertaken from a dual perspective: exploring how events which are sometimes private and not particularly socially significant become scandal in the context of football stories, but at the same time investigating some scandalous behaviours that warrant considered attention and ethical intervention.

To examine some of the ways in which football scandals play out publicly, as well as some of the cultural conditions that allow the events of scandals and misbehaviours to occur, is not by any means to be unnecessarily critical or to condemn team sports as lacking value, validity or integrity. As a social and political space, sport is highly favourable to the development of integrity[13] as well as to the broader promotion of health, fitness and community development.[14] However, while there remains a wide consensus that the participation in and spectatorship of team sports teaches strong ethical and community values, it is increasingly recognised that making either positive or negative value judgments about sports in general is overly simplistic and depends more on the way in which sport is played, taught and practised.[15] Australian sport in particular has regularly been *imagined* as an egalitarian field,[16] yet elite team sports are increasingly understood as lacking a spirit of inclusiveness,[17] favouring instead the marketability and celebrity of individual players. While these disjunctures establish the 'field' in which scandals emerge, they do not provide a standpoint for evaluating scandalous behaviour. Rather, sports scandals should be seen as indicators of the ways in which sporting culture has changed and developed in the context of wider social shifts, including the commodification of sport, changes in the presentation, performance and acceptability of certain kinds of masculinity, and in the development of neoliberal governance of elite-level sports.

Grounding Scandal: Culture and Identity in Australian Football

'Former St Kilda player Lovett raped woman while she slept, court hears'[18]

'Bingle sues Fevola over nude photo'[19]

'West Coast player fined, suspended for disparaging remarks over Demon player's mother'[20]

'Footy needs to clean up its act off the field'[21]

'Partying claims Dog Suns' Ablett'[22]

'I hit rock bottom: Fevola bares his soul'[23]

'Lovett charged with second count of rape'[24]

Australian Rules football is one of the dominant masculine team sports in Australia, played across most of the country, with a particularly strong presence and following in the states of Victoria, South and Western Australia. It is a major source of news stories relating to both on-field play and the off-field lives of its players, coaches, managers and other sports stakeholders. Its prominent place within contemporary national news routines is a significant factor in the public imagination of the game and this is inseparable from the factors which result in it being a major source for scandal reporting. The term 'Australian Rules Football' today is usually synonymous with the Australian Football League (AFL) game and its role as a sports entertainment industry; however, Australian Rules is much wider – and older – than the AFL which itself is a young organisation with a relatively short history. Where the AFL was once the Victorian state league as the VFL, the league has resultingly become a national competition which attracts wide-spread media attention and spectatorship, and places individual players in national public focus (where once VFL *teams* but not necessarily individual players, were recognisable across the country). The AFL is a successful managing organisation of the *business* of the sport[25] and provides a governance institution for on–field rules and codes of practice for footballers' off-field behaviour. Throughout this book, I will be focusing predominantly on footballers from the AFL teams given the high-profile of their players in media scandal reporting, although many of the issues also relate to what are informally thought of as the 'second tier' leagues such as the West Australian Football League (WAFL) and the South Australian National Football League (SANFL), as well as community and amateur teams where similar off-field behaviours and issues occur without necessarily attracting media attention and scandal.

One of the important ways in which the AFL and other national sports governing bodies contribute to the circumstances which make football scandals possible is through their role in shifting football from a recreational and community-oriented cultural formation into a professionalised and commodified high-profile institution. While the professionalisation of sport in terms of the sound codification of rules, representation and promotion of the game and policies designed to protect players and spectators are wholly good things, professionalisation also creates the possibility

for scandal through placing the game in the realm of entertainment and profit-making.[26] Although relationships between sports
governance bodies and journalists are not necessarily always
of mutual benefit as scandal reporting demonstrates, the larger,
professionalised relationship between the league and media
organisations is not only a financial one but exponentially increases
public interest in players themselves over and above the former
interest in teams – the technology of the close-up, the cross-over
and the live interview being major elements in this.[27] Naturally, as
on-field interest and recognisability of individual players increases,
so too does the public interest and capacity for reporting on players'
off-field activities as part of an 'overall package' of sports celebrity
reporting methods. With this in mind, it is important then to see
not only how scandal emerges through the *traditional* culture of
football codes but, in a modified form, through the contemporary
culture and governance arrangements instituted and maintained
by league organisations.

If scandals are the media construction of everyday events – and
sometimes crimes and seriously irresponsible behaviour – into
highly repetitive and often banal narratives that are marketed to
readers, why should they be interesting to research, study and
critique? In addition to the ways in which football scandals reveal
some of the tense relationships between players, governance
organisations, news routines and audiences, they also provide an
opportunity to understand how a significant cultural institution,
Australian Rules football, is itself responsible for the many events,
activities, attitudes and behaviours that lead to scandal. That is,
footballer scandals are formed from stories, events, gossip, ideas
and revelations that are more than just individual failings and
bad decisions, more than just the disclosure of an affair or illicit
behaviour or a crime. Rather, the behaviours, attitudes and
experiences which lead to scandal are culturally produced by
the circumstance of *being a footballer.* It is not just the high-level

publicity or lack of privacy accorded footballers, but the ways in which footballer identity is constituted within an existing culture of masculine football, reproduced over time, that is core to the events and allegations which become scandal.

Investigating scandals, then, helps us to understand how identities and behaviours are constituted and performed in the context of a relatively tight-knit, institutionally controlled culture – in this case, the masculine, team-based culture of elite football that plays a significant role in how the subjectivity of players is made intelligible, sensible and coherent across both on-field play and off-field social, personal and private activities. That is to say that footballers, like all other subjects, do not fully have agency over their representation, identities and behaviours, but are produced through the institutional culture that governs an array of aspects of footballers' lives, even if that governance is not necessarily for the benefit of players or even the game, but for the continuation of a highly marketable football 'brand'. When with great publicity Western Australian footballer Ben Cousins' use of recreational drugs became a significant talking point in media discourse and, subsequently, he was deregistered as a player, he was represented as a rogue, a one-off transgressor, an aberration among other better-behaved footballers in the clubs. However, in teasing out some of the ways in which footballer identities are formed, Cousins' off-field behaviours can better be understood as a *predictable* outcome of the ways in which the performativity of his identity is constituted within the culture of masculine team sports – as risk-taking, hypermasculine, high-energy and pleasure-seeking across the continuum from on-field to off-field contexts.

Thus, the behaviours and events that are reinscribed by media processes as scandals emerge as a result of the ways in which football culture produces particular ways and expectations of behaving. While the professional identity of footballers is strongly encouraged by commercial league organisations working with club management teams, the *residues* of older behaviours such as team bonding, binge-drinking and off-field pleasure-seeking in sociality that were part of football culture and the culture of team sports continue, and cannot be submerged despite the professionalisation of football.[28] Indeed, as I argue in this book, the professionalisation and commodification of football simply leads to greater media interest in what is perceived as a *disjuncture* between the claims to professional football and the risk-ridden off-field sociality — that disjuncture in its sometimes incomprehensibility is the source of many football scandals.

In discussing football scandals, there is no intention in this book to suggest that football teams or players are beset by scandal more so than any other masculine team sporting institution. Indeed, Australia's National Rugby League has likewise felt the impact of numerous ongoing scandals relating to player behaviour, including a number of group sexual assault cases, episodes of binge drinking and violence. The Australian cricket team has, similarly, been involved in scandals in both on-pitch and social arenas, including narratives around extra-marital affairs most markedly seen in stories about Shane Warne. British football (soccer) players are similarly involved in scandals around off-field behaviour, much like the high-level elite National Football League (NFL) and Major League Baseball (MLB) in the United States. However, Australian Rules presents an interesting case study for team-based sports scandals: partly due to its increasing ubiquity across all Australian states; partly because of its continuing centrality in *imagining* the Australian nation itself; partly because many of the exemplary scandals discussed here relate to the history of a sporting code and the growth of governance organisations including the formation of the AFL as the principal institution which defends against, yet sometimes is the subject of, scandal.

Another element in the materialisation of a scandal culture in football rests on how identity is constituted within that culture.

This book takes the view that identity of all subjects, including that which we can call 'footballer identity', is constructed and produced through the matrix of available cultural discourses in which that subject is constituted over time. Following the work of historian and theorist Michel Foucault, Judith Butler points to the fact that there is nothing innate or inherent about identity – behaviours do not emerge from some core essence in the body of the subject – but are performed over time, lending the illusion that there is an inner identity core that is fixed and unchangeable. That is, identity and selfhood are to be seen as normative ideals rather than descriptive features of experience; identity is the resultant effect of regimentary discursive practices which make certain ways of performing selfhood coherent and intelligible.[29] The subject, then, is performatively constituted by the very 'expressions' that, in everyday life, we usually assume to emanate from an inner self (for example, desires, behaviours, tastes and attitudes). As Butler writes, 'performativity must be understood not as a singular or deliberate "act," but, rather, as the reiterative and citational practice by which discourse produces the effects that it names'.[30] As performativity is tenuous, so too is footballer identity. If the discourses which produce the idea of 'footballer identity' can change, then so too the performances, behaviours and attitudes of footballers.

Understanding footballer identity as constituted at least partly in the culture of Australian Rules is important for making sense of scandal and scandalous behaviours. Firstly, because the off-field behaviours of footballers that become the subject of scandal are not just the aberrant behaviours of a few individuals or something that naturally emanates from tough men who happen to play a tough game, but are performances that make footballer identity recognisable and intelligible to themselves and to each other – expected and coherent within the *context* of football culture. So when members of a club go out binge drinking or causing public nuisance, such as occurred during the Hong Kong street antics of the Australian Western Bulldogs players in October 2010 which included jumping onto taxis and blocking traffic,[31] the performance is seen not only as acceptable to themselves because they are footballers, but as *necessary* for being footballers in a traditionally recognisable and coherent way. Therefore, it can be argued that not all actions and activities of footballers (or anyone else, for that matter) is something over which they have complete agency and control and it is not something for which they – or any other individual – are necessarily fully responsible (even if one should ask that people are held accountable for actions that hurt or cause violence to others). Rather, the behaviours or performances that are sometimes just annoying and at other times are genuinely problematic and the cause of injury, insult or violence to others are the product of football culture itself.

This is perhaps best understood in some of the ways in which the identity performance of footballers crosses from expectations for on-field success and pleasures sought in the group sociality after the game. One of the arguments presented in this book is that scandals emerge as a result of a little-understood and under-theorised *continuum* between on-field play and off-field behaviours. Footballers are expected to perform in a hypermasculine, competitive, team bonded and sometimes ruthless manner on the field and during the game. As importantly, there is also significant *pleasure* to be derived from playing football, despite the common rhetoric that refers to play as tough, hard, risky and injury-prone. At the same time, players express off-field pleasures as parts of teams whereby team bonding continues through sociality, through the (sometimes heavy) use of alcohol and recreational drugs, through sexualised behaviours towards women, and through sometimes disruptive or disrespectful behaviours such as street violence that are performances of the same kinds of hypermasculinity expected on the field. While it is the case that clubs and the league itself aim to foster a professional identity for footballers[32] that involves more respectful, less-damaging and less-risky behaviours, the fact that the problematic behaviours and attitudes are merely an *extension* or *continuation* of the on-field expectations of contemporary elite Australian Rules players makes it all the more difficult to prevent scandalous activities and thus the reporting of scandal.

Towards Ethics

'Charges dropped in pack rape case'[33]

'Nixon faces sex scandal inquiry'[34]

'Photo-scandal teen tackles Saints at new HQ'[35]

'Cousins banned after drinking binge'[36]

'Rape trial told Lovett felt entitled'[37]

'Brendan Fevola sacked by Brisbane Lions for "multiple" contract breaches'[38]

Exploring how scandals play out presents some important opportunities to think about ethics. For example, the relatively high number of scandals related to the sexual assault of women by footballers gives occasion to examine the ethical relationality between men whose identities are performed in the context of hypermasculinised cultural institutions and women who socialise with them on the fringes of that culture. Expectations, behaviours, attitudes and reasons that lead to the continued objectification and sometimes assault of women emerge through football culture as it is reproduced across generations and over time, despite club and league policies designed to enculturate respect for women and the concomitant penalties and sanctions that may interrupt or end a player's career. The failure of such policies and sanctions needs to be understood in ways which allow us to better understand why disrespectful, irresponsible or criminal behaviours emerge from football culture, and to explore alternative ways in which the culture of clubs, the league and its governance institutions can foster the development of an 'ethical footballer' whose on-field achievement is matched by the off-field attainment of ethical relationships.

If football culture, rather than any individual (whether a player, a club stakeholder, a coach or an agent), is to blame for the events that lead to scandal, then we are led to the question of how to change that culture in order that off-field behaviours *protect* against rather than *cause* injury, insult, violence or violation of women, bystanders, families and others, and that becomes a matter of ethics. As I argue in many chapters in this book, the attempts by clubs and league governance figures to professionalise footballers' public identities and ensure respectful off-field football behaviours through personal conduct policies, sanctions and penalisations for unsavoury or inappropriate behaviour is problematic in that such methods take governance over the entirety of football players' lives, both professional and private. More importantly, these methods have a tendency to fail because they do not ever address the root cause of scandal as being in the culture of the sport and in the performances of identity produced in that institutional culture. In many cases, policies, education programmes and the institution of player development managers to help govern off-field elements of footballers' lives operate as processes designed to prevent transgression as well as public relations scandal containment or mitigation strategies;[39] these too often fail to address the culture of football as the cause of unethical behaviour, the role of that culture in producing footballer identities and the concomitant problematic performances, and the environment of football as the site of unethical, disrespectful, risky or injurious behaviour found not merely in *individual* players but in the *bonded grouping* of teams operating in off-field sociality.

Strategies to prevent scandal and improper or violent behaviours that injure others in the off-field arena should be praised. That such effort goes into compliance mechanisms designed to produce a 'professional footballer' leads quite naturally to the question of ethics. Professionals in other career areas (doctors, nurses, teachers, academics, lawyers, judges, engineers and accountants) are often bound by ethical codes of conduct which are governed by professional societies – some of which require compliance with those codes and membership of that organisation in order to practice in that profession. In many cases, those ethical codes involve not just the 'workplace' behaviours and how individuals relate to each other in terms of the 'work', but also how one conducts oneself in pseudo-work related social activities. If elite footballers are to have a professional identity and, indeed, to work as highly paid professionals in a sporting career, then there is nothing unusual about the application of ethics and the questioning of ethical compliance through scandal reporting.

However, it remains the case that *addressing* the problematic behaviours that lead to scandal requires more than rules, penalties and sanctions. Rather, what is needed is the wholesale transformation of football culture and identity itself, and that requires a *critical* deployment of ethics as more than codes and standards of behaviour. I address the issue of ethics in relation to scandalous behaviours throughout this book and in some detail in the final chapter, drawing closely on the recent work of theorist Judith Butler who has advocated an ethics of non-violence through an understanding of the vulnerability and precarity of bodies.[40] For Butler, an ethics can operate through recognition of the vulnerability of the other, such as a bystander or non-footballer, leading to a reciprocal and responsible relationship. As I argue, footballers are in an excellent position to recognise such vulnerability given their own vulnerability to loss and shame and their bodily precariousness in terms of the very high risk of on-field injury. By transforming football culture in such a way that the hypermasculine inviolability of the body is shifted in favour of further recognising the possibility of injury, there is an opportunity for thinking a more ethical football culture, thereby a more ethical footballer and footballer identity, more responsible and less injurious behaviour, and thus a reduced risk of scandal for footballer's stakeholders.

Discerning Scandal

There is something remarkably disconcerting about being an outsider to football culture yet researching and writing about football scandals, identity and ethics. For much of my life I have followed a range of sports, and more recently become an avid, if unwitting, reader of football scandals, despite efforts to ignore other types of celebrity scandal reporting. In reading, researching and writing about football scandals, I am thus very much aware of my complicity in recirculating scandals that have previously been put to rest, in feeding a commercial media culture of scandal through readership and in taking a certain kind of pleasure in the stories as they unfold. However, by critiquing the cultural conditions of footballer scandals I do aim to distance myself at least partly from the more damaging aspects of unnecessary scandal reporting on the lives of footballers and their significant others; at the same time, I also maintain there is significant benefit in investigating scandals as a means of opening up the possibilities for reflecting on ethics, identity and the ways in which institutions and cultural groupings can be positively transformed. With this in mind, this book is not designed to list, categorise or quantify football scandals. Rather, I take up a handful of scandals from recent years as 'entry points' for the critical reflection on culture, identity and ethics.

The first chapter investigates some of the ways in which football scandals have shifted in recent years and, particularly, how wronged parties from outside football culture have, in rare cases, been able to find opportunities to respond to scandal, to represent their perspectives not as victims but complainants, and have made use of digital and online media to air grievances. I examine in this chapter the so-called 'St Kilda Schoolgirl' scandal of 2010 and 2011 in which a young woman who had been dating a footballer and then a footballer's agent revealed a number of cultural norms within footballer's off-field lives that have led to a sometimes dangerous misogyny towards women. By understanding how the young woman at the centre of the scandal maintained focus on herself through expert use of both traditional and online communication forms, rather than allowing herself to be represented through recognisable media scandal narratives, she has been able to highlight the mechanisms by which football culture objectifies women. I argue here that the young woman can be read as an unintentional gender activist, particularly in terms of the ways in which she made her case through a range of communicative forms, revealing to the public how the masculine exclusivity of football and the ways in which the sexual use followed by the ostracisation of women is unethical. I also investigate here some of the ways in which the public relations techniques deployed by the AFL and St Kilda Football Club during and subsequent to the incidents operated, particularly as they struggled to manage and contain the shifting elements of the story.

The second chapter provides an overview of the broader social context and some of the cultural changes in football organisation and identity that not only form the background to scandals but are active elements in the production of sports scandals as *cultural effects*. Using some of the incidents in the particularly notorious off-field life of former Carlton and Brisbane Lions player Brendan Fevola, the chapter works through the cultural foundations of elite-level Australian Rules footballers as community and national 'heroes', articulated through performances of particular types of masculinity and the ways in which these elements of footballer identity are re-packaged and commodified as aspects of celebrity identity in contemporary football culture. Important here is the argument that, contrary to much social commentary on football scandals, footballer masculinity is by no means 'hegemonic'. Rather, it is demonstrated here that off-field footballer performances are certainly 'hypermasculine' but they are forms of masculinity that are residues from the past and are, today, often out of step with contemporary standards and practices of masculinity. The disjuncture in gender distinction between broad social expectations and the masculinities found in football culture is a significant element in how particular off-field behaviours today are seen to scandalise the public.

Much of the off-field activities of footballers that relate to unethical practices and attitudes towards women occur in groups and team players socialising together, and these include some cases of sexual objectification and alleged assault. The third chapter examines a number of sex scandals, including allegations of group rape, and the ways in which public sphere debate tends to respond in a polarised way by either stereotyping the woman complainant as a gold-digger, liar or sexual predator or condemning team sports as rotten in and of themselves. Neither of these arguments is useful in comprehending how sexual violence operates in the context of football culture. I draw here on a reading of Judith Butler's theories of performativity and how identity performances can differ between individual selves and groups operating in concert as a way of understanding why women can be subjected to sexual violence or non-consensual sex by a group of footballers who, ordinarily and individually, would not be part of such a crime. If reducing the likelihood of scandal means preventing certain unethical behaviours and attitudes which objectify, use or are injurious towards women, then it is important to develop ways in which an ethics can be installed in footballers when acting not just individually in their private lives but in tightly bonded groups. An important point to be made here is that there is nothing wrong with team bonding itself, for this is necessary for on-field success. Rather, to avoid scandalous behaviour and ensure a more ethical kind of relationality with women, the team bond needs to be transformed into something which rests on rather than repudiates an ethical relationship with others.

In the fourth chapter I look at three interrelated compulsive behaviours that have been significant in numerous football scandals over the past decade: binge drinking, use of recreational drugs and compulsive gambling. Interestingly, all three relate to contemporary on-field and institutional questions of integrity, including alcohol advertising and sponsorship, use of performance-enhancing drugs, and the relationship between gambling and match-fixing. Research by Eric Dunning and Ivan Waddington[41] has demonstrated that although the notion of sport is governed by concepts of health, puritanism and stoicism, there remains a submerged tradition of off-field 'Dionysian' sociality marked by partying, pleasure-seeking and abandon. I draw on this research to point to a *continuum* between the act of pleasure in the game and the pleasure-seeking that marks the off-field activities of footballers, which includes the pleasures of alcohol, recreational drugs and gambling. By showing that both the pleasures and off-field activities are produced as an outcome of football culture, it is possible to argue that the penalisation of players as a response to off-field scandals in these three areas is problematic and wrongly assigns responsibility to the individual player while failing to address how the constitution of those individuals within the disciplinarity of football is causal.

In 2010 a scandal was caused by an opinion article written by Brownlow Medallist and former Western Bulldogs and Brisbane Lions player Jason Akermanis in response to the AFL and AFL Players' Association 'Inclusion and Diversity' campaign designed to combat the perception that Australian football culture is broadly homophobic in contrast to shifts in attitude within other, predominantly non-team sports. Although the campaign itself was highly problematic in using some outdated rhetoric and ignominiously avoiding the use of terms such as lesbian, gay and queer, Akermanis argued that queer players should stay in the closet rather than disrupt the bonds of a football team or make other players uncomfortable in the showers. Controversy lasted for several weeks while Akermanis at first denied he wrote the comments alone, then later defended them, contributing to his being sacked later that year by the Western Bulldogs. Chapter five examines this scandal by asking what it is about contemporary football culture that excludes non-heterosexuals, and how that fits with Akermanis' claims that the locker room is a naturally homoerotic space enjoyed by straight footballers. Questions around the ethics of a culture of exclusion are opened here in terms of the notion that the use of homophobic insult by players and coaches as a means of enhancing on-field performance is injurious to non-heterosexual persons, whether within or outside Australian Rules football culture.

The final, conclusive chapter focuses on the question as to what would constitute a more ethical Australian Rules football culture and a more ethical footballer immune to the sorts of scandal significant in the game over the past decade. Taking up some of Judith Butler's most recent work on how an ethics of non-violence is produced through the capacity to recognise the inherent vulnerability of others through our own bodily vulnerability, I explore a number of the reasons why football culture can sometimes be unknowingly without ethics, how this leads persistently to a range of scandals and, indeed, injurious behaviour towards others off the field, and why the production of a more ethical footballer would be advantageous to Australian society in general. Central to the suspension or disavowal of ethics among footballers is the culture itself which encourages a performance of inviolability, thus preventing footballers from recognising their own precariousness. In a sport in which injury is not only common but, indeed, likely, ethics can be fostered by asking that footballers recognise their own vulnerability to on-field injury in order better to relate ethically and without injury to vulnerable others.

Building on the insights of critical and cultural theory, *Vulnerability and Exposure* seeks to develop the sorts of debates that occur subsequent to footballer scandals into ones which avoid accusatory moralisations against either players or victims and instead consider the role contemporary football culture, football institutions and footballer identity each play in enculturating the behaviours that, whether innocent or injurious, result in scandal narratives. Doing so is not to undermine the importance and significance of Australian Rules football in contemporary society as a well-loved institution that has real and genuine meaning not only for its players but for its spectators and casual followers. Rather, it is to explore the possibilities of a more critical approach to the subject of scandal and ways in which more ethical relationships between footballers and others who find themselves on the margins of football culture can be fostered.

1

The 'St Kilda Schoolgirl': Public Discourse, Digitisation and Reconfiguring the Footballer Sex Scandal

Throughout much of the twentieth century, sports scandals relating to the off-field social world were generally limited to issues such as the occasional pub brawl, drink driving, fraud or financial wrong-doing. And that was only when such issues spiralled into scandal – in many cases they may have resulted in brief news reports and some minor disciplining, but were not necessarily considered scandalous. Other events in the social world of masculine team sports during the past century relating to the treatment of women caught up sexually in the cultural environment of sports teams and clubs sometimes *ought* to have become scandal but have more often remained hidden; at other times these scandals have emerged in ways which involve reportage that overwhelming – if implicitly – supports the perpetrators of sexual violence over women victims, survivors or complainants.[1]

By the start of the twenty-first century, sports sex scandals were being more widely reported, debated and determined by news routines and media commentary. However, most recently the way in which these scandals play out has shifted beyond the 'knowable' forms of media narrative as a result of the use of digital communication tools, social networking, YouTube, Twitter and other applications that 'give voice' to those who have been 'wronged' in a sex-based scandal. In Australian Rules football culture, this was most-readily witnessed in 2010 and 2011 in what became known as the 'St Kilda Schoolgirl' scandal, which involved players from the AFL's St Kilda Football Club, a young woman who had first encountered some of the players during their visit to her school, sexual involvement with several players, an alleged teenage pregnancy, a romantic involvement with a much older player-manager whose initial role was to resolve the scandal. The 'passing around' of a young woman football fan among players and club stakeholders is, of course, not in any way new. However, this scandal departed from the normative routine of sex scandals in that the young woman, Kim Duthie, was able to disrupt the standard sex scandal narrative that typically makes a young woman 'victim' or silences her altogether and, instead, maintain media focus on herself not as victim but as complainant.

What is new here is the fact that the communication involved in this scandal utilised both traditional news media and digital forms of dissemination to construct various accounts and positionings of both parties. The argument here is that the discourse around the incident or scandal is structured not solely by traditional media forms and not solely by the public relations histories and forms utilised by masculine team sporting organisations. Rather, the ways in which the scandal has been communicated publicly is governed by the intersection between both. What that produces is a set of shifts not only in how sports-player sex scandals are responded to publicly but in how a victim is positioned, addressed and has her story coded as legitimate or dishonest. However, as I will argue, these shifts are not wholesale but maintain certain continuities in the ways in which complainants within sex scandals have their story publicly articulated, and the new elements here on the one hand open possibilities for cultural or institutional change in the ways in which elite/celebrity masculine sports teams, codes, leagues and individual players demonstrate ethical responsibilities towards women, but on the other hand constrain those possibilities.

This chapter will start with a brief summary of the 'St Kilda Schoolgirl' story, before looking at some of the ways in which we can make sense of the shifts and new elements in footballer sex scandals. Important here, firstly, is considering how Duthie's use of digital media maintained her – as complainant and *not* victim – at the centre of public discourse rather than being subject to the traditional eradication or invisibilisation of those who have been assaulted or victimised by elite footballers. Secondly, I will look at the public relations mechanisms deployed by the AFL during and subsequent to the incident. These have included both engagement with news media and the use of digitally distributed text and video as part of a risk management strategy, the new element here being a direct address to the young woman through invoking a discourse of welfare and vulnerability that aims to mitigate the negative publicity brought about by the scandal. Finally, I will examine some of the ways in which the young woman's media activism opens the space for critique of the conditions that make 'scandalous' behaviour possible in the off-field environment of contemporary football in terms of the extent to which a broader groundswell of criticism by women would be helpful in bringing about cultural change to a more ethical football culture.

Scandal as a Narrative of Media Incidents

Sex scandals differ from other types of scandal such as fraud, political intrigue, back-room deals with public money and nepotism. Scandals relating to sex, sexuality and the outcomes of sexual behaviour are structured by a discourse of contemporary sexualised culture often preoccupied with sexual values and practices, the proliferation of sexual texts, a public and sometimes lurid interest in gossip and reports of unusual sexual experiences and arrangements, and controversies and panics around claims that older conceptions of sex and sexuality are breaking down.[2] Scandals typically centre on media-disseminated allegations that would ordinarily be damaging to an individual or organisation's reputation. In the case of sex scandals there is usually an element of sexual behaviour that is deemed non-normative – an affair, a substantial age-gap between the participants involved, sexual assault, among others. Sex scandal stories play out at the interface of that which is normally relegated to the 'private' and 'public interest'.[3] The series of incidents that became known as the 'St Kilda Schoolgirl' scandal bears the common tropes of sex scandal in regard to the non-normative or non-traditional values indicated in the narrative of scandal – a young woman who has had sexual relations with a number of footballers and a much older player-manager; the fact that her initial encounter with players occurred through a school visit; the fact she was under eighteen years of age at the time of the initial encounters; and the fact that she was alleged to have been pregnant to one of the footballers. These particular elements are neither atypical nor in any way matters of social shame for the individuals involved. However, the combination of the celebrity status of the members of St Kilda Football Club, and the discourse through which these incidents are available to be consumed as gossip provides them collectively with the status of scandal. At one level, this scandal allows new public relations mechanisms to come into play to protect the players and league stakeholders from criticism of wrongdoing. At another, it opens opportunities to engage critically with the sexual practices of elite masculine team sportsplayers and the institutional culture of Australian Rules football in regard to gender relations.

The series of incidents, stories and news items that comprise the cycle of scandal began in May 2010, when it was reported that two St Kilda footballers had been accused of having sex with a seventeen year-old woman who became pregnant to one of them.[4] It was noted that although the players had visited her school at which point they first came to her attention, she did not formally meet them until some weeks later in a Sydney nightclub on the evening of a win for the team. The report, which did not name the players, noted that Victoria Police and the AFL became involved after the pregnancy was reported to her school principal, that an investigation occurred but that the players had been cleared by both Police and the AFL of any wrongdoing. It was also inferred on the same day that the young woman may also have been sexually involved with a player from rival team Collingwood.[5]

Later in May 2010, *The Age* revealed knowledge that a photograph of the young woman had been emailed among past and present St Kilda footballers, staff at the AFL Players' Association, staff at the Department of Justice, the Transport Accident Commission (a major sponsor of junior football in Victoria) and the Melbourne Magistrates' Court.[6] Forwarded emails included suggestions that recipients visit her Facebook page to 'do your worst',[7] that is, punish her for her role in the first part of the scandal earlier that month. With her identity revealed, the young woman made a complaint to Victoria Police; the response of the AFL was to note that social networking privacy was problematic, that there would be no investigation of the forwarded image and identification of the young woman, and, as AFL chief executive Andrew Demetriou put it, children in any case should be discouraged from using Facebook.[8] By early June, however, Demetriou altered his position and stated that those forwarding the emails were acting distastefully, although there was some concern that what was distasteful in the view of the AFL was the fact that the email named the players involved, rather than expressing alarm that the young woman had been identified widely among the network of footballers, club and league stakeholders and associates.[9]

The next phase of the scandal occurred in December 2010 when Duthie posted nude and sexual pictures on Facebook and Twitter of St Kilda captain Nick Riewoldt and his teammates Nick Dal Santo and Zac Dawson. The first photograph showed Riewoldt standing naked, posed and holding his genitals next to a clothed Dawson who holds what appears to be a condom packet beside Riewoldt's genitals. The second image revealed Dal Santo on a bed with his penis exposed, appearing to masturbate. The images were overlaid with the phrase 'Merry Christmas courtesy of the St Kilda Schoolgirl' and were redistributed virally within a matter of hours. The club responded quickly with a press release stating that they were liaising with Victoria Police to have the photographs removed, and that they were concerned the images were obtained illegally. Victoria Police responded to queries stating that it was not a police but a civil matter for the two parties to resolve.[10] However, later the same day it was revealed that Facebook had been contacted and the young woman's account was forcibly closed while at the same time the Federal Court of Melbourne placed a temporary injunction against the further publication of the photographs.[11] Initially, Duthie informed the public through both interviews and statements on her Twitter account that she had been in the room when the photographs were taken, had been the only woman present, and that the players involved had been drinking heavily.[12] Statements of support for the footballers came from several spokespersons, although Riewoldt made his own statement declaring that he had never met Kim Duthie, that the photograph had been taken at least twelve months earlier by fellow player Sam Gilbert, and that he was angry with his teammate as he had asked at the time that the image be deleted.[13] It was then alleged by Riewoldt's manager Ricky Nixon that Duthie had been attempting to extort $20,000 in exchange for the photographs, and it was noted that an affidavit filed in the Federal Court by Sam Gilbert confirmed he had taken the photographs himself 'for private use' in Miami, with the young woman copying them later from his laptop in March 2010 without his knowledge or permission.[14] Later that year it was reported that her pregnancy with twins had ended in the miscarriage of one and the stillbirth of the other.

A controversial deal between the young woman and the St Kilda Football Club was made in January 2011, whereby the club would provide accommodation for her for some months in Melbourne in exchange for a list of assurances, including confirmation that no player from the club had approached her during their school visit, that no phone number of a player had been given to her at the school, and that she had met the players only at a social event in Sydney in March 2010.[15] During February 2011, debate on the scandal continued, with former Commonwealth Government treasurer Peter Costello questioning in an opinion piece if it was right that sportsplayers visit schools:

> Footballers are not chosen for their moral principles. They do not go into a national draft for budding philanthropists. They can run and catch and kick a ball. What are the clubs thinking when they send them to schools to give guidance on life skills? Any right-thinking parent would quake with fear to hear that footballers were coming to their daughter's school to give a little bit of inspiration.[16]

This commentary had the important effect of opening discussion on the role of the footballers themselves in the scandal, discrediting the previously unquestioned view that footballers are appropriate role models for motivating adolescent students.

On 18 February 2011 it was revealed that the young woman at the centre of the scandal was now involved with the forty-seven year-old married Australian Football League player-manager Ricky Nixon[17] who had been visiting her in a hotel room now known to be paid for by both St Kilda Football Club and, later, the *Herald Sun* newspaper.[18] Within two days, news stories stated that Kim Duthie claimed to have evidence of the affair with photographs and video footage that would confirm the relationship.[19] A former footballer who had played for Carlton, St Kilda and Hawthorn, Nixon was a significant stakeholder in Australian Rules football, running the sports management agency Flying Start, a regular radio commentator on sports, and had previously been the subject of a number of news stories after arrests for drunkenness and driving under the influence. Nixon stated publicly that he had not had sex with her, but that he 'had inappropriate dealings with her'.[20] This is a term of indistinct signification which was never explained or clarified. The scandal continued to unfold further over several days in later February with footage of Nixon's belongings in her hotel room and images of drugs present in the room which were alleged to have been brought there by him. On 22 February, Duthie was threatened with a warrant in order to be questioned by Victoria Police[21] over the presence of alleged drugs in her footage of Nixon which she had supplied to the *Herald Sun* newspaper and which had subsequently been forwarded to the police. She was released without charge.[22] At the same time, Nixon left the country for an overseas recruitment trip, although it was inferred that sources close to him suspected the young woman had been spiking his drink as 'his recollection of events is hazy';[23] nevertheless police intended to question him.[24] Indications that the scandal was beginning to affect negatively the broader public image of Australian Rules football emerged, with high-profile sports journalist Caroline Wilson objecting not only to the scandal but to discourses deployed by the AFL to mitigate rather than address the situation:

This ugly scandal symbolises Australian Rules football for those outside the industry and around the country. Right or wrong, Australian Rules football has been tainted. And the game should have taken a stronger stand by now instead of talking constantly and yet again about its concern for the girl who had sex with two St Kilda and one Collingwood footballer early last year.[25]

With several players no longer willing to work with Nixon[26] or, indeed, to risk being tainted by association, the AFL Players' Association appointed Melbourne QC David Galbally to investigate the circumstances of the alleged affair between Nixon and the young woman.[27] After returning to Australia in early March, Nixon announced he would check into a rehabilitation clinic to resolve his personal and drinking issues,[28] and that his actions in regard to the young woman had been the result of a substance abuse problem[29] which had ' clouded his behaviour over the past eight weeks'.[30]

On 6 March, Duthie was interviewed by Liz Hayes on Channel Nine's *60 Minutes* (Australia). The interview rehearsed much of the history and detail of the scandal to date, but also focused on her motivations for the release of the nude/sexual images. She explained that she was driven in part by vengeance after feeling hurt subsequent to having been suddenly excluded by players and others from the social world of Australian Rules football in which she had forged a sense of belonging. It was revealed she had lied about being pregnant to St Kilda player Sam Gilbert, confirmed that she had taken the images from Gilbert's computer herself, and footage of text messages between Nixon and herself was shown indicating that in the days following the revelation of the affair he had been on the one hand planning a future with her and, on the other, threatening her if she did not release a statement to the media exonerating him.[31] The following day, AFL chief executive Andrew Demetriou announced he had known previously that she was not pregnant.[32] Ricky Nixon's accreditation as a player manager was revoked for a two-year period, and the young woman responded to the news on Twitter with the statement: 'Satisfied. Told you so. #YouLoseRicky'.[33] Nixon did not appeal the two-year suspension, and by April 2011, he was stating publicly that he no longer wanted to be involved in football management or within the Australian Rules institutions altogether.[34] The scandal narrative continued to unfold during the month of April, in which Duthie's family revealed they had received death threats, with her father stating he had wished she had been kept home from school the day of the fateful encounter with the St Kilda footballers.[35] Duthie also appeared on the Seven Network program *Sunday Night* and underwent a lie detector test with the results agreeing with her assertion she had had sex with Ricky Nixon. Nixon was also interviewed by the program and announced he had continued to receive a barrage of text messages and emails from the young woman, and that she was stalking him at his Point Lonsdale home, complaining that 'the harassment is continual and has caused stress and anxiety to me and my family'.[36]

In mid-April, Nixon sought a court intervention order against Duthie[37] and it was revealed that he was collaborating with film-maker Deanna Zacek to produce a documentary about his time in the AFL and his involvement in the 'St Kilda Schoolgirl' scandal.[38] In late April, Nixon admitted publicly that he had threatened to kill Kim Duthie and himself if their relationship became public,[39] and in early May the *Sunday Night* program showed footage of Nixon walking out of an interview after being asked if he had an ethical duty of care towards the seventeen-year-old Duthie.[40] Galbally's report to the AFLPA was leaked in early May, revealing that police forensic experts had confirmed the footage of Nixon in his underpants in Duthie's room was authentic, and that Galbally's investigation concluded that Nixon had conducted a sexual relationship with Duthie, taken drugs with her, engaged with her in a threatening manner, and had taken advantage of her not only as a person who was in conflict with his clients but as a minor.[41] As the scandal narrative dragged on, an intriguing twist occurred when Duthie appeared on Channel Ten's *7pm Project* and recanted her claims that she had taken drugs and had sex with Nixon, publicly apologising on-air. However, immediately after the apology she spoke off-air while cameras were rolling and revealed that her recantation itself was a lie: 'You know. I can tell already that you know, that everything I just said I lied about'.[42] The producers broadcast this statement, although Duthie later stated on her Twitter account that she was aware the cameras were rolling. There was some media speculation that Duthie was under pressure from Nixon to retract her initial claims or that they had struck a financial deal for that retraction.[43] While some minor media and online coverage of Duthie continued, and Nixon's financial and institutional status were regularly reported on, including a violent assault on his ex-fiancée,[44] the scandal narrative wound down after it was revealed that no charges would be laid against Nixon in relation to sexual offences against Duthie.[45]

Media Activisms

Although filled with twists and apparent lies at times from all parties, this scandal demonstrates some of the continuing problematic ways in which women are treated in the context of the off-field celebrity social world of elite athletes as well as how they are represented and addressed in the circumstances of a media scandal. There is a clear argument that the policies and programs intended to counter the systemic value systems regarding masculine behaviour and objectification of women such as the AFL's *Respect & Responsibility* policy[46] are ineffective in preventing some of the more alarming cases of objectification, sexual violence and forms of emotional abuse such as social exclusion of those previously invited into the social sphere of footballers, and the mechanisms utilised to discredit the competency of a younger person to speak their view on events which impact on themselves as much as on footballers, clubs or the reputation of the league. There are, however, some grounds for considering how this specific scandal might foster some broader cultural change on gender relationality within masculine, homosocially oriented institutions. This is especially the case, given some of the new elements in how scandalous material was revealed, which include the ways in which Duthie was able to make use of digital media to speak and maintain her story, rather than rely on the more mundane and predictable narratives of the 'wronged woman' in traditional press environments.

The most important new element in this scandal is what we might consider Kim Duthie's 'media activism', by which I mean her utilisation of both traditional and digital media forms to convey a particular politicised message, not merely her views or revelation of gossip. To define her as a media activist is to point out that her use of digital media technologies is *tactical*. For Michel de Certeau, a tactic 'insinuates itself into the other's place, fragmentarily, without taking it over in its entirety, without being able to keep it at a distance...It must constantly manipulate events in order to turn them into "opportunities"'.[47] That is, traditionally football institutions have had some element of media control or domination of the narrative in cases of scandal management, whereas Duthie has made tactical use of their media terrain to assert her claims over footballer wrongdoings. At the same time, the use of digital media as a site through which to make her concerns known publicly can be understood as a formation similar to cultural jamming. For Mark Dery, the language which conceals and protects corporate capitalism is undone – effectively deconstructed – through the subversive promotion of a plurality of views,[48] which more recently has found its fruition in an interactive engagement of an online 'war of information',[49] and Duthie's use of digital media can be understood as an activism that presents such a plurality against the usually singular, united narrative dominated by the AFL in the management of a football sex scandal. Finally, some of the media activism here, including her initial defiance of the court order to destroy the images of Riewoldt, Dawson and Dal Santo, might be understood as a form of electronic civil disobedience.[50] Characterising her as a digital media activist is not, of course, to suggest that she is deliberately and self-consciously motivated by the same series of normative ideals that might typically encourage those we normally consider to be activists of the political and/or postmodern left. Rather, it is to point out that her actions in using digital media, the textuality of her statements, the digital recording and distribution of images are performative acts which are always out of the control of the author – the speech goes on to have a life of its own. In this perspective, her motivation and authorial intention is irrelevant, for it is in the reading, interpretation and cultural impact of her actions, distributions, digital texts and interviews that a form of media activism can be identified.

The young woman's activism has crossed both traditional media and digital/online communication. In the case of the first, she has accepted interviews and, apparently, made certain deals with the *Herald Sun* for the costs of her accommodation[51] and with Channel Nine who may have paid for her *60 Minutes* interview.[52] Indeed, it was also remarked upon that she quite expertly faced a media pack at Melbourne Airport on her return from Queensland just prior to Christmas 2010.[53] However, it is the speed and veracity of her use of digital tools and a range of social networking sites for conveying a message that is the more striking aspect over the period of the scandal, particularly from late 2010 until late March 2011. The young woman's use of digital media is, of course, partly generational: as a seventeen-year-old raised in a first-world Western region, she participates in a culture in which the internet has become the obvious site for a range of forms of self-expression,[54] many of which have their own codes of practice, textuality and narrative and ways of writing and speaking[55] which can at times be a performance that is self-consciously 'notorious, obnoxious or annoying'.[56] Such expressive forms also often facilitate a peer networked culture of mutual dialogue;[57] both the mutuality and the pestering her online expressiveness produces was clearly disruptive to AFL stakeholders who had not previously encountered such communicative forms by victims or complainants in a sex scandal. At the same time, Duthie's digital media activism mirrors some earlier feminist political actions which sought to name perpetrators of abuse as a means of restoring a construction of women's agency.[58] In acquiring and distributing the images of St Kilda players, she not only created scandal but named those who had participated in the perpetration of her exclusion from club sociality subsequent to their understanding she was pregnant to a player. According to the *60 Minutes* interview, she had been trusted to be in footballer Sam Gilbert's home alone during their brief relationship and at that time accessed his computer and downloaded the nude/sexual photographs that were later in 2010 posted online. She claimed that posting the images to cause embarrassment was a response to Sam Gilbert, St Kilda Football Club and the AFL for cutting contact with her and excluding her from their social activities. Feeling 'hurt and isolated' she stated that she was driven by power and the desire for an apology for the manner in which she was sexually used and then ostracised, cast aside.[59]

Although her Facebook account was suspended as a result of the image postings,[60] she transitioned easily to other Web 2.0 sites such as YouTube and Twitter in order to continue the campaign and maintain the distribution of the images until eventually prevented from doing so further by a court order. Subsequent posts on YouTube and Twitter resulted in a significant following through which she made a number of statements highlighting the culture of objectification among celebrity Australian Rules footballers. In December 2010, she used video site USTREAM to discuss and explain her actions and the reasons for posting the photographs online.[61] At the same time, she responded to queries from people posting to her online on both Twitter and Formspring,[62] the latter exemplifying Web 2.0 participatory culture as a question-and-answer interactive site which has been operating since late 2009, allowing users to discuss issues and link commentary to other social networking environments. Later, it was digital footage taken surreptitiously from a mobile camera of Ricky Nixon's presence in her hotel room, apparently with illegal drugs, that she was able to present to the *Herald Sun* newspaper as part of the ongoing campaign alerting the public to the ways in which Australian Rules football stakeholders act in regard to women. During her *60 Minutes* interview, it was a digital archive of emails and text messages from Ricky Nixon both wooing and threatening her that provided further evidence of the cultural problems in the treatment of women by footballers.

There is one important and very significant effect of what we can refer to as Duthie's media activism that produced a change in the discursive, historical and cultural manner in which media scandals over masculine team sportsplayers' sexuality and objectification of women play out. This is that the use of digital tools, supplemented by her interviews in broadcast news media, have provided the objectified woman at the centre of a scandal the opportunity to have voice. Regardless of motivation, Duthie's use of both digital and traditional media maintained focus on herself not as *victim* but as *complainant*, overcoming the explicit and implicit silencing that is experienced by most women involved in a masculine group sex scandal,[63] and ensured that the issue of ethical behaviours in terms of footballers' attitudes remains one grounded in gender relationality. This is a significant shift in how sex scandals involving elite team sportsplayers address and respond to those involved. In earlier scandals, an impressionable young woman used sexually by multiple football players finds her own story is given little media coverage and often her reports to the police do not result in charges – that is, organised actions of masculine institutional hegemony position the woman at the centre of a sexual scandal as the absent other,[64] unable to assume the position of the speaking subject within a given discourse.[65] Without the discursive or communicative opportunity for voice, a victim of a sex scandal is thereby available to be coded either in reporting or by interpretation of readers as either the gold-digging vamp or the wronged virgin, typically the former.[66] Often, the woman in a sex scandal is only able to speak her story later, and only through banal, mundane narratives in a magazine 'tell all' that positions the woman as victim and the reader within the context of audiencehood for scandal,[67] but never addressed through the media engagement of an organisation or institution to which perpetrators of the scandal belong. For example, of a woman who was sexually assaulted in 2002 by up to twelve members of the Cronulla Sharks while on a pre-season tour in New Zealand – when the scandal erupted in Australia in 2009, player Matthew Johns made a statement on *The Footy Show* and discussed the anguish the incident and its revelation had put his wife through. In contrast to the concerns for Johns' wife, the victim remains absent from the rhetoric deployed by the institution that protects the perpetrators of the act, as presenter Sarah Ferguson pointed out in her *Four Corners* documentary of the incident: 'But neither he nor any of the players we contacted asked about Clare'.[68] In the context of finally being able to speak her story in the documentary, however, she is positioned through specific questions, editing and the standardised narrative of revelation as 'victim'. In the case of the 'St Kilda Schoolgirl' incident, the discourse of footballer sex scandal has been subverted by her persistent use of digital media, circumventing the traditional and recognisable channels through which the perceived 'vamp' attempts unsuccessfully to tell her story 'as victim', effectively demanding and forcing the AFL and the club to address her instead as 'complainant' in ways in which women in previous scandals have not been.

Again, this is not to claim Duthie is an intentional and self-conscious gender activist, although it is important to point out that her motivations should not be wholly excluded from considering the politics of the effects of her actions, as there is an identifiable politicisation of the issues of footballer treatment of women that can be teased out in her statements on motive. In an interview with journalists at Melbourne Airport on Christmas Eve, she stated the following: 'I'm not looking for money. I'm looking for a deal to tell my side of the story';[69] ensuring that her story is told in a particular way – not necessarily fully within her control, but actively disrupting the narrative of footballer sex scandal – has been central to both her motivation and the effect that her story has produced. At the same time, the impetus of her actions was known to be one of vengeance, although the key factor here is not revenge *per se*, but revenge over the ways in which she had been positioned early in the scandal. In discussing her reasons for distributing the nude photographs, she stated in a December 2010 interview with Western Australian media personality Howard Sattler: 'Basically I want the players to know how it feels to have your reputation ruined, as I had mine ruined'.[70] As importantly, her vengeance appears to have been related to her exclusion and ostracisation from the celebrity world of elite football to which she was once permitted access. As she put it of her time socialising with the players during 2010: 'I had a taste of that lifestyle and even more when I met the AFL players...It gives you that sort of buzz being around them...I just couldn't step down from being up that high'.[71] Certainly it is possible to read such ostracisation and exclusion, particularly of someone who was invited into the sociality of a peer group, as acts of bullying.[72] Arguments have been put forward, including by a former director of Essendon Football Club, that the exclusion of the young woman after her affairs with football players was an act of mistreatment,[73] and one which is common to masculine, homosocial institutions in which an in-group/out-group economy actively excludes women through a range of mechanisms including the implicit and the linguistic but also the ostensible and the physical.[74] Additionally, the masculine values traditionally applied to team-based sports add a further form of automatic exclusion of women by positioning them as *other* within the context of on-field and off-field sporting engagement and masculine team bonding.[75] By intentionally combating that ostracisation, she has drawn attention to elements of bullying in the culture of masculine team sports.

At the same time, it is important to understand the transition between motivation and effect of this arguable media activism by teasing out some of the less ostensible issues of gender relationality from her statements and interviews. She has made a number of statements about the ways in which women are treated by footballers and athletes: 'I think they treat girls pathetically. It's not right at all'.[76] Importantly, the rhetoric appears almost innocent, as if a discovery rather than a rehearsal of prior utterances by those who have spoken out against the treatment of women by celebrity sportsplayers. Attending a St Kilda training session in mid-January 2011, Duthie hung a poster that read: 'RESPECT. AFL can you please spell that for me?',[77] a reference to the Aretha Franklin 1967 song 'Respect' which served as an anthem within 1970s feminist political activism. A mediation session between St Kilda Football Club and the young woman resulted in an initial arrangement for a series of mutual apologies. The mediation session was ordered by the Federal Court hearing over the release of the nude photographs, although prior to the session the young woman pointed to the inequity in the difference between requirements for herself and for the club members: 'They've said "If you apologise to Nick publicly, then we'll apologise to you privately", but if it's private it's as though they've done nothing wrong. I want them to be public about it, that's what we're sort of trying to mediate'.[78] What is produced here is a critique of the inequity between how one is required to respond operates within a dichotomy of gender and, simultaneously, a dichotomy of the institution versus the private individual, the irony being that the private individual must apologise publicly, while the public, celebrity institution makes its contrition only in a private forum.

Maintaining public attention on herself as complainant through bypassing the traditional narratives that make public a wronged party in a sex scandal, the young woman has effectively produced a response to the ways in which exclusion and 'othering' of women occurs as well as the problematic and inequitable relationality of gender in sports institutions, prompting some women stakeholders in clubs to speak out,[79] and subverting the routine and recognisable discourse of scandal to one which has the capacity to address the issues she has raised. Ultimately, by allowing her story to be told through a matrix of partial items online that in the formation of scandal filter into news, supplemented by her own broadcast audio and video interviews, the young woman has been effective in tactically disrupting the traditional and mundane course by which such scandals play out through exclusions, de-legitimations and refusal of victim authenticity, pointing to a number of ethical gaps in the ways in which institutions respond to the complainant in a sex scandal, and opening the opportunity for exploring alternative forms of ethical engagement around the culture that makes a footballer sex scandal possible.

Public Relations and Risk Management – The Discourse of Welfare and Mental Health

Victims of rape, sexual assault and women who are objects of political and celebrity sex scandals are traditionally cast as either 'virgins' who, lacking autonomy, have been mistreated or had their consent to sex misread and misunderstood, or as 'whores' who have manipulated or lied and ultimately put an 'innocent' perpetrator at risk.[80] In some cases both have been applied to the same subject in media discourses. Writing about the United States sex scandal involving televangelist Jim Bakker, Joshua Gamson notes that the woman involved, Jessica Hahn, was positioned by news stories and particularly claimants defending Bakker simultaneously through the dual discourses of virgin and vamp: 'Good girl and her evil twin, trusting, naive, ruined woman and calculating, sex-drenched gold-digger, victim and vamp'.[81] For the greater part, broadsheet news media in Australia represented best by the Fairfax group of online and print newspapers (*Sydney Morning Herald, The Age, Perth Now* and *Brisbane Times*) have been relatively balanced in their coverage of the 'St Kilda Schoolgirl' story, refusing either explicitly or implicitly to code her as either innocent victim or predator across more than eighty news articles on the topic published between May 2010 and July 2011. At the same time, articulations of wrongdoing on the part of the players has also not been made explicit in the writings of journalists, although some opinion-columnists in those papers did make statements to the effect that cultural change in the ways in which sportsplayers treat women was required.[82] However, from articles as far back as May 2010, questions over the capacity of the young woman to tell the truth about the incidents were raised subsequent to the revelation that she had lied about her age to St Kilda players from the beginning – claiming to be nineteen years old.[83]

Some of the shifts in the ways in which the public relations strategies of the AFL and St Kilda Football Club that occurred during the scandal may well mitigate the benefits Duthie's activism brought to public debate. In the early stages of the scandal in May 2010 when it was known that a young woman was pregnant to a player whom she had initially met during a school visit, the AFL's public relations strategy was to focus on the players and the club's management of public events, with operations manager Adrian Anderson stating 'The AFL's concern in relation to this matter was whether any AFL player had acted inappropriately during the course of a school visit. This was not the case'.[84] This strategy repeats the standard approach of rejecting the opportunity to address the nature or event of the scandal, or to acknowledge the complainant, and instead focusing on how any internal investigation will ensure no wrongdoing on the part of the institution or its internal culture, and to promote the strength and solidarity of the organisation and its members.

The AFL Player's Association response to the release of the nude and sexual images of Riewoldt and Dal Santo was initially to make a defensive statement that did not mention Duthie, but instead stated that 'Players are outraged at the gross invasion of privacy committed today…They are sick and tired of being seen as "fair game" by some in the community…[and] subjected to these kinds of seemingly malicious actions'.[85] As Will Brodie put it, the St Kilda Football Club's approach to the nude photographs scandal was initially to follow '…the script: we are the wronged parties, our club is strong and united, there is no damage done, the photos were taken from Gilbert's computer without his knowledge or consent'.[86] A few days after the initial release of the images and two days after her series of radio interviews and Twitter and Formspring statements and online videos, Duthie was required to attend the Federal Court in Melbourne. Unable to represent herself at short notice while still holidaying with her parents in Queensland just before Christmas, it is St Kilda Football Club which begins to acknowledge her directly, with club vice president Ross Levin referring to her as 'a malicious troublemaker who was delighting in the distress she was causing'.[87] This is the first media statement in print in which Australian Rules football stakeholders address or acknowledge that there is a complainant at the centre of the scandal, and this is arguably the result of the inability to maintain a clear and networked media risk management strategy leading – in a tone that appears frustrated and angry – to accusatory statements of a kind rarely witnessed in elite football teams' professional public relations approach over the past half-decade.

As the story unfolded in late 2010, the AFL's response to the scandal continued to shift strategy, with a renewed and more extensive focus on the young woman. Rather than silencing or ignoring, the AFL and the integrated public relations strategy of other stakeholders has repeatedly been to argue that their actions around the scandal are grounded in their concern for the 'welfare' of the young woman, utilising a discourse of vulnerability as a means by which to frame her and her actions. In an opinion piece in *The Age* in February 2011, Chief Executive of the Australian Football League Andrew Demetriou stated that the AFL has 'offered her support and we have also at various stages been in contact with the Education Department, Department of Human Services Child Protection, welfare support services and Victoria Police to see what assistance they could offer'. He also stated that as 'a vulnerable teenager, indeed child, it is her welfare that is paramount', and that the AFL's concern is for 'particularly those who may not be able to help themselves, including this young girl'.[88] Subsequent reports and stories about the scandal have reiterated the AFL stance that the young woman was herself 'vulnerable and has serious issues',[89] indicating the initial effectiveness of the AFL's public relations position on the scandal. During the *60 Minutes* interview and report on the incident in March 2011, Demetriou's position that the AFL had not failed in a so-called duty of care towards the young woman was repeated: 'Certainly not with this girl. We've always taken the position that the girl's welfare is paramount. And anything we can do to assist her we've tried to do'.[90] The discourse of vulnerability and the welfare motif were articulated in order to justify a controversial arrangement made between St Kilda Football Club and the young woman, in which the club would provide her with accommodation in exchange for assurances and confirmation that she had not met players from the team during their visit to her school. The club announced that the arrangement included providing housing for her for a 'few months in order for her to gain stability back into her life'.[91] This new strategy, reinforcing and strengthening the statement of 'concern' thus again maintains focus upon the woman at the centre of a football sex scandal, contrasting with older approaches in which the discourse addressing a scandal centres on the damage done to the team, the game, to individual players and their families.[92]

Effectively, this strategy is an attempt to reframe the scandal by de-legitimating the young woman in a new way. A discourse of vulnerability here is one which articulates a victim as at risk of being wounded in some form, or having already been, and being susceptible to further hurt, lacking the resilience to avoid such exposure or weakness. It is not a response to vulnerability in either actual or philosophic terms, but a framed use of the signifier of vulnerability to do injurious damage to the reputation of a young woman in order to dispel the potency of her complaints about the behaviours towards women which stem from Australian Rules football culture. Demetriou's statement positions her not as vulnerable to the players or as a young person victimised, sexually used or objectified by the players, but as vulnerable to herself and her own actions in regard to discussing her stories at large; effectively she is depicted as an at-risk child, incapable not of responsibility but of making responsible adult decisions. Indeed, the vulnerability motif has been utilised to depict her as self-destructive, whereby the distribution of the photographs, revelations of the affair and other information shared by Duthie both online and in interviews impact on the club, individual players and stakeholders and the AFL more broadly are to be viewed as collateral damage within the perception of a young woman who is at risk of self-annihilation. For example, subsequent to the revelation of the affair with Ricky Nixon, players whom he represented including Riewoldt, 'were sticking by him in the belief that he had become the victim of a 17-year-old ticking time bomb'.[93] While press coverage of the latest stage in the scandal openly questioned the appropriateness of a player-manager either having sex with the young woman or even being unchaperoned in her hotel room, depictions of her in news-writing ostensibly draw on the broader discourse of vulnerability, with references to her as a 'damaged 17-year-old',[94] 'unreliable and dangerous',[95] in need of 'counselling support',[96] and 'troubled and troublesome'.[97]

Importantly, the concern-for-welfare strategy of the AFL was supported more widely, with Victoria's Child Safety Commissioner Bernie Geary stating in late December 2010: 'This child is in danger, this child will be left at the end of this situation as a vilified person'.[98] Alarmingly, child psychologist Michael Carr-Gregg stated in a radio interview that 'the teenager exhibited grandiose, self-destructive behaviour indicating she had a "serious psychological problem"'.[99] In both cases, the AFL strategy was reinforced by the denotation of Duthie as a *child,* therefore sexually precocious, therefore dangerous to herself and to others. There was also clearly some need for the football club and AFL more broadly to develop a new strategy, as the legal approach was not operating to prevent the scandal from continuing or to justify their position as wronged party. As St Kilda pressed for further court orders to seek destruction of the images, club vice president Ross Levin stated that the players 'intended to sue for damages, for breach of copyright, breach of confidence, mental distress and trespass'.[100] On Christmas Eve, Justice Shane Marshall responded to the request for destruction as 'fairly draconian', stating that he was unwilling to make an order in the teenager's absence, indicating a lack of support by the courts for the fast-paced legal tactics to contain the scandal. In the unworkability of this approach, the discourse of vulnerability was deployed to frame the story so as (a) to depict the organisational structure of Australian Rules football as *both* strong and caring, and (b) to de-legitimate the strength and efficacy of her complaint.

However, the utilisation of the discourse of vulnerability as a mitigation strategy that aimed to provide what Deb Waterhouse-Watson has referred to as footballers' 'narrative immunity' in sexual assault cases[101] did not go uncontested: Beverly Knight, a former director of Essendon Football Club, condemned this approach in saying, 'I think football's tried to make her…into a nutcase and it hasn't come out in support of its policies, and it needs to do that with voices'.[102] Her statement points to the ways in which the AFL distanced itself from its usual approach of maintaining focus on the strength and solidarity of its own organisation and the effectiveness of its policies; in the failure of legal mechanisms, actions to silence or ignore the young woman as complainant and the risk of the *Respect and Responsibility* policy being characterised as irrelevant and ineffective, the discourse of vulnerability was the more efficient means by which to attempt to make the young woman's statements and the issues surrounding the scandal illegitimate. Thus the utilisation of a discourse of vulnerability here is an act of wounding in itself, as it de-legitimates not just Duthie's claims but her voice.

As a public relations strategy that does more than simply refer to the young woman as a liar or a sexual predator, it rejects the more introspective option of offering to examine institutional or cultural problems in the gender relationality through which such vulnerabilities are produced. Rather, it presents the 'problem' of the scandal in neoliberal terms as an individualised one. For Foucault, a neoliberal governance framework individualises risk and vulnerability, requiring the management and mitigation of these to be handled by individuals in contrast to that which neoliberalism rejects, being the socialisation of welfare and the

collective approach to risk.[103] This acts to decouple the events
of the scandal from institutional structures and the problematic
culture of gender relationality within football clubs, and instead to
view the issues as having arisen from the acts of individuals, cast
as the result of the instability of a troubled young woman, and
needing to be managed and mitigated on an individual basis. At the
same time, footballers and league or club stakeholders' behaviours
are also individualised: Ricky Nixon's behaviour is put down to
alcohol and drug problems, much as Brendan Fevola's problems
were put down to his individual gambling addiction[104] rather than
exploring the culture of gambling among elite team sportsplayers.
Importantly, there is a significant gender distinction through which
this individualisation of responsibility occurs. For footballers and
for Ricky Nixon, the causes are external to the body, much like
the drug which is commonly perceived in contemporary culture as
something 'not real' that comes into the body but can be rejected
and eradicated,[105] or dealt with in a rehabilitation clinic. The
notion that the causes of the scandal are external and eradicable
was presented by Nixon as the solution to the problem of his
relationship with the young woman.[106] But for Duthie herself, the
individualised causes are presented as *internal*: her mental health
and her inability to make responsible decisions. This is a discursive
positioning that is strengthened by the attempt to read and depict
her online YouTube video-logs (vlogs) and her short Twitter
commentary as ranting and incoherent – a strategy that aims to
use these as evidence of her instability rather than a particular
form of online cultural expression that mirrors the ways in which
many YouTube uploaders and Twitter commentators work within
a particular set of codes of performance online. Her narrative of
anger was, of course, presented in the framework of *digital language*
and not that of the professional public relations door-stop nor in the
standardised narrative form of the vulnerable victim in a scandal.
By depicting her as vulnerable and allowing her 'online work' to

be read through instability and incoherence, her statements become the evidence and reinforcement for the very code by which the AFL's public relations strategy has characterised her to be read.

The Digitisation of the Public Relations of Scandal Responses

In addition to the deployment of a discourse of vulnerability as a new type of strategy that aimed to immunise the league and its players in this scandal, a second new public relations tactic used by both St Kilda Football Club and the AFL's organisational management was to follow Duthie's lead and make substantial use of digital and online tools. These were utilised specifically to mitigate the poor public perception of the club and the league that resulted from the off-field scandals over the Southern Hemisphere's summer of 2010–2011. One example of this was the production of a short AFL Media documentary on the St Kilda Saints. Produced by film-maker Peter Dickson, *The Challenge* was narrowcast on saintsfc.com.au on 23 March 2011, and available through both St Kilda Football Club and AFL websites. As Geoff Slattery explained in an online article about organising approval for the filming of *The Challenge*:

> We covered our reasons for wanting to shoot St Kilda, from the inside. To show the humanities of a footy club – any footy club, not just one under pressure – to allow the players to have their say, freely, without prejudice or manipulation or spin. And to name the show *The Challenge*, a title that would cover both on–field and off–field issues.[107]

Explicit here in the motivation behind the documentary is that traditional media processes and news values are untrustworthy or manipulative, and will particularly focus on revealing scandalous events rather than representation of the club or its players. Secondly, it can be read in this testimonial that other persons such as the young woman making statements online can prejudice the public perception of the club and players in ways which are not palatable to its own goals of protecting the image of the 'brand'.

The Challenge is a professional piece which focuses on St Kilda's new headquarters and facilities, the role of coach Ross Lyons in overcoming the club's grand final loss of 2010 and how he has attempted to keep up motivation of the team for a future grand final win. Briefly, it addresses some of the scandals that occurred over the summer, including the behaviour of members of the club while on tour in New Zealand with a breach of curfew and misuse of prescription drugs.[108] The 'St Kilda Schoolgirl' scandal is alluded to only very briefly, with none of the details of the events, pregnancy or the young woman's media statement discussed. In a very brief scene, an image of the *Herald Sun's* 21 December 2010 front-page headline stating 'Saint's Naked Fury' is shown while Nick Riewoldt's voice over discusses his view that the public are smart enough not to believe 'everything that's said in different mediums'. Another scene has Sam Gilbert and Nick Riewoldt sitting together in a locker room, Riewoldt's arm around a shirtless Gilbert, both confirming that while they fell out over Gilbert's failure to delete the nude image of Riewoldt, they are now 'alright' with each other. Riewoldt commented:

> Obviously there was that period at the start where there was a bit of friction, but we've got a good history together both on the Gold Coast and the same club; I don't know, I feel that if anything it's brought us closer together, we've been really honest with each other and talked about our feelings and emotions.

Although the statement makes clear the scripted form of the documentary, it is delivered in a tone of seriousness and reflection, working within a discourse of gentle sensitivity that mitigates elements of the hypermasculinity normally associated with masculine team sports.[109] Hypermasculinity marks football culture as the primary form of footballer gendered identity, despite the fact that such hypermasculine performance is currently out of step with contemporary forms of normative masculine behaviour which increasingly reflect a softer, albeit still–dominant, identity no longer marked by aggression, toughness, inviolability or violence. Although there is considerable masculine homosociality in the description of Riewoldt and Gilbert discussing 'feelings and emotions', the script appears to be one designed to inoculate against the possibility of a public perception that, through the nude images of homosocial partying and the scandals over the summer, riotous hypermasculine and sexual behaviour are part of the club's culture. Ultimately, it is coach Ross Lyons who reveals the purpose of the documentary as a media mitigation strategy against the poor publicity emerging from the players' off–field activities over the summer when he states:

> Understand this: whatever's been written and said, we've gone into action and we're not going anywhere. Okay, so we're in control again. We get to create and write our own story.

That is, it presents a claim to taking control of the scandal's narrative, even though this did not occur, as Duthie was ultimately more extensive in her use of digital tools to manage the narrative and ensure her capacity to speak. In using digital media as a channel for distribution, Saint Kilda Football Club returns to the traditional public relations method of addressing a sex scandal in the refusal to address or refer to the complainant, and promoting the solidarity and strength of the institution in both the on–field arena through showing how the club plans to build towards a grand final win, and in the off–field environment by demonstrating the camaraderie and unity between team members who had been known to have fallen out through the scandal. So it is in the newer environment of digital media distribution that the traditional methods of publicly mitigating scandal occur, while in the more traditional channels of public relations interviews, press releases or responses to news media queries, a discourse of vulnerability that discredits and de-legitimates the complainant is deployed.

Conclusion: Authorising Activism and Cultural Change

The question remains as to whether there can be any change to the problematic gender relationality in the off-field social world of masculine team sports through the two shifts in the narrative of scandal – Duthie's digital media activism and the St Kilda and AFL strategy of invoking the notion of vulnerability while shoring up through traditional discourses of solidarity. Does this open the space to work towards a new or renewed ethical position that protects those who come into contact with footballers from being used, hurt or put at risk, even if such injury is through exclusion and ostracisation? And is there any evidence that it has opened the possibility for cultural change? The St Kilda Football Club and AFL's strategy has been effective in mitigating the scandal and the onslaught of information that occurred online through bypassing and thereby transforming the recognisable narrative of the sex scandal. At the same time, however, the media activism of the young woman has altered the structures of address and response and the ways in which a complainant in a sex scandal can be identified and articulated by working at the interface between the traditional news media and online, participatory forms of dissemination and deliberation, perhaps transforming forever the ways in which a footballer sex scandal can occur.

While the situation and the differential use of media tools will indeed change the formation of scandal, the more necessary changes to gender relationality are less knowable, and that is because the effects of different forms of activism are not knowable in advance, particularly when that activism centres on the work of a single individual. In other words, it may be tactical in disrupting some of the structures that prevent change, but whether that produces change itself is questionable. Some years ago, a number of theorists debated Judith Butler's very brief analysis of Rosa Parks who has often been accorded responsibility for significant civil rights changes in the segregationist south of the United States by refusing, in December 1955, to give up her seat on a bus to a white passenger as she had been required to do. While her activism was highly symbolic on an international scale, it has also been criticised for representing the 'heroic individualist narrative'[110] in which a marginalised person is depicted as having had enough, refusing to comply with systemic inequities and thereby unwittingly launching a social movement. Judith Butler discusses the Rosa Parks case only very briefly, using her as an example of a form of agency: 'In laying claim to the right for which she had no prior authorization, she endowed a certain authority on the act, and began the insurrectionary process of overthrowing those established codes of legitimacy'.[111] In other words, what Butler has argued in her brief analysis is that unlike other transgressions which work within an existing system and often do not produce change as agency is typically only an effect of power and thereby constrained, Parks' transgression occurred without that cultural or institutional legitimacy; as an act, it produced its own authority. Butler has been heavily criticised for this comment, including from those who are usually well-aligned with her theoretical and political stance on subjectivity, agency and discourse. The main criticism centres on Butler's claim that Rosa Parks' refusal to give up her seat was itself an act of authority and not only of defiance attributed to some quality inherent in Parks' individual performance of refusal.[112] Critics have suggested that an element in the activism that has been missed in Butler's analysis is that Parks herself did not simply perform her defiance in a random moment of having had enough, but that she was already active in a complex arrangement of civil rights associations, including the National Association for the Advancement of Colored People (NAACP) and the Highlander Folk School in Tennessee which trained activists in civil disobedience.[113] That is, her activism had prior authority through her institutional connections to other activisms. Secondly, her resistance did not take place in a vacuum, as there was already a groundswell of resistance to segregation which can be seen if one looks at the specific historical conditions of possibility for such resistance.[114] Indeed, the Civil Rights movement was already emerging with significant activity in Montgomery and other places,[115] and there was an enhanced mobilisation of the movement in the South in the years just prior to Parks' refusal.[116] Finally, the transformative political agency that was produced by Parks' refusal to move from her seat also involved a retrospective authority, with the activist community in Montgomery accepting Parks as 'a suitable standard-bearer' for the cause,[117] the groundswell of which gained traction in the months and years afterwards. While Parks' activism was of enormous significance for civil rights changes, it thus was not without prior authorisation or occurred outside of the cultural shifts that were already producing that change.

I do not wish to suggest that the young woman at the centre of the St Kilda football sex scandal is by any means necessarily an activist of the same kind of importance as Rosa Parks, nor to make the claim that her online activism will produce changes as sweeping as those of the civil rights movement in the United States. But the question of the effectiveness of her activism can be understood through the critique of the individual hero that emerges in the discussion of Butler's claim around Parks' self-authorisation and agency. The young woman's activism as a complex of statements, videos, distributions of images and broadcast interviews is an act of defiance and resistance of the ways in which women are depicted in the context of sex scandals and the ways in which women and others are treated in the environment of elite football. The form of activism is new, even though, as I have argued, it is possible to see a gender politics among her motivations which indicates at least a tacit prior authority giving the acts legitimacy, or availability to be read as legitimate and perhaps even inspiring. But the true authority of the activism will be retrospective, and only if it produces an ongoing groundswell of defiance and critique over the ways in which women are positioned within the on-field and off-field environments of elite team sports. Former Essendon Football Club director Beverley Knight's call for women stakeholders to speak out on the issue indicates at least some institutional move towards the call for an upsurge of the sort of criticism necessary to undo the mechanisms that protect masculine homosocial environments from being condemned for the ways in which women are positioned or excluded,[118] although that call is yet to be met in any meaningful way. Duthie's actions may be contributing to that initial groundswell, but she is not producing the performative act through which there is a sudden and maintained shift in momentum towards change in Australian Rules football culture. Whether the strategy of the AFL and St Kilda Football Club in depicting the young woman as vulnerable and unstable has been enough to reduce the possibility of her becoming a standard-bearer for a cause does, of course, remain to be seen in the longer term.

2

Situating Scandal: Footballer Masculinity, National Heroism and Celebrity Culture

In the previous chapter, I discussed one of the more recent Australian Rules football scandals that centred on the gendered relationships between players and outsiders and the ways in which the common scandal narrative and codes of response had been transformed by the 'St Kilda Schoolgirl's' use of digital media. Before addressing in depth some of the other scandals that have emerged from Australian Rules football and uncovering some of the ways in which ethical behaviours can be understood in masculine team-based football, it is important to make sense of the institutional, cultural and gendered contexts in which the off-field 'footballer scandal' commonly and repetitively arises. Many contemporary scandals involving footballers are produced through a combination of *hypermasculinity* in a culture in which masculinity as a facet of identity is in flux, the traits and stereotypes which allow footballers to be seen as local or *national heroes*, and the contemporary status of footballers as *celebrities*. Together, these three elements form not only the backdrop through which footballer scandals occur, but are the framework which convert both public and private behaviours, incidents and acts into communication which is produced into scandal. That is, footballer scandals are an effect of the cultural situation in which footballers find themselves within today's commodifying and neoliberal formulations of elite-level professional sport.

Celebrity itself is closely figured within the contemporary tabloid taste for scandal, with both professional artists and amateur reality television celebrities represented in scandal narratives, typically related to gender, sexuality and relationships. Scandal shifts information about well-known figures from the private to the public through a narrative framework of 'uncovering', and the labour of that uncovering is part of the entrepreneurial activities of newspapers, magazines and celebrity websites. However, the figures chosen for scandal are routinely those who themselves profit from publicity, and this now includes those within football culture which is, since the 1980s, located within a neoliberal, profit-making professionalisation of sport. The implication, then, is that the league organisations, clubs and governance arrangements have a certain accountability in the production of footballer scandals by encouraging the marketing and commodification of the game and its players. I argue in this chapter that a range of shifts in how masculinity is perceived, the role of the footballer in the national context, and the relationship between sportsplayers and organisations that have recently begun to produce footballers as celebrities are primary in establishing and maintaining the situations through which scandals arise. I discuss each of these three areas individually before expanding on some of the ways in which this scenario situates the responsibility for scandal and the accountability for scandalous and sometimes unethical behaviours. Unlike other chapters which undertake a closer examination of footballer scandal incidents and events, I focus here on the broader social background and some of the cultural changes that are not only the backdrop to off-field football scandals but are active in the production of sports scandals as *cultural effect*.

Football Culture and Masculinity

Whether football scandals centre on sex, sexual assault, violence, drugs, alcohol or gambling, they are almost always inflected by the culture of masculinity that is endemic to contemporary male team sports. However, the ways in which gender is the focal point of scandalous behaviours need to be teased out, as masculinity is often the unstated, invisibilised norm of football culture. Increasingly, the discourse of footballer scandals has indeed allowed the question of masculinity to emerge, with a number of commentators now often discussing the fact that teams involved in scandals are held together by bonds not just of teamship or mateship but, specifically, of *masculine conduct* that push on-field and off-field group behaviours from being relatively harmless bonding activities to actions which impact negatively on others and on the players themselves.[1] Where issues and behaviours related to masculinity result in scandal and negative reporting, there are numerous examples. These include violence and fighting, risk-taking in the excessive use of illicit drugs, significant use of alcohol and binge drinking, group sexual assault of women, and other behaviour that can be considered disruptive, unethical or providing football more generally with a negative reputation.

The culture of football is one particular *site* in which players undertake gendered identity work. Within a cultural studies understanding, one does not take the approach that players are masculine to begin with, join the team and the culture of elite sports and that their inherent, individual manliness might contribute to some of the bad behaviours that are taken up by contemporary media and commentators as scandal. Rather, all persons perform gender as part of an ongoing process that involves the relationality of persons to each other and of one gender to another. In other words, performing masculinity involves more than just having a male body and male genitalia, but is a social process undertaken in a variety of scenes and contexts across all of a man's life in order to present one's gender as coherent, intelligible and recognisable.[2] It involves repeating sets of meanings and behaviours that are 'already socially established'.[3] However, the ways in which masculinity is performed differs in different contexts and environments, and there are particular ways in which the masculinity of footballers is performed, held up and reinforced in contemporary football culture where one set of meanings and behaviours are socially established. These differ from how those same players might perform their masculinity in other contexts, for example, in the family home or in the context of a heterosexual romantic relationship. Within contemporary masculine team sports culture, this gender identity work may include risk taking,[4] the rhetorical and material marginalisation of women from masculine sports,[5] physical strength, toughness and competitiveness,[6] heroism, aggression and bravery in the face of physical injury risks.[7] It is when such behaviours – all quite normative within football culture – are exacerbated or taken to hypermasculine extremes in the off-field environment that the possibility of unethical behaviour and scandal arises. Importantly, this is to argue that there is a continuum of gendered behaviours that extends from on-field play to off-field social behaviours; where masculine team behaviours that are considered normative in the context of the game are enacted off-field, there are consequences that result in scandal. For example, there is a link between on-field bravery in play and risky illicit drug use, between competitiveness and excessive alcohol consumption, and between the marginalisation of women from men's sports and sexual use and objectification of women.

A number of sports researchers have referred to the idea that sportsplayers and/or the site of masculine team sports express what is referred to as 'hegemonic masculinity'. For example, Davis and Duncan discuss the sport domain in terms of it being a major site that reinforces hegemonic masculinity 'by creating and recreating what it means to be a man through masculine interaction'.[8] Wheaton has pointed out that a number of scholars see men's sports as celebrating hegemonic masculinity through physical dominance,[9] while Nylund found that hegemonic masculinity is reinscribed in sports talkback radio.[10] A number of other scholars have made assumptions that team sports such as Australian Rules football (or soccer in the United Kingdom and gridiron and baseball in the United States) are prevalent sites for the performance and maintenance of hegemonic masculinity.[11] While it is certainly the case that some aesthetic and performance elements of extreme masculinity play out in football both in on-field and off-field social settings, one of the problems with the assumption that football is predominantly a culture of 'hegemonic masculinity' is found in the fact that the term hegemony here is misused, and that what is problematic about the performances of footballer masculinity is not necessarily hegemonic in contemporary culture, nor is it necessarily deemed acceptable or even tolerated by the majority of men and women outside of football culture.

The term 'hegemonic masculinity' was popularised by sociologist R. W. Connell whose important work demystified masculinity and maleness and made a significant contribution to showing how masculinity was not an essential, fixed and unchanging set of behaviours that emerged from a person being a man, but is socially constructed through gender relations. Connell pointed to the fact that there are multiple masculinities that are hierarchically determined in relation to each other, whereby hegemonic masculinity is a contestable *dominant* form of masculinity that subordinates both women and other men who do not fall into that category.[12] Furthermore, Connell claimed that the culture of sports was the 'leading definer' of masculinity, supported by the linkage between skills, strength and masculinity in the embodied footballer.[13] For Connell, hegemonic masculinity is thus legitimated through a range of practices, which includes the practice of sports.[14] Usefully, the concept draws attention not only to the constructed nature of masculinity but to the fact that there are multiple masculinities that are not equally valued[15] such as, to some extent, gay men, 'geek men', and so on. Connell also noted that hegemonic masculinity, as the dominant social form of masculinity that subordinates others, is historical, contingent and can change and evolve with changing social circumstances and new social ideals such that what was hegemonic in the past may be subordinated under a different or new form of hegemonic masculinity today or in the future.[16] It is certainly the case that footballer masculinity subordinates other men, such as was seen when it was alleged in September 2013 that a Brisbane Lions player had abusively taken control of a man with a disability in his wheelchair[17] or, also that month, when a St Kilda player set fire to dwarf entertainer Blake Johnston during a Mad Monday celebration.[18] However, while that behaviour might remain normative among some players, the hierarchy of subordination that actively demeans those with disabilities or those with a different body size is no longer broadly unquestioned (hegemonic). Connell's concept of hegemonic masculinity has been problematically applied in the critique of team-based sports through the *isolation* of hegemonic masculinity from broader social and cultural processes. Sportsplayers' specific type of masculinity – physical, aggressive, tough, competitive, muscular and expressing bravado – is seen to be the 'type' of masculinity that dominates all others in contemporary Western culture. This is not the case.

There have been a number of critiques of the use and misuse of the concept of hegemonic masculinity over recent years. Important in driving this critique has been the work of Christine Beasley who argues that the concept of hegemonic masculinity has been used to stand in for 'a singular, monolithic masculinity, a global hegemonic form on a world scale'.[19] Beasley argues that the term hegemonic masculinity tends to slip between, on the one hand, referring to a political mechanism related to gender dominance and, on the other, referring to dominant 'versions of manhood' to, finally, referring empirically to specific and actual groups of men.[20] Problematic with the latter two categories is that it associates hegemonic masculinity with the idea of actual men exhibiting a list of specific characteristics and personality traits, thereby losing the social malleability of hegemonic practices.[21] Beasley's answer to these problems is both to narrow the definition and to expand it. In reading this, it is useful to pay attention to her point that masculinity can be produced as a mobilising cultural ideal separate from those who actually wield power – for example, muscular working-class men who do not wield significant institutional power and therefore are not members of a dominant masculine group also represent a cultural ideal intended to invoke multi-class recognition and solidarity around masculinity.[22] The distinction between actual men and cultural ideals allows for a narrower, more theoretically sound conception of hegemonic masculinity that is discursively produced regardless of individuals who benefit from those perceptions. At the same time, Beasley multiplies the concept of hegemonic masculinity, arguing that while men's studies assumes there are multiple masculinities, it tends to presume there is only one, monolithic hegemonic masculinity where there may in fact be a range of dominant masculine performances, codes and behaviours.[23] Thus in the case of footballers, in Beasley's framework, the muscular, fit, and athletic masculinity may be produced as a cultural ideal that upholds and reinforces particular forms of gender relations, but this does not necessarily mean that footballers are in a position of dominance over all other men expressing different masculinities, nor that even if these ideals are hegemonic that they are the *most* or *only* hegemonic form.

Despite the usefulness of this refinement of the theoretical notion of hegemonic masculinity, it remains an awkward concept to apply today to a discussion of football culture and footballers' gendered identity. One of the issues for a cultural perspective on athletes and masculinity is the need to unpack the important term 'hegemony'. Too often, the concept of hegemony in the context of hegemonic masculinity remains undefined and under-theorised, tending to be only a synonym for dominance, whether that be the dominance of an ideal or a group. As Richard Howson has argued in discussing the debates around hegemonic masculinity, there is a need to critically engage with the term hegemony, particularly in terms of the use and meaning given to it originally by Marxist theorist Antonio Gramsci.[24] For Gramsci, hegemony referred to the process by which a dominant class or group in a given society is able to maintain and reproduce its dominance by gaining the consent of the dominated; this occurs through the dominated coming to feel that the domination of a group is either natural or in the best interests of a whole society.[25] Hegemony, then, is a set of processes by which a range of values and beliefs permeate a full society, come to be seen as 'common sense' and thereby support the rule of one class or group – that is, achieving relative consensus of all in the interests of the few.[26] Hegemony in that sense is what Fred Inglis has usefully referred to as a 'saturating omnipresence of the way things are',[27] produced in such a way that it constructs consent for the whole complex of 'lived culture' of the masses.[28] That is not to suggest that hegemony is never uncontested or absolute, for full consensus can never be achieved; it is thus always open to challenge by alternative social forces and counter-hegemonic processes.[29] What is particularly useful about Gramsci's notion of hegemony is the fact that it critiques essentialism – that is, the structure of society or the domination of a particular class is shown up through analysis to be not at all natural, but a *process* which must be constantly renewed and reinforced.[30] Hegemony is thus located within networks of knowledge, truth and power that actively and materially constitutes particular identities and govern the way in which subjects perceive their own sense of agency.[31]

When recent Gramscian approaches are taken into account it becomes possible to see not only that particular cultural ideals of masculinity are not necessarily always or unthinkingly held up by those in dominant positions. Rather, what constitutes hegemonic masculinity is that which has the *consent* of a widespread population; that is, the forms of masculinity that are respected and seen as natural, appropriate, proper and that dominate are not necessarily the toughest, roughest or most sporting forms of masculine behaviour. I am thus not convinced that footballer masculinity any more than warrior masculinity or other ideals of masculinity with their concomitant traits are necessarily hegemonic today. Rather than assume that football culture is the site or expression of 'hegemonic masculinity', it is important to acknowledge that it is, rather, a *non*-hegemonic masculinity, an *outdated residue* of the past, absolutely *out of step* with the forms and performances of masculinity that dominate in wider society. Elements such as on-field strength, toughness and competitiveness may be a cultural ideal, but numerous old-style masculine behaviours in the off-field environments such as excessive and competitive drinking and objectifying behaviour towards women are not things to which society widely consents but are, in fact, widely contested. In saying that footballer masculinity is out of step with dominant forms of masculinity elsewhere is *not* to suggest that footballers are misogynists and men in other social contexts are not. The marginalisation of women and of femininity continues across society, although in ways which today are far more subtle and insidious than they have been in the past. This marginalisation is, indeed, found in footballer misogyny and other behaviours which relegate and/or demean women and femininity, including less-masculine men, gay men and those fellow players whose on-field performance has not been up to scratch. Gramsci's Marxian approach to hegemony is not wholly different from Foucault's approach to disciplinarity and discursivity[32] in which accepted norms are understood to be enculturated within institutional environments and through institutional bonds. Hegemony can be read from this perspective as always contingent, available for polysemic interpretations and multiplicities of meaning, but active in the ways in which the micro-power of disciplinarity expressed through passive surveillance, supervision and the production of docile bodies produces a range of conformities without force.[33] Sporting teams and clubs, in addition to the school and community environments from which elite players are drawn, are highly normalisational sites in which their entire aim is to produce particular conformative bodies and their concomitant behaviours (whether on-field or off-field). Hegemonic masculinity as an available, reified and sometimes transformable discourse thus produces gender identities and gendered relations, but produces them variably and differentially in different contexts. There is nothing particularly unusual about some disciplinary institutions operating outside of wider cultural norms and values and thereby producing particular forms of gendered behaviour that differ markedly from those that have emerged as normative more broadly.

Although it is the case that there are multiple masculinities, and these are not equally valued, there have also been articulations over the past two decades that masculinity is in crisis, with anti-feminist groups arguing that women and others who have questioned masculine dominance have effectively feminised men and/or somehow 'wounded' men to the point that a sense of masculine dignity has been lost, concurrent with calls for a return to 'traditional' or 'authentic' masculinity.[34] While such anti-feminist claims assume that highly patriarchal forms of masculine identity are timeless and ahistorical (and, apparently, both ethical and 'right'), the other side of the coin is that the claims to a crisis in masculinity point to how it has changed over recent decades in broader sociality. This includes the production of the new masculinities which, although they participate in the subordination and/or marginalisation of women, are a softer, less ostensibly harmful form of masculine identity and correlative behaviours. They include what has increasingly come to usurp older ideals of masculinity: what David Buchbinder has referred to as *new man*, a subject who is 'less convinced of the authority and rightness of traditional male logic, and more amenable to alternative ways of thinking'.[35] The disavowal of machismo and the increasing reification of pro-feminist, queer-affirmative discourses,[36] the repudiation of blatant misogyny,[37] and the increasingly outright opposition to male violence and sexual violence in public sphere discourse also form part of this more recent shift in what is considered a more *accountable* masculinity.

Even more recently, the increasingly dominant, hegemonic, expected and consensual form of masculinity is becoming closely aligned with the formation that has been termed metro-sexuality, representing the heterosexual, fashion-conscious, grooming-conscious urban male. Mark Simpson, who coined the term metrosexual in 1994, describes this increasingly common formation of masculine identity as follows:

> The typical metrosexual is a young man with money to spend, living in or within easy reach of a metropolis – because that's where all the best shops, clubs, gyms and hairdressers are. He might be officially gay, straight or bisexual, but this is utterly immaterial because he has clearly taken himself as his own love object and pleasure as his sexual preference. Particular professions, such as modeling, waiting tables, media, pop music and, nowadays, sport, seem to attract them but, truth be told, like male vanity products and herpes, they're pretty much everywhere.[38]

Metrosexuality is not unlike Buchbinder's description above of the new male, nor other descriptors of new masculinity: as an *inflection* of men's identity, it frequently involves a disavowal of misogyny and sexism, physical violence and aggression. But it does not mean that it – or men in general – have shaken off other, subtler elements of hegemonic masculinity such as competitiveness and the subordination of women and other men. Rather, it is a means of performing masculine identity with an increasingly heavy emphasis on consumption of clothing, fashion, grooming products, digital and mobile technologies and other goods and services coded as 'aesthetically sound', a part of the general shift in the performance of identity from any claim to an inner authenticity towards – although not wholly – the fluidity of consumption as the means by which performance is made in late contemporary capitalist cultures.[39] Through promotion and marketing, taste cultures, white collar employment and increasing financial affluence, the new masculinity – distinct from the more ruffian, larrikin or laddish masculinity of team sports – has dominance, competing with older forms of masculinity which no longer have broad social consent and the behaviours of which are no longer deemed acceptable within a widespread social, mediated and discursive framework.

In other words, what we have experienced in contemporary Western culture is a shift in what constitutes hegemonic masculinity as the forms of masculinity which, while dominating, are consented to socially across a range of institutions from the legal to the political to that found in entertainment media and thereby deemed socially acceptable. This is perhaps best exemplified by an example of a person who benefits significantly from hegemony within a masculinised political profession: former federal treasurer, Peter Costello who, in 2011, presented a relatively scathing attack on footballer masculinity in an opinion piece in *The Age*. Costello questioned the wisdom of having Australian Rules football players present inspirational and motivational speeches in schools, stating that any 'right-thinking parent would quake with fear to hear that footballers were coming to their daughter's school'.[40] What this indicates is a significant distinction between a man who, symbolically, represents transnational business masculinity – a formation which a number of masculinities scholars have argued is the contemporary, hegemonic form of masculinity in the globalising context[41] – and the form of hypermasculinity that is represented by (at least in Costello's view) the footballer that can lead into situations of scandal. That is, the masculinity reified within football culture in both on-field and off-field contexts is no longer commensurate with hegemonic masculinity, as the masculinity that finds *consent* in broader society. Football masculinity is *not* hegemonic, in that sense, even though it may well be argued to be *hypermasculine* in trait, style and effect where hypermasculinity is understood to be symbolically represented and fetishised through attempts at dominance via competitiveness and heroism,[42] muscled bodies, roughness and ruggedness[43] and testosterone-driven sexuality,[44] potentially (but not always) lacking in sexual self-control and capable of becoming violent.[45]

Where, then, does this hypermasculinity sit in terms of broader cultural understandings of masculinity and hegemony? It is possible to argue that the hypermasculinity of football culture is a *residue* from the social past that is reproduced and reinforced in the specific site of football culture (and other, similar realms such as the military). Cultural theorist Raymond Williams presents a useful way for understanding how there can be disconnect – albeit interrelated – between forms of masculinity operating in different contexts and spheres with his approach to cultural 'structures of feeling'. For Williams, culture is understood as a complete 'way of life' for an identifiable group of people,[46] although it is not static and unchanging, despite the common claims to, say, British culture or working class culture or ethnic culture; rather it is always a process.[47] Structures of feeling is a concept used to understand the ways in which a culture is operating at a particular historical moment, which includes common perceptions and values articulated in politics, art, media, textuality and forms of communication. Within the structures of feeling of a particular society is his articulation of 'dominant, residual and emergent' elements which operate as stresses and tensions in the context of culture as a persistent process of change. What is dominant in a culture is that which occurs through hegemonic processes. Contemporary late capitalism, neoliberalism, an ethic of work and – importantly for this study – cosmopolitan white-collar consumer masculinity can be considered elements of the dominant. The emergent refers to new meanings, values, practices and relationships that are continually being created – not as an isolated process for they emerge from within culture but may be oppositional to that which is dominant or hegemonic even though they are often incorporated into it as the most direct means by which dominance maintains itself against the visibility of alternative and oppositional elements.[48] The beginnings of Gay Liberation in the 1970s or the early appearance of the metrosexual male in the 1990s might be considered examples of emergence that have now been incorporated within contemporary neoliberalism.[49] Finally, there is the residual, which Williams describes as being usually somewhat distanced from the effective dominant culture, but at the same time also a part or version of it. That which is residual is formed and rightly belongs in the past, but remains *active* in the cultural process, and is comprised of 'certain experiences, meanings, and values which cannot be expressed or substantially verified in terms of the dominant culture, [but which] are nevertheless lived and practised on the basis of the residue – cultural as well as social – of some previous social and cultural institution or formation'.[50] In contemporary culture, this would include royalty and monarchy – not belonging within contemporary late capitalist cultures but remaining active in the cultural process. In the case of gender and gender relationality, I am arguing here that *footballer hypermasculinity* can also be understood as residual: neither hegemonic, as I have been arguing, nor part of dominant culture as it does not in itself and alone serve neoliberal consumption, but remaining active in the process by which gender is made sensible. This is not to suggest that on-field hypermasculinity does not have broad appeal for spectators – it does, in much the same way as the war film can appeal to those who would never conceive or be capable of going to war.

In this, Williams opens up an important critique of hegemony by articulating the point that no 'whole way of life' is without 'its dimension of struggle and confrontation between opposed *ways* of life'.[51] In the case of masculinity, not only is it to be understood that the cultural experience through which masculinity is performed and plays out is not determined by a singular discourse, but that the multiplicity of masculinities to which men's studies scholars later referred is one which operates not only through processes of hegemony and domination but through struggle and confrontation. Thus, when anti-feminist commentators and activists concerned that masculinity has lost its authenticity refer to a contemporary crisis in masculinity, what they are in fact doing is taking note of the ways in which that struggle and confrontation peaks at various historical moments and through a range of contexts. The struggle between the more dominant, hegemonic forms of masculinity produced through consumption in opposition to types of residual masculinity performed through violence, intensive homosociality or hypermasculine misbehaviour is one such site of struggle. When hypermasculinity is understood as a residue of older formations of masculinity that are no longer hegemonic, a struggle can be discerned that occurs not only between different masculinities but between the valuation of different symbolisms of masculinity. The struggle is, as I have indicated, one well represented by former

Treasurer Costello's attack on footballer masculinity. Similarly, in discussing how masculinities are represented and performed in different media sites, Darnell and Wilson analysed the depiction of hypermasculinity in men's talkback radio programs, labelling such hypermasculine articulations as 'unapologetic'[52] and thereby indicating that this residual gender performance has, indeed, a responsibility for apology – at least in terms of more recent articulations of masculine gender norms. A key argument here is that such contestation, confrontation and struggle between residual, dominant and (potentially) emergent formations of masculinity are not only the common experience of contemporary culture, but are a significant causal factor in situations that result in scandal.

Public interest in footballer scandals are just as much about the distinction between different forms of masculinity and are, in fact, an interest in the competitiveness of residual and dominant masculinities more so than in the individual case or details of the scandal. To consider this in practical terms, it is useful to look to former Carlton and Brisbane Lions player Brendan Fevola as an example. Fevola's body shape – considerably muscled, six feet three inches in height and weighing one hundred kilograms (according to a Wikipedia page), generally sporting either unkempt or very short-cropped hair, appearing partially unshaven – is an exemplary image of hypermasculinity, in contrast with the current hegemonic and dominating image of groomed masculinity. His on-field success with Carlton Football Club, which was not apparent early on but became notable by the middle of his career, help position him as hypermasculine through competitiveness and sporting achievement. His off-field behaviours likewise are representable through hypermasculinity, particularly his media appearances on *The Footy Show* utilising a less-than-cerebral demeanour, his involvement in a number of altercations and violent incidents including one in Ireland in 2006 in which he was described as having 'acted like a right thug and was very drunk',[53] and the misogyny apparent in his affair with Lara Bingle that led to the breakdown of his fourteen-month-long marriage,[54] followed by his involvement in the distribution of a nude photograph of Bingle,[55] and the fact he allegedly exposed himself to a woman in public[56] are all traits that align with the description and depiction of hypermasculine behaviour. But can Fevola be considered to represent forms of hegemonic masculinity? As a player who has owned a South Yarra restaurant, he is in a power position as an employer and, in terms of the aesthetics of restaurant and club ownership, this might align with some of the depictions of contemporary hegemonic identity. However, the fact remains that both during and subsequent to his football career, his hypermasculine behaviour has not accorded him a position of masculinity that is consensual with contemporary attitudes, thus not hegemonic. His hypermasculine behaviours may have been forgiven, and his position as a hypermasculine sportsperson may have protected him from criminal charges at times, but he does not represent, belong with or reinforce a masculinity that can be described as hegemonic or part of dominant culture. Rather, Fevola's performance of masculinity is residual, something which may have been considered and consented to in the past, but which does not position him broadly and generally with respect and accord. Indeed, his hypermasculinity has been described as out of step with broader social attitudes in a scathing attack on his character in an opinion piece by Rohan Connolly. Connolly refers to his behaviour as representing that of a relic from the past, with 'a mentality stuck firmly in the 1970s' but notes that Fevola has been blind 'to the march of time…the difference [being] that most of the other dinosaurs in football actually did play in the 1970s, and certainly aren't part of a modern, professional club'.[57] In other words, Fevola's hypermasculinity is characterised through *struggle* between residual and dominant/contemporary forms of masculine identity.

There are two additional points that need to be made about footballer masculinity. While I have been arguing that the culture of masculinity that is witnessed in Australian Rules football and the ways in which it is represented through contemporary media scandals is, in general, hypermasculine but not hegemonic, it should not be assumed at any stage that this represents the complete gendered identity of individual footballers. All identities are, as Judith Butler has argued, multiply-constituted,[58] incomplete and always in process. That is, all identities are constituted within ambiguities, incoherences and inconsistencies, but for the sake of coherence we are required to disavow, suppress or reinscribe in order to perform as an intelligible and coherent self.[59] This is no less the case for the masculinity element of identity or subjectivity than for any other aspect of the self, although there are two reasons why this is not often discussed. Firstly, there is the pedestrian idea that masculinity is derived from biological manhood and is thus fixed and innate − in this view, masculine behaviours and traits stem from the body, sex and chromosomes, and the view remains popular despite its simplicity. Secondly, in using the notion of hegemonic masculinity, scholars have not only equated hypermasculinity with hegemony, but see this hegemonic form as singular, monolithic and overriding of other elements of the self.[60] However, masculinity operates different and variably within football culture − it is always multiple. All subjects are complex (including, of course, the subjectivity of footballers) and this complexity means that different elements of masculinity will be performed in different contexts. The multiple masculinities embodied by a single, individual footballer-subject will include not only the forms of hypermasculinity endemic to contemporary team sports, but other performances occurring both within and outside of the site of football: the player who provides home care for an ageing parent, the player whose relationship with his wife is not one of active subordination, the player who works for anti-violence campaigns, the player who acknowledges his own vulnerability even within masculinity. Thus there is the point that football culture may be, on the one hand, a site of hypermasculinity that produces excessive and sometimes dangerous behaviours resulting in scandal as we saw with Fevola's range of off-field incidents and, on the other hand, an array of masculinities both within the subject in various contexts and across whole teams and the league itself is to make a political statement that is not intended to be an apologist testimonial for those excessive behaviours. Rather, it is to follow Richard Pringle's point that reductively conceiving of sportsmen through simplistic arguments about masculinity 'makes it difficult for researchers to recognize admirable or positive practices within male sporting cultures'.[61] The politics of this point is to say that there are indeed useful, disruptive and anti-hegemonic forms of masculinity that can be discerned in football culture, and attention should be paid to these as much as to the hypermasculine and homosocial aspects that tend to govern the drawing of footballers into scandal. Indeed, Fevola himself represents some of that complexity and the multifaceted forms of subjectivity: in early 2011, he revealed in an interview on *The Footy Show* that he has suffered from Attention Deficit Disorder and depression, has had a number of severe financial losses, various addictions and attempted suicide.[62] What this reveals is that, in contrast to his hypermasculine behaviour and the troubles and ultimately social marginalisation it has caused, there is a vulnerability that is not at all aligned with the sort of masculine demeanour we are used to seeing from him. These revelations, effectively, allowed a more complex representation of Fevola to emerge than is usually depicted among footballer hypermasculinity with its inviolability and toughness. Sadly, scandal narratives tend to represent the worst – not best – traits of masculine identity.

Secondly, it needs to be borne in mind that not all footballers actively express hypermasculinity but, much as the 'new masculine' that comes to dominate in broader contemporary culture through neoliberal consumption, many footballers – at least individually, less so in the homosocial grouping of the team – have come to articulate a metrosexual masculinity, likewise through consumption. David Beckham has long been considered the epitome of metrosexuality in European soccer, although not all commentators and scholars agree that similar examples are found in Australian team sports.[63] Others have, however, argued that this shift is seen locally and, indeed, physically, with Filiault and Drummond making the point that among footballers there is increasing evidence of a toned, smooth, bodily aesthetic,[64] in contrast to the beefier, rougher, less-groomed embodiment of footballers that was better witnessed two or more decades ago. Warwick Capper, with the Sydney Swans and Brisbane Bears in the 1980s, was an early example and might be considered a forerunner. At the same time as we see an increasing masculinity produced among footballers through conspicuous consumption, it should also be remembered that footballers themselves are a commodity that is consumed. This consumption ranges from the ways in which gossip magazines and websites foster the consumption of personal lives and rumours about individual players to the consumption of the game to the fact that footballers are increasingly under the gaze of others – including a male–male consumptional gaze[65] – and are increasingly aware of it, hence responding through forms of metrosexuality. Again, this is not to suggest that football teams of the culture of the AFL itself are no longer the site of hypermasculinity for, as I will argue in the next chapter, this is clearly apparent when team members act in concert in off-field sexual behaviour including in group sexual assaults. But it is to point out that in discussing masculinity as the 'problem' of football culture, one needs to acknowledge the sheer complexity of the ideas behind masculinity, of the ways in which masculinity is performed in complex ways by all subjects, to avoid stereotyping all footballers, and finally to overcome the myth that footballers represent a dominant form of masculinity across all society.

National Heroes and the Nation

I would like to turn now to a different but related topic in how the framework for scandals comes about for Australian Rules footballers: the role of the footballer as local, community and especially national hero. Sports in general have maintained a particularly crucial role in the formation and maintenance of a sense of national identity. The place of team sports in the nation is extended and maintained by national media coverage – including both the regular broadcast of competition and the mass audience spectatorship of major games such as premiership grand finals which gain significantly high participation through viewing and discussion as 'a major national event'.[66] Much of what has been described as the corporate nationalism of contemporary sports was reinvigorated in Australia in the early 1980s subsequent to a perceived drop in the role of sports as contributing to the national image and character during the 1970s.[67] The significance of sport to the Australian nation is perhaps best represented by the marketing chant 'C'mon Aussie, C'mon' used in selling Australian cricket in particular.

The functioning of contemporary sport organisations and governance bodies contribute significantly to the continued *nationalisation* of sport in Australia, and thereby to the production of the sportsplayer as national hero. Riding on the national popularity of Australian Rules football and its role in national identity and pride, the Victorian Football League, which was first established in 1896, was effectively able to nationalise Australian Rules football with itself as the central 'node' in an interstate league. This was not, of course, a shift whereby the AFL actively comes to usurp a central role as an Australian sport in the nation contra the wishes of the broader population, but one brought about by a number of cultural changes in Australia at the time, including the increasing capacity of media to broadcast and report upon Victorian football events across the country. Indeed, I recall well as a child in the 1970s and 1980s in Perth that while most of us were aware of the VFL teams and the successes of each, Western Australian Football League (WAFL) dominated discussions and rivalries over sport. This was not a specific Western Australian pride or an attempt to differentiate between Perth and an East Coast (Victorian) sporting environment; rather it was the effect of Australian regionalism produced through distance and size of the land mass, as well as the intellectual and affective relations these produce. However, from 1980, the VFL match of the day was being broadcast across the nation, increasing the interest in all states in Victorian football. This permitted the VFL to respond to the growing national interest with plans to expand the league on a national scale, occurring subsequent to the appointment of Ross Oakley as VFL chief executive in 1986. With South Melbourne's move to Sydney and the formation of the Sydney Swans in 1982, the precedent was set for interstate clubs to be formed, and this allowed West Coast Eagles and Brisbane Bears to be founded in 1986 and permitted to join the league on payment of costly licences, with both beginning play from 1987. Adelaide followed in 1991, Fremantle Dockers in 1996, Port Adelaide in 1997 and most recently, in 2011, the Gold Coast Suns. This influx of interstate teams resulted in the push to rename the league the Australian Football League in 1990, the final act in what had been a dramatic shift in the *place* of Australian Rules across the 1980s from a suburban competition to a national one with a combined multi-million dollar turnover.[68]

This shift, of course, impacted significantly on the state-based suburban performance of Australian Rules football. The VFL name was adopted by the former rival Victorian Football Association

(VFA) in 1990, with their games broadcast on ABC during a period in which the national Seven Network had exclusive AFL broadcast rights. Throughout much of the 1990s, the former VFA and now VFL clubs began a process of alignment and mutuality with AFL clubs, improving their financial viability, attracting AFL fans and providing an additional source for AFL player drafts. In Western Australia, interest in AFL and the new West Coast Eagles team competed for spectator interest with WAFL, and by the mid-1990s it was culturally understood that WAFL was a second-tier *regional/state* competition in contrast to the now clearly *national* AFL competition. Similarly, the South Australian National Football League (SANFL) suffered throughout the 1980s with high-performing players shifting to VFL clubs. With match attendance dropping throughout the 1990s, SANFL too was no longer the premier football event in South Australia. In 2008 there were reported claims the AFL was encouraging SANFL to change its name and drop the 'national' from its title,[69] indicating the extent to which AFL has become *the* central Australian Rules football competition in the Australian nation. Name changes that reflect the shifting relationship between Australian Rules football and the nation have not been uncommon. For example, the less-celebrated Queensland Australian Football League, which has been the Queensland Football League (1903–1927), the Queensland Australian National Football League (1927–1964), dropping the 'national' in 1964 to become the Queensland Australian Football League until 1996. Then the Queensland State Football League from 1997 to 1999, reflecting AFL rules as the AFL Queensland State League from 2000 until 2008, and finally reverting to the Queensland Australian Football League from 2009, participating from 2011 in the North East Australian Football League along with AFL Canberra.

With the AFL centralising Australian Rules football in practice and code, the game and its participants and stakeholders become centralised in the national imaginary, leading the way for high-potential or high-achieving players to shift from being local community heroes to heroes on a national scale who support and reinforce the nationalism of the nation. This occurs, of course, in the context of international sports such as the Olympics in which nations compete with each other,[70] but this is no less the case with sports that are played competitively wholly within the nation. In the nineteenth century emergence of modern sport in Europe, players and participants had close links with local communities, and were seen to represent communities specifically as members of teams (not necessarily as individuals), embodying urban and suburban population groupings, with strong ties between teams and local communities.[71] Where broadcast media, corporatisation on a national scale, codification of rules and the de-regionalisation of particular sporting codes centralises a sport within the nation, the local sportsplayers' community ties gain another layer, positioning the team and its constituents simultaneously to be read through discourses of national heroism. They are the product not of being 'taken up' by the nation, but a tool of nationalism that builds, reinforces and maintains a sense of national identity.

For Benedict Anderson, the nation itself is *imagined* into being as a political community and unity – that is, there is no fixed 'object' that is the nation on which a national identity is over-written. It is imagined as a community (often a masculinised one) through the myth that the nation is the site of a deep, horizontal comradeship and fraternity.[72] Certain elements that make the Australian national identity plausible – although never uncontested – operate simultaneously to produce the sportsplayer as national hero. For example, the ceremonial reverence of that other masculine figure, the *unknown soldier* operates to produce an unnamed hero of the nation as a quasi-religious figure available for the discursive centralisation of the nation as an embodied entity in competition with other nations and requiring defence from the external.[73] A shared language too is part of what constructs a nation,[74] but this is not limited to scripted or spoken language but to cultural symbols and shared understanding of them. In the case of Australian Rules football, this is the *shared language of spectatorship*, the generally friendly rivalry between spectators of different teams, the general population's awareness of the rules of the game and the achievements of various teams. Finally, the internal competitiveness that is part of the Australian national identity, not oppositional to but occasionally juxtaposing national fraternity and comradeship, plays into the situation that makes sporting *competition* between teams the site from which the team sports hero emerges.[75] The sporting hero is thus fabricated from within a context in which sports represents particular values that are central to the nation and to nationalism.

Within the construction of the Australian national imaginary are a number of persistent figures that operate, much in line with being a cultural residue from the past, as folk heroes. These are military officers, surf lifesavers, certain athletes in non-contact sports such as marathon runner Robert de Castella[76] and cyclist and *Tour de France* winner Cadel Evans, in addition to the Australian Rules footballer. National heroes are not individual 'names' as such but *figures* – stereotypes that work linguistically and culturally to link a set of 'expected behaviours' to an 'identity category'.[77] The stereotype of the national sporting hero is, in part, a masculine one, the outcome of the fact that masculinity has for more than two centuries played a central role in the construction and imagination of the contemporary Western nation, whether that be the United States of America, the United Kingdom or Australia.[78] Riding off the fetishisation of hypermasculinity throughout much of twentieth century the footballer in general and not necessarily as an individual is accorded the role of masculine local, community and national hero, although not all sporting heroes are necessarily men – Cathy Freeman is a good example of a woman who gained national hero status after her wins in various late-1990s championships and the Sydney 2000 Olympics. The production of any sporting hero occurs through historical narratives emerging from discourses of the past by which acts of commemoration accord the figure or type of hero a particular status.[79]

Although national heroism and the traditional links between sports and communities has usually been built around teams, for a number of reasons which I will outline later below, the sports hero has been more recently individualised, producing national heroes as sportsplayers in their own singularity rather than as relatively nameless figures within the relationality of the team, code, sports or nation itself. Part of that product has been the stereotypical signification of the national hero through a discourse of Australian 'larrikinism' which, as Elspeth Probyn has noted, emerges through a particular history of Australian masculinity and has become endemically reiterated in the context of sports media.[80] As a white, Anglo-Saxon form of 'being Australian',[81] it is not dissimilar from sportsplayer laddishness – a British signification, but in this case formed through historical discourses of masculinity and sports in the specific Australian context. The larrikin has been described as being marked by a flaunting sexuality, wittiness, willing engagement in physical and verbal violence, licence to exceed conventions, charisma, roughness, romantic attachments to the working class and a commitment to drinking alcohol in public spaces.[82] It is, as Turner and Edmunds have pointed out, part of a populist ethos in which one disavows elite, upper-class, overly sophisticated or highbrow tastes and behaviours.[83] As an iconic image of Australianness, perhaps best remembered in Paul Hogan's depiction of masculinity in the 1986 film *Crocodile Dundee,* but also built on the everyday Australian stories of the diggers of the First World War and soldiers of the Second World War and even earlier depictions of men on the 'colonial' Australian frontier, it remains in the public imaginary a figure of *heroism*: badly behaved but not criminal, tough yet capable of folk-like practical ingenuity, irreverent and anti-authoritarian but not an outright revolutionary, mischievous but performing acts which usually can be forgiven. In the case of footballer identity, the portrayal of footballers as irreverent, homosocial, forgivable and mischief-making larrikins situates the 'character' at the centre of one significant and persistently reinforced discourse of Australian national identity. Connolly has remarked that larrikinism has been a particular trait of Brendan Fevola, particularly in his media performances on *The Footy Show*. He notes that what some will read as 'yobbo' behaviour is understood by others as that of a 'loveable larrikin' harking from a time when 'misogyny and public indecency was "being a lad"'.[84] It is the fact that much of Fevola's misbehaviour resulting in persistent scandal and negative reporting was available to be read through a discourse of larrikinism through which he was able to remain not only a football hero but a national hero for such a long period. In combination with sporting achievement as well as the centrality of sport in the national imaginary, then, the individualised footballer becomes more firmly representable as an Australian national hero, thereby receiving spectacular, individualised media coverage and being available for the sort of reporting that can result in scandal. The larrikinism of footballer masculinity becomes, however, not the focal point of scandal but scandal's *excuse*. Again, this is something that is witnessed in the fact that despite a series of drunken brawls, public violence and other misdemeanours, Fevola avoided for a long time any police charges (although most of us who are not national football heroes recognised through Australian larrikinism would be charged for the same offences). While footballer masculinity might be shifting towards metrosexual or softer masculinities in representation and self-presentation off-field, this softer, non-nationalistic masculinity is not excluded from national discourses of manly heroism but incorporated, such that off-field sports scandal becomes the mechanism through which the blurred areas between hard and soft masculinities are policed.

From Hero to Celebrity

In order to appreciate the cultural context in which footballer scandals become both thinkable and broadly excusable, a third area involving the production of sports and footballer celebrity needs to be unpacked. Such celebrity arguably emerges in the context of the increasing professionalisation of Australian Rules football and within a media management framework in which both media and the AFL public relations machinery are, on the one hand, antagonistic in the event of scandal but, on the other and more broadly, operate for mutual benefit through the promotional potential of celebrity stories. The footballer as celebrity is somewhat different from the perception of the footballer as community or national hero, particularly in terms of the media separation of footballers into individual personages outside the context of the team which is more properly found in the discourse of heroism. However, the construction of footballers as celebrities does contribute to the production of sportsplayers as individual heroes, but not through the traditional larrikin status. In arguing that footballers have adopted a celebrity style of off-field presentation and representation is not intended to imply that individual footballers consciously and actively seek to *be* celebrities. Some do, of course, and we might include Jason Akermanis among those, given the outspoken and often non-endorsed views he has expressed in media interviews and newspaper columns which are sometimes shamelessly or unthinkingly controversial, and more likely than not designed to spiral into further media coverage – a sort of celebrity trouble-making that has, ultimately, impacted negatively on his sporting career but kept him known-for-being-known. However, other footballers who have 'become' celebrities are frequently positioned to be so as a result of the ways in which Australian Rules football under the governance of the AFL operates, in conjunction with media interest in the personal, the private and the individual.

The idea of celebrity is not new, but it is only relatively recently and in accord with the increasing massification of media that we see the rise of the notion of the celebrity as a person who has been positioned or is viewed to possess the quality of being able to attract attention.[85] Operating through the contemporary media depiction of spectacle, celebrities 'exist to act out various styles of living and viewing society – unfettered, free to express themselves *globally*'.[86] What is well-recognised about any celebrity today is that they are not simply well-known or recognisable, but are a product of a cultural industry that fabricates the interchange-ability of celebrities and with the capability of producing, often instantly, more persons as celebrities through communication strategy, attention and focus.[87] Scholars have noted that celebrity culture reflects a cultural shift from the valuation of *character* and *achievement* to that of *personality* (a fabrication, usually, in itself) and that celebrities are often problematically promoted as role models while not being necessarily figures of authority.[88] In the case of footballers who are produced through media focus and attention as individual celebrities, the celebrity status is accorded them by virtue of being a footballer, not necessarily by being a footballer of great achievement. That is why a rookie recruit can be as much a celebrity as a long-term player or Brownlow medallist in the final stages of an illustrious career.

It is the reification of the visual image that makes possible what is clearly a shift from the heroic national fame to celebrity among sportsplayers.[89] The capacity of spectators to watch from home with increasingly better close-ups of play, post-match interviews with footballers, the growth of television programs about football and the ways in which gossip magazines have increasingly focused on sportsplayers in the same way as they have film and television stars has been a significant factor on the wholesale commodification of sportsplayers. Sports celebrity began with a small handful of international significant 'names' such as those of Michael Jordan, Tiger Woods and David Beckham,[90] but there is some clear evidence that all footballers are available for the same process of commodification through initially becoming known through sports journalism and football reporting. Chris Rojek suggested four additional reasons for the rise of sportsplayer celebrity, these being (1) the growth of satellite television since the 1980s; (2) the increased concern with health and fitness in popular culture which has benefited sports by increasing the focus on healthy activities; (3) the adoption of sportsplayers as a counter to the so-called crisis in masculinity, and (4) the increasing economic power of the sports sector through sponsorship, prize money and high salaries.[91] What is perhaps most interesting about these four reasons in addition to the increased visualisation of football is the fact that none of them imply that players themselves have been *responsible* for the situation in which they are produced as celebrities. While some players may take advantage of the cultural, economic and communicative opportunities that come from celebrity status, the fact remains that in many cases players do not have agency over this process, and that does open some ethical questions as to whether or not players should be considered solely accountable for some of the problems that arise as a result of being figured as celebrities (a point I take up again in later chapters).

While it would be common sense to suggest that media industries act to commodify football players, seeing them as a basic raw resource that can be refined, fabricated, manufactured and sold to audiences as celebrity, this would be a significant oversimplification. Rather, there are two factors in addition to media sourcing that have contributed to the shift from national hero and the community location of the team to individualised celebrity that results in the commodification of footballers in spectacle and scandal. The first of these is the *professionalisation* of contemporary sports. Sports in general have evolved from play and from a nineteenth century participatory and routinised orientation to an establishment that, as Frey and Etizen have suggested 'resembles a corporate form guided by the principles of commercialism and entertainment'.[92] Professionalisation has produced a situation in which elite AFL footballers are now professional footballers as opposed to earlier models of participation that were amateur, that involved players who had other careers or at least ambitions for later careers, and where play was about dedication to a team and athletic prowess rather than salary and contract. This contributes to celebrity status in several ways. Firstly, players can expect greater media scrutiny than amateurs, as membership of an AFL team is now a high-profile 'job', not an act of partaking within a spirit of community. Secondly, because so much depends for the team and the spectators on contracting the right players, football culture becomes further individualised as attention is focused on the capacities and abilities of individual players to fulfil that contract (within, of course, the context of teamwork), again allowing greater attention on the player and greater media attention on the elements of that player's private, social and non-sporting life that *might* impact on ability. Finally, professionalisation of Australian Rules football has meant that there is always some suspicion that the values of players may have shifted 'from those based on self-development and satisfaction to those of entertainment and self-interest'.[93] Again, this increases the value in surveillance and scrutiny, in much the same way that politicians (another, albeit distinct, form of celebrity) are surveiled for the possibility that self-interest might govern intent and outweigh contribution. Through professionalisation, then, the celebrity footballer is further opened for media scrutiny which then results in the fact that non-sporting and off-field activities are stumbled upon and can result in the stories that spiral into the spectacle of scandal.

Correlative with the professionalisation of sports is the professional 'other work' of the sportsplayer. While various leagues and teams place some restrictions on what a player can do and say in public, particularly when the opportunity to do or say these things stems from being part of that league or team, the 'work' of being a footballer is the work of performing as a celebrity beyond the actual activities of the game – a task undertaken well by players who maintain themselves in the public spotlight through scandal, but not one in which we can say is well-achieved if part of that work is to be a role model. This work allows player celebrity to extend beyond the specific sport itself and the act of being a sportsplayer, and for many it is the process of product endorsement in advertising campaigns that not only becomes a result of celebrity but contributes to the ongoing increase of publicity that further cements celebrity status.[94]

The second element that promotes the celebrification of footballers is the structural arrangement of contemporary football culture itself. By this, I am referring again to the governing body of Australian Rules football that is the AFL, operating as with other similar bodies in other sports as a corporate organisation[95] and, in this case, with a notably high-paid and high-profile chief executive. Although, as I have been arguing, there is a matrix of links between the AFL as a governing organisation and, on the one hand, the production and protection of an older, residual form of (hyper)masculinity and, on the other hand, the centralisation of football within Australian national identity and pride, at the same time the AFL operates as an organisation within a neoliberalist framework which participates in the construction of celebrity. Neoliberalism is the contemporary governing arrangement in Western countries, operating as an organising force for governance that works by deploying power mechanisms of the biopolitical and security, allowing the measurement, rating and commodification of all that can be commodified. In Foucault's work, there are two contemporary forms of power at play, both dovetailing into each other and both at work for economic rationalisation and the production of the economic man. The first, slightly older form is discipline, which is connected with but often exceeds institutions. It is a mechanism of power enacted through surveillance and regimentation of the body and focusing on individualisation and normalisation as the primary outcomes.[96] This is witnessed in the production of the footballer *as* a footballer – discipline, training, the surveillance of the body, the checks and assurances on the peak fitness of the body, including through drug testing.

The other form of power operates at a broader social level, and this is what Foucault referred to as the biopolitical and sometimes as security or national interest.[97] It is a form or 'technology' of power that addresses whole populations through regulatory practices that seek to ensure an economic, cultural and political status quo in order to aid the free enterprise culture of neoliberal society. As Foucault put it in his 1975–76 lectures at the *Collège de France*, like

> disciplinary mechanisms, these mechanisms are designed to maximize and extract forces, but they work in very different ways. Unlike disciplines, they no longer train individuals by working at the level of the body itself…It is therefore not a matter of taking the individual at the level of individuality but, on the contrary, of using overall mechanisms and acting in such a way as to achieve overall states of equilibration or regularity.[98]

Both operating alongside with and distinguishing itself from the power formation of disciplinarity expressed through surveillance, supervision, inspections and the production of docile bodies,[99] biopolitics governs through investigation, assessment and examination at the level of the demographic and statistical; it intervenes and regulates where necessary for equilibrium and balance and social modification thereby producing a subject which is both in flux, flexible, and available for commodification.[100] Biopolitical power is thus a framework for the production of particular identities that occurs in ways different from disciplinarity's normalisation while operating alongside it.

As we know from Foucault's articulation of the biopolitical and his divergences into governance and the constitution of both the state and the self, the biopolitical framework constitutes subjects who will exist as good economic citizens for the ends of neo-liberalism; free citizens who engage in the market and act as entrepreneurs of the self.[101] This is a formation of the subject who is defined through self-interest and who, in the economic theory beginning in the eighteenth century and grounding today's neoliberalism, is seen to have actions that have a multiplying and beneficial value through the intensification of that self-interest.[102] That is, the application of economist rationality to the very idea of the human subject whose activities are for the benefit of the market. For Foucault, the market comes to act not only as a free corollary within governance, but as a regime of truth which co-ordinates a whole set of practices establishing a particular type of reality.[103] While the AFL does not perform all such biopolitical functions of governance itself, its operating strategy is one which fits within neoliberalism, capitalising on the game, producing it and its players as commodities to be 'sold on' to spectators, advertisers, endorsers and media broadcast for a fee. Indeed, its mission is that of most contemporary sports governing bodies being to manage, regulate and promote sport as a commodity by re-packaging play and players' lives as spectacle.[104] Turning football and footballers into that which serves neoliberal ends is not necessarily a fully conscious, deliberate act, but the result of economic and cultural factors operating both nationally and globally as the context in which Australian Rules football operates as a contemporary public cultural institution. It is thus part of what Rojek has referred to as 'the sports industry' which, he argues, requires the idealisation of sports celebrities as the means by which the sport can be sold into popular culture.[105] This is not to suggest that the AFL or individual clubs are themselves solely responsible for the celebrification of sportsplayers, because, at the same time and acting like so many other corporations, they seek to ensure that Australian Rules is promoted, and protected not as a *game* but as a *brand*.[106] In this, they further make use of disciplinary processes of normalisation to curtail the celebrity status of footballers and ensure that the brand is not damaged by the fame and focus given to footballers outside of the context of play. In order to do so, the public relations machinery, its promotion of footballers publicly, and its encouragement of footballers into particular communitarian roles and role-modelling is deployed – not for the benefit of the community but for the ends of financial frames through which sport is a late capitalist commodity. However, by converting players from a raw resource into a commodity that has individual celebrity status, this is not always well-controlled.

Where footballers are commodified through celebrity status, it is not solely about their on-field activities. Rather, celebrity is utilised in media as a means by which to commodify a fabricated image of the whole subject – private life, social activities, relationships, opinions and political views. These become the topic of media reports, and the means by which celebrity status contributes to the situation of footballer scandal. Celebrities serve as a focal point for gossip and information exchange,[107] and much of that information exchange is between the reasonably private and the public. Scandal works through spectacle around the private, the secret or the hidden, usually with claims or evidence (not always unexpected) that marks the subject of scandal as having behaved in a manner considered in some way deviant. The question of privacy is central to the ways in which spectacle operates in news media. Stories of deviancy written through a mode of spectacle operate as forms of entertainment. Entertainment, of course, is only marginally legitimated as an ethical reason for a breach of privacy, on the basis that 'the public is interested in knowing – not that there is a public interest in knowing, but just that most people would like to know and would derive some pleasure from knowing'.[108] However, it is the case that newsworthiness is increasingly justified by entertainment value.[109] The spectatorship and, indeed, consumption of the commodified footballer celebrity within the forms of spectacle and scandal can thus be understood as being about readers' pleasure, rather than information. At the same time, the revelation of private matters is an important element in journalistic practice which, at an ethical level, will often reveal private information that has afforded an individual personal power as part of a Power Transfer from the private person to the public.[110] Usually, a process of Power Transfer operates as an ethical justification for journalism where revealing information about a protected official such as a politician or a senior executive helps to redress the power imbalance, for example, where such a person has failed to disclose a conflict of interest or will benefit personally from a public act. However, sports celebrities are not such persons and usually do not wield power in the traditional, governmental or executive sense. While the revelation of off-field activities and behaviours performed by footballers is news and is in the public interest – for example, participation in a group sexual assault – the framework through which such scandals are revealed and read is one in which players' personal or private activities as opposed to their public, work or sporting activities are revealed as part of the ongoing process of commodifying that whole person.

Conclusion

Having worked through the three areas that situate footballer scandal – masculinity, national heroism, and celebrity status – it is important finally to ask what is scandal in the context of the discourses which produce the footballer as subject. It is too simplistic to suggest that scandal emerges because media set upon footballers' public, private and social lives and convert information into a story; too simplistic because for that to work there needs to be an audience interest in such stories. As I have been arguing, that broad popular interest in footballer's lives, behaviours, attitudes, interests, mess–ups and mischief arises through a combination of three cultural elements: firstly, the questions around footballer masculinity and the perception of a crisis in masculinity whereby footballers are seen to be part of that crisis – sometimes too hypermasculine, at other times felt to be representing an authentic, traditional masculinity. For scandal, it does not matter what sort of masculinity is really being performed – issues related to masculinity such as violence, risk-taking and sexuality only come to matter to a broader culture as a result of the framework of shifting concerns around masculinity and where footballers might, today, fit in with those shifts. Ultimately, contemporary footballer identity is built from uneasy relationships between masculinity, community or national hero and celebrity. The older forms of hypermasculinity and national heroism became transformed as part of a 'package' of the promotion of footballers as spectacle. But this merging of elements in the package is neither seamless nor coherent, hence the opportunity for scandal to arise when the disjunctures arise between, say, hypermasculine behaviours off-field and celebrity expectations.

The role of footballers as national heroes produces an increased focus on the footballer; in Australia, this is at least in part the result of the deliberate nationalisation of Australian Rules. Finally, the production of sportsplayers as celebrities opens the media pathway for the incorporation of footballers' lives as a commodity utilised to sell media time. This occurs predominantly through professionalisation and the shift in governing bodies such as the AFL from a role of game management and regulation to one of promotion, public relations and brand management. Indeed, it is the neoliberal framework in which the AFL operates that unwittingly encourages the marketing not only of players, but the commodification of, on the one hand, the older forms of masculinity I have been discussing and, on the other, the national heroism with its conservative but recognisable production of football culture through larrikinism. While both of these are residues from a cultural past that do not fit neatly into contemporary neoliberal discourses, such residual cultural elements remain available as an 'expected' performance for commodification.

When one considers the ways in which the contemporary neoliberal framework that allows and encourages the sports governance machinery to commodify football players and the residues of hypermasculinity and national heroism into packaged celebrities, despite strategies for limitations, it becomes necessary to ask whether Fevola can be held responsible and accountable in terms of the scandals that marked much of his career. Given the ways in which celebrities' private lives become available for media consumption in ways which did not affect the footballer of the past as 'hero', it is possible to argue that there is absolutely no public benefit to some of the transfer of information from Fevola's private life. For example, the breakdown of his marriage after his affair with Lara Bingle, the distribution of the Bingle photograph and many of the issues around his gambling are interesting and sometimes intriguing to read. But are they of value to the public in regard to Fevola's status as either a national hero or as a footballer? These incidents are not. In that sense, one does need to ask if the AFL governance and the Brisbane Lions themselves bear some responsibility *not* for the scandals or for Fevola's off-field behaviour, but for the *situation* in which it becomes thinkable and plausible that Fevola is a resource available to media for scandal reporting. The Lions did not view themselves as having a responsibility, particularly in implying in regard to Fevola's problems that 'the club is not a rehabilitation facility'[111] The situation that is produced, then, is one in which scandal emerges through the production and consumption of information about footballers, but this is usually something over which footballers themselves, individually and even collectively in teams, have no control. Rather, it is often an unfortunate cultural condition that governs how players are perceived today. At the same time, and as I will go on to show in later chapters, the revelations through scandals are not necessarily a bad thing, for they do draw attention to irresponsible and sometimes harmful behaviour, and to some very important ethical questions over responsibility and accountability.

3

Bad Bonds: Group Sexual Assault, Gender Relations and Group Identity

Recently men's sports in Australia and in particular elite-level team sports have been a subject of considerable public scrutiny around the sexual behaviour of players, team members and stakeholders towards women. A series of instances of sexual violence against women has put in doubt the reputation of masculine team sports, casting such sports as a site of dangerous risk-taking, criminal irresponsibility and disrespect for the rights of others.[1] These scandalous events are marked by sexual engagement that is group-based, involves multiple team players and occasionally players from more than one club, and forms of identity and identification that encourage a suspension of ethical behaviour towards women as football's 'external other'. This has included cases such as accusations of sexual assault by members of the Australian Rules team St Kilda Saints;[2] a Montmorency Football Club member involved in an alleged gang rape in October 2009;[3] and the more recent scandal involving Andrew

Lovett and claims made of non-consensual sex occurring with a woman during a party at another player's home. Scandals of this nature also include the 'St Kilda Schoolgirl' case discussed in chapter one, particularly in terms of the ways in which the young woman at the centre of events stated she was pregnant to one player, passed around among others and finally involved with the players' manager, former footballer Ricky Nixon. The response of the codes, sponsors and governments has increasingly been to condemn such actions by team players, although only when specific fault can be determined and the public profile of the sport is in question,[4] and sometimes to institute or remind the public of policies and programs intended to counter systemic value systems regarding masculine behaviours which encourage group and individual violence. However, given the frequency and veracity of media scandals involving Australian Rules football, it is clear that policies designed to mitigate scandal are having limited effect in changing the institutional and cultural practice of this brand of masculinity which supports and protects sexual and violent misbehaviour of men in teams.

Ethics of sexuality and sexual violence are strongly linked with sports, although this is by no means ahistorical. In addressing ancient Greek and Hellenistic attitudes to sexuality, Foucault pointed out that it was 'well known that one cannot win a contest at Olympia unless one has led a particularly chaste life'.[5] Received wisdom throughout much of the twentieth century was that sexual activity prior to a sporting match impaired performance, despite the lack of physiological evidence that sex in the days before a sporting event has any impact on athletic ability.[6] Given the number and profile of sex scandals over the past decade in Australian masculine team sports, it would appear celibacy and abstinence are not a part of the ethical order of contemporary team sporting culture; rather there is a notable tension between the practice of off-field masculine group behaviour and the discourse which upholds the place and distinction of masculine sportsmen within nationalist cultures. This tension presents several opportunities to reconsider how an ethics of vulnerability and an approach to masculine 'localised' group and institutional sexual (mis)behaviour can be developed with a view towards intervention, prevention and institutional/cultural change. This chapter looks at some of the ways in which scandals around group sex and sexual assault play out and highlight possibilities towards cultural change through nuanced approaches to understanding group identity behaviour and ethics.

I will begin with a brief overview of some Australian Rules sex scandals to show how public sphere discourse of group sexual violence is marked by continuities in public sphere debate which polarise to prevent a critical engagement or intervention. Secondly, this chapter draws on a reading of Judith Butler's theories of performativity in order to develop a means by which better to understand the *group identity* of football teams and how these operate differently from individual subjectivity in the context of team-player off-field bonding that can, in extreme instances, lead to sexual assault. Finally, drawing again on Judith Butler's more recent work on developing an ethics of non-violence that is derived from her readings into vulnerability, the precarity of bodies and recognition of the other, I will argue that sportsplayers are, indeed, well-placed to recognise the vulnerability of women complainants in a sexual assault scandal through their own on-field vulnerabilities to loss, shame and injury, thereby recommending some possibilities for new approaches to policies, intervention and prevention of masculine group sexual violence. However, as I will show, the particular site of the group sexual encounter or the team bond through which women are objectified, passed around and made use of sexually by more than one player indicates some of the ways in which a *group subjectivity* suspends or counters the ethics by which players, acting individually, typically govern themselves. Utilising Butler's work as an approach to furthering the understanding of sexual violence has significant relevance for football sex scandals, given her earlier work points to the discursive constitution of gendered identities in terms of categories and norms that are performed over time, while in her more recent work she has elaborated an ethics of non-violence that operates within a context of subjectivity and recognition.

Of the Australian Rules footballer scandals I have been studying, those related to sexual assault, group sexuality, the objectification of women or the assumption that women can and should be shared sexually among players are the more alarming, particularly because there is an identifiable 'other' to whom violence is done. This may not necessarily be the physical violence of forced sex or rape (although clearly it sometimes is), but the violence of coercion into sex with single or multiple players and the many violences which occur subsequent to the act, such as the injury of condemnation, the unwillingness to hear the woman's story, or allowing the common and widespread social response that the woman who became involved with a group of footballers at a party 'deserved it'. As importantly, the issue of group violence against women and group-based sexual assault and coercion are significant when they emerge as scandal, partly because scandal itself may not necessarily operate to mitigate the reproduction of the behaviour by others outside football culture. Notable is the fact that there has been an increase in group sexual assault and group rape by young men under the age of twenty-one years in the broader population. Co-offending in sexual assault has been reported as more prevalent among juvenile than adult offenders, with most gang rapists in their late teens or early twenties when convicted,[7] and some indication that the mean age of offenders has dropped from about twenty-two years prior to the 1980s to between eighteen and nineteen years in the period 1990–2001.[8] Such cases have included a fifteen-year-old schoolgirl in California gang-raped over a period of two hours by several of her classmates after a school dance, while passers-by and others from the dance were aware and failed to report to security or authority figures just inside the school.[9] In Australia, this has recently included charges against a group of four boys aged eleven, twelve, thirteen and fourteen who sexually assaulted six women (aged sixteen to sixty-seven) over a forty-eight hour period.[10] Risks for young women of being gang-raped by recently graduated school boys after drinking at 'schoolies' events (post-secondary graduation celebratory trips) became known to be considerably high during the late 2000s.[11] While such juvenile offences occur in circumstances markedly different from those of elite, celebrity adult sporting teams, the involvement of footballers under the age of eighteen is also notable. For example, the Montmorency Football Club scandal in which up to thirty players were accused of gang-raping an eighteen-year-old woman during an end-of-season football trip included one seventeen-year-old who had to be scheduled for trial in the Children's Court,[12] although charges were eventually withdrawn. What these alarming cases point to is that the ethical problem is not limited to the violence done unto the individual woman in a football group sex scandal, but the ways in which it may sponsor younger persons to behave similarly and perpetrate correspondingly. Whether or not Australian Rules football does, in fact, reproduce or foster group sexual assaults among much younger persons is currently unknown, but would be an important area for further research. Thus, while looking at the broad cases drawing on professional, celebrity and elite-level Australian Rules football group sexual assault scandals, the aim is to begin to develop ways of thinking that can also be applied to the significant issue of group sexual assault in general, including those that occur in contexts where high-profile media targeting does not normally act as a potential safeguard to prevent the rape of young women.

Australian Rules, Group Sex and Media Scandals

The Australian Football League (AFL) has been instrumental in formulating and managing programs of violence prevention and the promotion of good off-field conduct. The AFL's *Respect and Responsibility* initiative, launched in 2005, provides an education program for all AFL club players and new draftees. The National Rugby League (NRL) has similarly initiated education models designed to address violence against women through their *Playing by the Rules* program. Other Australian rules organisations including state-based leagues and community football leagues have developed codes-of-conduct to address on-field and game behaviour, although there has been less emphasis on responding to off-field (mis)behaviour among school-aged, community and non-professional football teams. This is due, in part, to the lower risk of media attention towards misbehaviours among non-celebrity players, although the risk to women, bystanders, others and ultimately to the players, teams and code stakeholders remains the same. However, given the ongoing frequency and veracity of media scandals among elite Australian Rules football players in Australia over the past decade, there is some question as to the extent to which such policies are producing genuine institutional and cultural change in terms of gender relationality and protection of vulnerable others during sports teams' on-tour and off-field bonding social activities.

Scandals of this sort are produced through a combination of sex and spectacle. The celebrity formation of footballer identity effectively 'authorises' news media conventions to disseminate information gathered about private, off-field and non-sporting activities of players, whereby the information forms a commodity to be sold on to readers and viewers. At the same time, issues around non-normative sex and sexuality – such as group sex and sexual assault, form part of a public, albeit media-generated, fascinated with sexual stories,[13] thereby exacerbating the circulation and consumption of such scandal stories. Unlike other scandals, these media narratives also circulate through legal and criminal reporting, which is a genre usually distinct from celebrity scandal. Given the repetition of scandalous stories related to footballer sexual activities, the scandals operate on the one hand as a form of 'shock knowledge' designed to interest, intrigue, titillate or outrage readers and viewers. But at the same time, as with many scandals involving celebrities or well-known persons, the information and the way in which the stories play out is banal and repetitive of earlier examples of scandal. This has the effect of linking football culture and footballers themselves with the scandals which become 'stock knowledge' on footballer behaviour – a form of stereotyping (which is not to say the stereotype is necessarily 'wrong' or 'untruthful'). For example, in discussing the prevalence of group sexual assault among young school-leavers at 'schoolies' events in Queensland, director of the Gold Coast Centre Against Sexual Violence, Di Macleod, drew parallels between these events and football culture, indicating the extent and veracity of the 'common knowledge' of footballer group sexual behaviour:

> In some cases these assaults can involve the style of gang-rapes associated with the nation's football fraternity. "It's certainly not unique to football, it's certainly not unique to any football code, and it's certainly not unique to sports heroes," Ms Macleod said.[14]

Thus, the genre of scandal as a combination of news events, stories, gossip and commentary comes to produce a particular idea in the public imagination of football culture which can, effectively, aid the reproduction and continuation of that element of the culture over time.

Footballer scandals occur, in part, because of the high rate of team or 'group' activities, whereby fellow players are involved in the private, off-field, social and/or sexual activities of other players, typically from the same team. A cursory examination of an online Wiki list of Australian Rules football media scandals between 1990 and 2011 indicates that of those which were about sex or sexual assault fifty-four per cent involved *groups* of players, usually from the same team. Of media reports about Australian Rules football players and non-sexual violence, forty-three per cent involved more than one player in the same incident; thirty-six per cent of the remaining 'individual' violence reports involved violence against women, the majority of which was a domestic violence attack on a players' own girlfriend/wife or ex-girlfriend/wife.[15] Indicating that the emphasis in scandals on group-based violence, sex and sexual assault is not endemic solely to Australian Rules culture but to masculine groupings and masculine team sports more generally, it is worth noting a comparison with the culture of Australian National Rugby League and related scandals: in a similar online listing, fifteen incidents of sexual assaults were reported in the news media between 1990 and 2011, with fifty-three per cent of these involving groups of NRL players and a single victim of the assault. Group-based non-sexual violence was slightly lower in the case of Rugby League, with only eighteen per cent of incidents involving more than one player.[16]

The majority of news reports across both sporting codes occurred after 1999, when four Brisbane Lions players were accused of rape in the United Kingdom during an end-of-year trip, without charges laid after players insisted to British and Australian police that the sex was consensual. As a form of footballer scandal, group sexual assault is thus relatively new. The media focus on masculine team sports and group sex/rape began in earnest in February 2004 with the allegations of six Rugby League players from the Canterbury Bulldogs involved in sexually assaulting a twenty-four-year-old woman at a New South Wales resort.[17] No charges were laid. Subsequent scandals include a 2009 revelation of a 2002 incident when three rugby league players from the Cronulla

Sharks engaged in group sex for two hours with a nineteen-year-old woman while on tour in New Zealand, with reports that up to twelve players were in the room. No charges were laid. As Deb Waterhouse-Watson has recently pointed out, of several dozen individual players accused of sexual assault either in solo or group situations over the past decade in Australia, only two were ordered to stand trial,[18] an outcome which has, on the one hand, mitigated scandal by suggesting that the allegations either were untrue or that the activity was, after all consensual and, on the other hand, sometimes exacerbating the scandals by opening the question as to why so few charges are laid or why so few cases arrive in court.

Momentarily, I would like to focus on the scandalous 2009 revelations about the NRL Cronulla Sharks' incident in New Zealand in 2002 because it provides a framework for understanding the media and public response to the spate of later sexual assault scandal reports among AFL footballers. While this did not involve Australian Rules footballers and while this book is focusing predominantly on the culture of Australian Rules, it is worth noting some of the details of this scandal given the important role it has played in 'framing' subsequent masculine team sport sex scandals, group-based sexual assaults and other footballer sex stories in the media. According to reports, a woman was invited to a hotel in Christchurch in which several Cronulla players were staying while on a pre-season tour of New Zealand. At least twelve players and staff were in the room and it was stated that six or more players had been having sex with the woman known as Clare. Initially denying any involvement in the act in May 2009,[19] alleged ring-leader and participant Matthew Johns later apologised publicly, although insisted the woman was a 'willing participant'.[20] As with many other group sexual assault incidents, the claim that the act was consensual on the basis that there was never a statement of 'no' was once again debated in the media, with commentators emphatically confirming the legality and the interpretation of the point that: 'A woman too drunk or too asleep to object to sex is not consenting. Saying yes to one act, or one partner, does not imply consent for more acts, for more partners'.[21] Thus there is a clear public perception on one side that the act is scandalous because it undertook violence against a vulnerable individual, even though that violence occurs within a framework of the complexity of consent and the ignorance around the notion that a failure to fight back or being too drunk to consent reasonably is not an implication of being a willing participant. On the other side of the public debate around the scandal was the hailing of Matthew Johns as victim of the woman involved. In considering aspects of the public response, David Sygall wrote: 'Like sporting villains before him, Johns will tap into an aspect of Australian culture that permits, or even applauds, bad behaviour, rewards a courageous apology and even portrays him as a victim'.[22] What is demonstrated through the narrative of the scandal is the wholly unethical act of objectification of Clare in which the young woman was sexually assaulted by multiple players at the same time, with her vulnerability or, indeed, her wishes failing to be recognised by the group of players present – whether the players sexually assaulting her or those spectating or otherwise in the room. But what is also demonstrated not just in the scandal but through the ways in which the narrative played out is the additional violence of exclusion and erasure. The initial denial of Clare's story by Matthew Johns[23] indicates the ways in which scandal around team sportsplayers' involvement in group sex relegates the woman involved to an otherness, an objectified position for which a genuine responsiveness is disavowed. This is further shown by the fact that when the scandal erupted in Australia in 2009, player Matthew Johns made a statement on *The Footy Show* and discussed the anguish the incident and its revelation had put his wife through. However, as presenter Sarah Ferguson stated in her *Four Corners* documentary of the incident, 'neither he nor any of the players we contacted asked about Clare'.[24]

While this scandal frames the contemporary response to mas-culine team sportsplayers, sexuality and relationality with women in Australia, and was certainly the most extensive and notable scandal in Australian sports related to sexual assault, there is a wide range of individual examples in recent years of group-based sexual behaviour, typically involving no consent, among Austral-ian Rules footballers. Early among these was an October 1999 incident in which four Brisbane Lions players were accused of raping a young woman after partying in London. The scandal emerged through a report and interviews on *Four Corners* in 2004.[25] The young woman, Sarah, who was from Australia and living in London was a friend of one of the players. After an evening of drinking in a local bar, Sarah was in no state to make the two-hour journey to her home, so was invited by one of the players to stay in their hotel. As Sarah relates in the interview, she was asleep for possibly three hours before waking up to find Adam Heuskes on top of her; realising soon that there were at least four other players in the room watching and two players on the bed with her. Not unlike other rape cases, it took Sarah several weeks to report the incident to the British police – despite a substantial investigation in which the players were regularly represented by a club lawyer, the British Crown Prosecutor dropped the case in August 2000. However, that month, according to the *Four Corners* report, Adam Heuskes, who was by then playing with Port Adelaide, was accused again of rape by a twenty-year-old woman referred to in the documentary as 'Jane'. In circumstances remarkably similar to those of the London case, this incident allegedly involved the young woman drinking heavily, and other players co-perpetrating in the act, including Port Adelaide player Peter Burgoyne and Sydney Swan Michael O'Loughlin. Taken drunk from the bar to a nearby park, the three players sexually assaulted her. According to *Four Corners*, Jane indicated that 'her clothes were ripped off, her bag thrown away. She was forced to the ground, tossed around like a rag doll and raped…by Adam Heuskes and Peter Burgoyne and that at one point, Heuskes and Michael O'Loughlin were masturbating close to her face'. Friends of Jane found her, dishevelled and abandoned in the park, and took her immediately to the police, resulting in charges against Heuskes and Burgoyne. However, the charges were dropped after Director of Public Prosecutions, Paul Rofe, stated there was 'no reasonable prospect of conviction on any criminal charge'.[26] However, Port Adelaide fined Peter Burgoyne $5,000 for being 'in an inappropriate place' that night, although it is unclear how this relates to the lack of criminal charges. As the scandal played out, a similar situation as the NRL group sex scandal becomes noticeable in which denial of the incident and the blurring of the question of consent is the response given by players, clubs and the league governing body; that is, blurring the response to the question of consent through arguing around 'the fine line between seduction and rape'.[27] Part of the blurring of consent relates to the fact that gang rape and group sexual assault rarely utilise violence or force in the manner more commonly recognisable in single-perpetrator rapes.[28] Indeed, as the *Four Corners* interviewer found in discussing the incident with AFL chief executive Andrew Demetriou, it was difficult not just to have a response but to have a *respondent at all*:

Andrew Demetriou, AFL Chief Executive: You'd have to direct those questions to the Port Adelaide Football club.
Ticky Fullerton: They've directed us to you.

At the same time, the capacity for the young woman to make a reply to a response is limited in the case of Jane, with suggestions made by *Four Corners* of a possible payment of 'hush money' accompanying her signing a confidentiality agreement that prevented her from speaking out on the incident.

In a March 2004 Australian Rules sex scandal, St Kilda players Stephen Milne and Leigh Montagna were investigated initially by the club and then by the police. Two women had reported being raped by the two players at the home of one player.[29] Importantly, this scandal emerged less than a month after allegations of the rape of a woman in Coffs Harbour by several Canterbury Bulldogs players, marking an early peak in public focus on group sexual assault perpetrated by players in the context of masculine team sports. Not dissimilar from other cases, alcohol was involved as the players had been drinking at an AFL family day, and the sexual assault involved a group-based form of relationality between the men, with reports stating that 'It had been alleged that one of the women was later sexually assaulted when the players attempted to swap partners'.[30] In May 2004 it emerged that the players would not be charged, with the Victorian Director of Public Prosecutions concluding 'there was insufficient evidence to launch a prosecution against Milne and Montagna'.[31] Most football scandals play out over days, weeks or perhaps several months, and in the case of the latter they peak and wane in line with news cycles and new revelations. Unusually, the Milne/Montagna sex scandal was relatively quiet for the extended period from 2004 until June 2010, after which two former detectives who originally investigated the case admitted publicly that senior police officers had put pressure on the detectives to ensure the case would be dropped.[32] Former detective Mike Smith stated that the urging from senior officers was 'more along the lines of "Don't do the job as best you can"'…It was "Come on, they [the players] haven't done anything wrong, really"'.[33] This opened significant questions as to the network of relationships both within and on the fringes of Australian Rules football culture which actively work to mitigate scandal and the laying of criminal charges in the case of sexual assault. The fact that, in April 2010, Collingwood Coach Mick Malthouse during a verbal clash with Stephen Milne referred to him as a 'fucking rapist'[34] so many years after the charges were dropped raises further questions as to the extent to which senior AFL stakeholders are aware of the background of scandal events that had, at least publicly, been denied. At the same time, it demonstrates the extent to which scandal information, whether or not true, sticks and remains available for re-articulation even within football culture. In the re-emergence of the scandal, the team-based sexual sharing of a woman was again highlighted as new statements came to light, including former lead investigator on the case Scott Gladman revealing there were text messages from Milne and Montagna to the two women that, if the case had been permitted to proceed, would have formed part of the evidence against the players. According to a *Herald Sun* report, Gladman stated that: 'Montagna allegedly sent a message saying sorry, and that he had thought the woman knew it was Milne… And Milne sent a text to the woman's friend, saying sorry about the mix-up, and that he hoped she had a good time'.[35] These further point not only to the possibility of criminality in the case and that the woman's claims should involve a serious investigation, but to the role in footballer sex scandals of an objectified sharing of women without necessarily their consent.

Against the grain of the trend in which footballer sexual assault accusations rarely result in charges, in this case Stephen Milne was charged with four counts of rape in June 2013, nine years after the alleged incident, with police believing they had enough evidence to reopen the case subsequent to the public statements of interference in the original investigation.[36] Importantly, the decision by St Kilda Football Club and the AFL to suspend Milne from play in what was expected to be his thirteenth and last season was considered controversial, with the AFL Player's Association claiming the club was putting 'the interests of its brand before the interests of its player'.[37] What this response points to is the tension that emerges between on-field and off-field in the context of scandal. As journalist Caroline Wilson noted: 'Sport is just a sideshow to this unfortunate and devastating story but in the wider context of football's relationship with society the St Kilda Football Club has done the right thing in removing Milne from the field of play'.[38] Here, the conflict between the on-field and off-field worlds is one in which some argue for their wholesale separation such that the charges against Milne should have no bearing on his capacity to participation in a high-profile game while others, such as Wilson, rightly indicate that the culture in which sexual assault scandals emerge is a culture that is inseparable from the on-field performance of players and the club environment. Indeed, the fact that the incident involved more than one player in a social context points to the wholesale inseparability of on-field play and the club's social environment. It also signifies the educational role football culture plays, whereby this is not merely the case of a public figure engaged in a dispute over a matter within his private life but one in which the sport and its players are deemed to be representative of the capacity to adjust or solidify social norms. To allow a player arrested and charged with rape to play is not simply a response in line with managing and protecting the brand but one which has substantial repercussions for how rape is perceived publicly and the extent to which perpetrators are deemed responsible for sexual assault. Despite these tensions, Milne's enforced withdrawal from play was rescinded in July 2013, after he had been bailed with instructions to appear before the Melbourne Magistrates' Court in the following September.[39] What might be inferred in such a decision is that the public relations response to a player's involvement in a sexual assault scandal is aligned with the measurement of a public's capacity to become 'used to' the knowledge of a scandal – any outrage subsides after peak moments in a scandal, and the length of time between charges and a committal hearing permit the more ethical response of the club and the league to be retracted.

What is significant about the sexual assaults narrated through many of these scandals is the way in which group sexual behaviour occurs. In some cases, it is articulated as the performance of a gang rape; in others it remains group-based through partner swapping or the 'handing over' of a partner from one player to another (often without consent, as in the Milne and Montagna allegations), thereby also making the sexual assault about a relationality between the players rather than with the woman involved. This was also the case in the more recent Andrew Lovett rape incident in which he was charged by police over a claim of rape by a woman at an apartment in December 2009 subsequent to a night of drinking with teammates.[40] Subsequent to the laying of charges, St Kilda Football Club suspended Lovett indefinitely which resulted in the former player making a substantial compensation claim against the club, arguing that 'by deliberately excluding Lovett from the main playing group and denying him access to the club's facilities and resources during his period of indefinite suspension' laws protecting employees from workplace bullying were contravened.[41] Lovett was charged with a second count of rape in May 2010, relating to the same woman who, it was revealed at this time, was 'the former partner of a Melbourne-based AFL footballer'.[42] Details of the incident emerged just prior to the committal hearing in August 2010, in which it was revealed that the woman had met players Andrew Lovett and Jason Gram just before Christmas 2009, had accompanied them back to Gram's apartment in a significantly intoxicated state, and believing she would be having sex with Gram. According to reports, Gram placed her on his bed to let her sober up, and they kissed. The woman's friend, also at the apartment drinking at the time, stated Gram's housemate and fellow player Sam Fisher arrived home, found the woman near the doorway sobbing, accusing Lovett of having entered the room and assaulted her, with the phrase 'I was asleep and he pumped the shit out of me'.[43] Again, there is the involvement of alcohol and the sharing of a woman by players, even though in the reports on this case consent was granted neither by the woman nor by Jason Gram that Lovett should be permitted to have sexual intercourse with her. Andrew Lovett stated in a formal police interview that: "'She seemed to be enjoying it. I was enjoying it. And we were kissing each other still passionately, at different stages'".[44] While the indication of a performance of pleasure is not, of course, an indication that consent can reasonably have occurred, the key issue in this scandal is that the woman has persistently stated that she thought she was having sex with Jason Gram. Indeed, according to the same report, St Kilda football manager Greg Hutchison testified he had discussed the issue with Lovett very early on Christmas Eve (the morning after the incident and had asked Lovett if the sex was consensual. 'Lovett's reply was, "Yes, but she may have thought I was Grammy'".[45] Of course, that indicates that she was *not* consenting to sex with Lovett and was therefore raped. However, the case went to trial in mid-2011 with Lovett's plea of not guilty; it was revealed during the trial that other players who were present, including Sam Fisher, Adam Schneider and Adam Pattison, had each stepped over the sobbing complainant without asking if she was okay – this, at least tacitly, indicating the way in which Australian Rules team culture regards a woman who is clearly articulating vulnerability and injury. However this is not necessarily a universal position of all players: to their credit, Andrew McQualter and other unnamed players who were present angrily attacked Lovett, asking 'How could you bring the club down like this?'[46] and demonstrated some concern for the woman, offering to take her home.[47] The jury acquitted Lovett in July 2011, of all counts of rape,[48] and it is understood that the defence case that a jury could not be 'satisfied beyond reasonable doubt as to the prosecution's allegations' resulted in a verdict of not guilty on each charge.[49] It should be noted that in less than a month after the case Lovett was again the subject of a police investigation after a different woman had contacted police earlier in the year alleging she had been sexually assaulted by him in 2009.[50]

There are two common responses to the off-field sex scandals, violence and misbehaviour of sports teams (seen both in Australia and elsewhere) in public discourse on the topic, in part directed by the tone of news stories and opinion editorials, although an analysis of blogs, online news responses and online debates demonstrates the polarisation around the issue into two discursive categories. The first *focuses on the victim*, although typically excludes any possibility of speech or response beyond the initial accusation. In addressing her, accountability is assigned and she is depicted as responsible for her own vulnerability: the skirt was too short, she consented to group sex and is now attempting to capitalise on it, she was herself the sexual aggressor victimising the men/team;[51] she allowed herself to be made vulnerable by drinking too much, she is lying about the assault or did indeed consent to sex but has later changed her mind; she acted in a predatory manner and is thus complicit in the violence enacted towards her.[52] The second *focuses on masculine team sports* and its culture as the problem and source of both the scandalous behaviour and the protections enjoyed by players: the sport itself is deemed culturally rotten or, as a team sport, compares unfavourably with non–team sports and healthy exercise such as tennis, swimming, jogging and use of gyms;[53] misbehaviour will happen but the players require ever-greater discipline both on-and-off field (including increased curfews, sanctions, drug and alcohol testing, supervision in public); masculine sportsplayers expect sex from women as a reward for their celebrity status;[54] the bonding of the team is problematic with hypermasculine bonding that places others in danger when carried from on-field to off-field; the intensive homosociality of men's sports promotes extreme and sometimes criminal sexual behaviours;[55] off-field misbehaviour will happen but should be stemmed through greater penalisation including exclusions from on-field activity, fines, suspensions and permanent bans; the misbehaviour will happen but the players require greater preventative training as a risk management strategy, with the expectation institutional change will trickle down. While there is clearly a shifting balance, it would appear that the first group of responses (blaming or disbelieving the woman who has been sexual assaulted) remains the more common *public* response, as witnessed in commentary, replies to online news articles, blogs, conversations and some considerable citizen journalism.

Neither of these responses, of course, promotes an adequate framework for addressing men's team behaviour. Rather, they both reproduce the unproductive assigning of responsibility to *individuals* within a liberal-humanist framework[56] rather than looking to the ways in which football culture structures the situation in which unethical behaviours occur. In the case of responses which assign responsibility to the woman, she is individually accountable for the behaviours of the footballers towards her. In the case of footballers, inappropriate behaviour is put down to a handful of 'wayward individuals',[57] not to the culture that produces such behaviours. Although there are alternative responses to a footballer group sexual assault scandal, including those by sports journalists and commentators which critique gender relationships within sporting culture,[58] the two common rejoinders continue to dominate public discourse on such scandals, becoming the automatic responses which play out repetitively each time similar narratives arise. The debate polarises on either the complainant as responsible for her own vulnerability or as not having really been vulnerable in the first instance, or on whether or not masculine team sportsplayers are 'any good' — the less-popular argument, given the cultural links between elite sporting competitions, masculinity and the nation.[59] In the case of the first, complainants, bystanders and those who might participate in group sex or social activities with footballers need to have their vulnerability acknowledged and recognised by members of the teams. This has not been the case, indicating clearly the gender relationality through which such public debates play out, whereby the voice of the complainant is excluded or erased.

For example, the response of the AFL to the claims made in 2010 by Lara Bingle that a nude photograph of her had been taken by player Brendan Fevola, circulated among other footballers for their gratification and ultimately finding its way into publication in *Woman's Day*, was to dismiss her claims to having been sexually objectified and to argue that she was failing to co-operate by refusing to participate in the AFL's private, internal investigation rather than making her claims through the public institution of the courts (and, here, the institution of the media). In the case of the second category of public responses, increased discipline appears not to be making an impact, as seen recently in the case of Australian Rules team St Kilda's riotous misbehaviour while touring New Zealand, quickly on the heels of earlier scandals over the summer.[60] Problematically, this response group consistently signifies risk as risk to men or to the game (whether from the harm caused by the teams' misbehaviour, or the harm caused by the victims' accusations). The polarisation of public discourse that becomes more concrete during the emergence of a group sex scandal establishes an impasse preventing critical public engagement in cultural, policy and prevention techniques. In this persistent rehearsal of the polarised debates, women remain representable only within a virgin/vamp dichotomy,[61] thereby reproducing the stereotyping of women involved in football culture by only allowing the possibilities of an 'authentic' or 'inauthentic' woman, rather than allowing the complainant to be addressed as subject. As importantly, both of these responses involve the assignation of responsibility through judgment which, as Kathy Dow Magnus has pointed out, is antithetical to a critical approach which investigates the 'social conditions that induce individuals to act as they do'.[62]

There are two ways in which to begin developing alternative approaches to the broader cultural transformation necessary to intervene critically and pragmatically in sports-based group sexual assault, which I will address in the remainder of this chapter. Firstly, the possible array of responses to gang rape that have developed in recent literature must be critiqued from an approach that explores the dynamics of group sexual assault from the *dual* perspectives of gender relationality and masculine bonding. Secondly, and following this, it is important to address the event of group sexual assault from the perspective of how an ethics that recognises the vulnerability of others, including victims, is currently stemmed by *group* identity. The aim is to develop ways in which group homosociality in high-level team bonding environments can be transformed into a site for ethical behaviour by exploring the performativity of subjecthood between individual selfhood and group identity to determine the site of an ethics that has both pragmatic preventative and cultural transformative potential. Important here is to bear in mind the complex array of group dynamics that are at play in a sexual assault scandal, ranging from the greater likelihood of sexual engagement involving multiple players to the supportive bonds among a team and its stakeholders subsequent to the revelation of scandal in which various protections are offered. In the ongoing Milne/Montagna case, the bonds between players in a sex-fuelled evening in which the allegations of non-consensual partner-swapping have emerged are part of this; so too is the controversial evidence that emerged in reports that in late 2013 during the committal hearings senior St Kilda players and prominent supporters were approaching sponsors to help finance Milne's legal team.[63] While the cultural perspectives of sexual assault can be read from a number of perspectives on ethics, responsibility and gender relationality, it is instructive to consider these in the context of varying masculine group bonds.

Teams, Masculinity and Group Identity

Current approaches to group-based sexual assault need to theorise further the formation of groupings of men as well as the production and performance of identities as integral and combined elements in the phenomenon. Usefully, some prior study has explored the ways in which male homosociality has operated to exclude and objectify women and marginalised others as a means by which male bonding is enacted.[64] Homosociality is the non-sexual organisation of relationships among men which, effectively, produces not only segregation of gender identities within institutions,[65] but organises forms of sexual relationality between genders such that the objectification of women is undertaken for the benefit of men in their relationships with each other.[66] Understanding Australian Rules sex scandals from the perspective of homosocial bonding highlights the structure of the team and its on-field behaviours through the relationality of gender which, subsequently, governs the ways in which off-field bonding behaviours are performed and the ways in which scandals erupting over those behaviours are discussed publicly. In this framework, group-based sexual assault is, then, a problem which emerges not through individual or group acts in and of themselves, but through the ways in which contemporary masculine footballer identity is performed as an identity which demands for its coherence an exclusion of women as other and a directing of performance to the recognisability by other men. That is, masculine footballer identity is at least partly constituted by definition of what it is not – woman – thereby articulating a performance of identity that 'others' through exclusion and objectification, and the prioritisation of male-male bonds over women who can be part of sexual but not social activity in strongly homosocial environments and contexts.[67] But to understand the centrality of homosociality in the context of group-based sexual assault requires further investigation of the mechanisms by which homosocial behaviours are performed and upheld through group sexuality.

There have been a number of under-theorised accounts of group-based violence and sexual assault which have either articulated the root cause within a framework of 'peer pressure to conform' to group behaviours,[68] low self-esteem among group members as pivotal in violent and aggressive behaviours towards others that result from identifying with a meaningful group,[69] or by arguing that group dynamics in violence and sexual assault depend on a division of men into followers and leaders, with the subordinated followers acting along with dominators of the group 'lest they be branded as non-masculine, risk expulsion from the group, or, in extreme cases, become victims themselves'.[70] Such archetypes of participants and perpetrators in group sexual assault have also been articulated in fictional accounts of gang rape, with a common perception that within the united and bonded group there are those who are the core and aggressive members initiating the rape, those who are reluctant participants going along with it after initial hesitation, and those who refuse to participate.[71] Unfortunately, none of these approaches are particularly useful in understanding the *specificity* of group violence and sexual assault among elite footballers: while there needs to be more work on the relationship between these behaviours and self-esteem of footballers – particularly those who are under persistent media scrutiny and whose reputations are maintained only as long as they sustain on-field success. It is doubtful if these successful, celebrity and often wealthy individuals are subject to the same conditions that produce losses of self-esteem among other men and boys in contemporary society. Peer pressure to conform to group behaviours is also not a significant factor, as sports teams are already subject to various structuring acts and performances of group bonding – both on-field and in off-field environments – that are not necessarily predicated on the need to maintain belonging in the same way as might be experienced by other groups (for example, where ostracisation or expulsion can occur more easily).

In the case of the leaders/followers discourse, there is some recent evidence that in group sexual offences, there may be less distinction between leaders and followers or between initiators and imitators than previously thought,[72] thereby indicating greater equality and sharing of the perpetration of the act by the participants.

One of the problems with the study of group rape in general is that, despite its prevalence, it is rarely examined as a phenomenon distinct from *other* forms of sexual assault, violence and crime.[73] That has left much of the existing literature without the capacity to understand some of the ways group bonding not only enables the act or crime through addressing shifts in the performativity of identity, but can be investigated as the site for intervention and prevention (rather than through addressing individuals). What is needed for an approach that can consider the relationship between group sexual assault, identity and ethics is an investigation firstly of the notion of the *group* before the idea of *sexual assault* or *violence*. Much of the study of group sexual assault and violence that has indeed explored the group element has focused on United States college fraternities, and this has shed some light on the processes by which sexual assault occurs in the context of group behaviours. Importantly for the study of scandal, cases of group sexual assault on university campuses received high-profile media coverage and airing of public attitudes from the 2000s, while in the 1990s and earlier the idea of gang rape was relatively side-lined in reporting;[74] mirroring the period in which Australian Rules and Rugby League scandals around sexual assault emerged in Australian news reporting. Erhart and Sandler's 1985 study of campus rape found that a number of conditions made gang rape of women by fraternity men both feasible and probable, including excessive alcohol use, isolation and protection from external monitoring, and behaviours which treated women in general as prey in addition to intensive competitiveness with other fraternities sponsoring the frequency and extent of group sexual assaults.[75] Among the more useful accounts of group bonding and its relationship to group sexual assault is the work of Peggy Sanday who undertook a significant study of group bonding and sexuality in United States university college fraternities. Sanday demonstrated the ways in which notions of fraternity, brotherhood and the group bond can produce an intragroup aggression whereby reasonable individuals will 'gang up sexually on one woman and honestly believe that she can physically withstand multiple sexual activity with many men'.[76] Central to Sanday's account is the way in which a sexual culture emerges on North American university campuses that makes a gang rape feasible, permissible, acceptable and often unchallenged by authority figures.[77] The sexual culture is driven by the homosocial bonding of the group, but it is also this bond that makes participation in a rape possible, whereby the emotional bond forged through pledging and initiation rituals provides a sense of invulnerability (including invulnerability to the law) that would otherwise not be felt by young men acting individually.[78] Thus the bonding between perpetrators rather than *individual intent* is central to making such acts possible.

For other writers, it is the institutional group environment of fraternities as organisations in addition to the absence of university or community oversight that creates 'a sociocultural context in which the use of coercion in sexual relations with women is normative and in which the mechanisms to keep this pattern of behavior in check are minimal and absent at worst'.[79] The practices of bonding through a notion of brotherhood presents the localised context by which the crime of group sexual assault can occur, particularly through the rituals of group protection, secrecy and loyalty.[80] For Nina Philadelphoff–Puren, the institutional problem of group sexual assault in fraternities (and other masculine-bonded sites) is in the re-identification of individuals with the organisation which begins with initiation:

the initiate is both annihilated (with the feminine) and then reborn into his new identity as a fraternity member. The structure of the initiation ensures that this new identity is not only antithetical to the feminine but literally predicated on its destruction. Moreover, during this process, law, identity and authority are displaced from their centre in the wider culture and refocused on the group: it is the group that makes the law, the group that provides the identity and the group that is the centre and measure of values.[81]

The strand of the study of group sexual assault examining fraternities has thus examined some of the behaviours from the perspective of the group, although such findings are not, of course, fully translatable to the environment of football team group mis-behaviour, as fraternities and team sports are considerably different, albeit both masculine and homosocially oriented, institutions. Fraternities have greater structural and institutional secrecy[82] and certainly less media coverage than that experienced by footballers and other team sportsplayers; most elite-level footballers have been brought up in team environments from an early age and at least since adolescence, whereas admission into college fraternities has very specific points of entry and initiation, including age, adulthood, the transition from school to university life and the transition often from a family household to living away. Nevertheless, this literature points to the centrality of group bonding as that which makes group sexual assault possible.

To understand the homosocial bonding between masculine team sportsplayers that makes sexual assault not only possible but permissible as a ritual of group behaviour requires, however, a more nuanced account of the discursive processes of selfhood, masculine identity and group subjectivity. Using Judith Butler's theory of performativity, whereby subjects are constituted and re-constituted in particular ways according to pre-existing discourses (as opposed to being driven by assumed biological needs or drives) is a useful way in which to understand the behaviour of masculine bonded men operating in a group context such as in a sporting team in an off-field environment. Masculine identity is not, in Butler's post-structuralist formulation, a naturally occurring or essentialist subject, but a set of performances citing culturally given norms of masculinity and played out in such a way as to lend the illusion that these behaviours are the emanations of the identity, not the means by which it is constituted. That is, in performing masculinity – which is never a conscious or voluntary act – one cites and repeats the name or category; such performances come to stabilise over time, retroactively producing the illusion of a fixed, inner core from which behaviours, attitudes and actions are felt to manifest.[83] That is, actions, attributes, behaviours and performances do not stem from an inner, fixed essence but constitute it. Following Nietzsche, she points out that there is no 'doer behind the deed', that is, no static sexual subject (being) revealed through behaviour or desire (doing). Rather, identities are performed *over time* in accord with discursive expectations and cultural demands for coherence, intelligibility and recognisability, in order to maintain social participation and belonging.[84] Identity is the compulsion to reiterate 'a norm or set of norms' which 'conceals or dissimulates the conventions of which it is a repetition'.[85] The expression of masculinity thus occurs through performances, attitudes, attributes and desires that constitutes the masculine subject. For Butler, identity – and gender identity – is manufactured in the languages, concepts and ideas available to a culture at a specific point in time, meaning the notion of gendered behaviour as fixed, natural and dichotomous is historical and ultimately unstable, even if reproduced through an array of cultural, institutional and discursive methods. That is, all identities are constituted within ambiguities, incoherences and inconsistencies, but for the sake of coherence we are required to disavow, suppress or reinscribe in order to perform as an intelligible and coherent self.[86]

As the repeated stylisation of the body,[87] the performance of masculinity among footballers cites various cultural norms that construct a particular form of coherent masculinity. However, what comes to constitute masculinity for footballers (and particularly for elite teams of footballers) is not necessarily the same masculinity which circulates through other scenes and practices of masculine performativity. Rather, it is important to consider not just how masculine identity is performed within a reified set of norms that are recognisable broadly and culturally, but to consider how *localised* groups of subjects may perform a particular brand of masculinity that relates more closely to the institution, the environment or, in this case, the sport, the code and the team rather than to masculine norms as they may circulate more broadly. In contrast to Connell's hegemonic masculinity thesis by which the masculine cultural production of domination is produced and legitimated,[88] the particular forms of violence and domination align with a hypermasculine machismo that, as recent writers in theoretical criminology have argued, is external to the dominating but not physically violent forms of masculine practice found more broadly in neo-liberal contemporary Western culture.[89] That is, while violence and sexual assault are performances of masculinity, they are not necessarily performances most recognisably aligned with the hegemonic norms of domination in which the subordination of the other is steadily more subtle and often more insidious. Rather, these particular performances of masculinity are produced through the *local* culture of contemporary team sports which inflect elements of broader masculine identity but which would not necessarily be forms fully acceptable outside of the network of sports teams, leagues, codes and their related institutions. This is not to imply that the relationship between elite masculine sports and national identity does not provide a mechanism to protect such behaviours.[90]

But what – and who – then are these identities in the scenario of a group sexual assault or group violence? To assume that group-based violence occurs through a set of masculine individuals who have come together and behaved criminally or brutally to subordinate a woman or another subject cast as 'other' would be to restore intent and to argue that (masculine) self-identity precedes the acts and performances.[91] Instead, I am arguing that the identity performances at stake in group violence and sexual assault involve a *suspension* of the constructed masculine individual identity in favour of *group subjectivity*. That is, masculine group sexual assault focused on the semi-present woman or violence against the marginalised other is a performative and embodied act of *collective identity* in which integral elements of individual (masculine) subjectivity are sidelined in favour of a form of subjecthood that is represented through performances of engagement of the bonded group. For example, the narrative (whether truthful or not) of the assault of 'Jane' by Adam Heuskes, Peter Burgoyne and Michael O'Loughlin can be understood not as the acts of three individual footballers but as the act of a bonded group performing a sexual assault on a semi-present (semi-conscious) woman collectively. The sexual engagement that occurs in this narrative in close proximity to one another in combination to the shared goal of 'getting off' dislodges the individuality of the players in favour of a collectivity, a shared subjectivity that is more than just three men individually identifying with one another but constituted in this specific context as a *group subject*. Indeed, some literature on group sexual assault in particular has pointed to the (literal) performance nature of group rape, in which the turn-taking at sexual engagement with the woman becomes ritualistic, and by which the victim becomes a dramatic prop, with the collectivity of the group bonding through the symbolic act of sharing.[92] The argument here, then, is that rather than investigating and intervening in team-based group sexual assault of women from the perspective of *individual* men, it is necessary to develop a theoretical approach that addresses the performativity of the *group as subject in itself*, separate from its individual members. This is a group identity or subjectivity that peaks in particular contexts and scenes, that has its own set of coherent performances and its own codes of ethics that may be significantly different from those of the individual players.

Subjectivity and Individuality versus Group Identity

Butler's theories of identity performativity point to the relationality that governs the ways in which identities are articulated towards coherence and intelligibility, although that has tended to give precedence to the role of social discourse in subject formation and the norms that structure a subject's interpellation, rather than to the specific intersubjectivity that can occur between members of a group, community or institution.[93] What has not been fully explored in theories of performative identity and identification is the way in which such identifications and performances that constitute identity intersect with the citation of *localised groups* such as teams. That is to say, that the masculine identity of footballers that is under question here is not built solely on the identification with broad, hegemonic or non-hegemonic-but-violent masculine norms given discursively, but on several intersections of identity that present masculine coherence and intelligibility in various contexts. The fact that no individual masculine sportsplayer (or other subject) is solely constituted by a singular and coherent set of norms, but through a complex array of mechanisms that produce the subject variously and in different context. Indeed, as Butler has argued, to 'prescribe an exclusive identification for a multiply constituted subject, as every subject is, is to enforce a reduction and a paralysis'.[94] Rather, there is an identification with the team of – at most – a few dozen players and related stakeholders (coaches, reserves, junior managers, rookies, etc.) as a homosocial masculine environment that may work in tandem with – and sometimes against – the citation of broader cultural codes, norms and categories of masculinity in the performance of male selfhood.

While variants and strands of masculine norms make possible the objectification of women and others *for* the acts of forging group identity, it is through identification with the 'masculine, homosociality of the team' in both on-field (sport) and off-field (social) environments that group sexual assault and violence become feasible. If identity is constituted in performances that occur through the citation, reiteration and stabilisation over time of a set of recognisable norms,[95] then among the multiple identifications[96] that are cited and repeated is the discursive arrangement of the team bond itself. Where the act of group rape or sexual assault is often coded by participants as recreation rather than crime,[97] such bonded activities are social performances of the group, not of a cluster of individuals acting in concert. In other words, to assume that the perpetration of sexual assault is the responsibility of individual players driven by the codes and norms of masculine individual identity precludes the centrality of the homosocial bond that is maintained through group identity and the collective performance of the act. This is not, of course, to imply that just because a sexual assault is the subjective performance of group identity that the players themselves are not responsible and accountable for their participation. Rather, it is to say that intervening to prevent group sexual assault requires intervening with the group *as a group*, and not the individual players simply as *members* of a group.

To fully understand some of the ways in which sporting teams can be transformed from a site of risk for vulnerable others into ethical environments that recognise vulnerability involves understanding further the ways in which group identity is performed. That is, while much of the literature on group sexual assault in United States college fraternities indicates the centrality of masculine homosocial group bonding to the perpetration of violent sexual assault, it is in looking to the ways in which group identity is performed, stabilised and establishes the ethics of the behaviour that can enhance the study of this masculine environment. Within cultural studies and much work around gender analysis, the performativity of identity has been discussed in terms of relationality to groups as communities, usually anonymous, geographically dispersed and imagined into being. Indeed, for those who work with concepts of identity performativity, underlying the performance of culturally recognisable gender identities is the motivation to be coherent and intelligible in order to maintain social participation and belonging.[98] That is, masculine identity requires identification with the array of concepts, norms and values of masculinity – or at least some parts, styles and forms of masculinity. Performativity theories point to the relationality that governs the ways in which identities are articulated towards coherence and intelligibility, although that has tended to give precedence to the role of social discourse in subject formation and the norms that structure a subject's interpellation, rather than to the specific intersubjectivity that can occur between members of a group, community or institution.[99] In her later work, Butler strongly emphasises the ways in which subjects are formed in the context of relations with others, and such subjectivity (as well as life itself) depends on the relationality of that self that is produced in the context of relating to others.[100] As she poignantly asks: 'The subject is always outside itself, other than itself, since its relation to the other is essential to what it is…So the following question emerges: how do we understand what it means to be a subject who is constituted in or as its relations, whose survivability is a function and effect of its modes of its relationality?'.[101] In the case of footballer identity, what is indicated is that identification and subjectivity are constituted not solely in a sense of similarity among footballers, nor solely in the taking on-board of behaviours and attributes that make footballer identity coherent, intelligible and recognisable, but that it is through a range of (sometimes pre-determined) ways of relating to others, *both* within football culture and external to it, that makes 'footballer identity'.

Importantly for understanding group sexual assault within Australian Rules football culture, it needs to be noted that Butler's theorisation has yet to be applied to the context of relationality among the small, local group in particular contexts or scenes. The context or scene I am thinking of is that of the off-field partying of a group of footballers in which shared sex with a woman is initiated. This temporal scene produces particular ways of being, particular intelligibilities of footballer identity and thus particular ways of performing and relating to the woman in that scene as football's other. Notably, such ways of performing in that temporally finite context are distinct from the ways in which the footballer's identity and sexual relationality to others might be performed when *away* from the team or group. It is in literature from social psychology that the distinction between individual identity and group identity has been quite well explored, although from a perspective that needs further adaptation to be understood within theories of masculinity, homosociality and the performativity of group bonding. Much of this work has been derived from Henri Tajfel's 1978 theories of social identity,[102] whereby all individuals are seen to be undertaking identity work as members of social groups; this is informed by the three processes of social categorisation by dividing persons into positive and negative association; social comparison which involves assessing one's own group in terms of relative status to other groups and, thirdly, psychological group distinctiveness which involves the ideology of the group in terms of what it seeks to preserve or sometimes change about itself.[103] Psychosocial theories of group membership have pointed out how collectivity is valued in different ways, such as when a sports team has recently had a win,[104] and this is seen to impact on both the integration and distinction between personal identity and group membership. More recent research in this field has indicated that while individuality and group identity are not independent but negotiated,[105] no sense of solidarity is simply imposed on persons, but is achieved through intragroup interaction which does in fact include forms of group diversity, heterogeneity and individuality.[106] In articulating these approaches from the perspective of the performativity of identity, it is important to input the factor of *temporality* in order firstly to avoid falling into the trap of assuming that small, localised group bonds are developed progressively and in a linear fashion towards solidarity and secondly to assume that group identity and bonds are maintained equally across all social, physical and temporal contexts.

In the case of masculine homosocial groupings such as Australian Rules football teams, it can be argued that group identifications operate as an element in the performativity of the perpetrating subjects in a manner that *peaks* and *falls* at particular moments and times, but are not necessarily maintained in constancy subsequent to those events. That is, at times the codes of coherence of individual selfhood are performed; at other times, it is the norms and attributes of the collective group or team that not only dominate but impede other performances which would be intelligible in other contexts. One of those moments in which the group peaks would appear to be in the context of the game, in which a team performs strongly with players acting in seamless collectivity and relationality to each other. Another of those moments in which we see group sex and sexual assault occurring through the suspension of ethics in that site would appear to be team partying and sociality off-field (frequently involving the consumption of alcohol). The incident involving Heuskes and Brisbane Lions players in London occurred in the late evening after football players were out together partying. The Heuskes, Burgoyne and O'Loughlin incident, as reported, was also after an evening out drinking. Likewise, the attempted partner-swapping in the controversial Milne and Montagna scandal was similarly after an AFL party event. So too the Lovett scandal, in which several players had been out drinking and were continuing to party (with the complainant present) at Jason Gram's apartment afterwards. Indeed, in some ways it might be quite productive to consider the peaked moments of group bonding that might occur both in on-field sporting activities and in off-field (mis)behaviour such as group sexual assault or violence as, following Nietzsche, a Dionysian abandonment of the self in a madness. Nietzsche felt such abandonment was, indeed, rare in individuals, but 'in groups, parties, nations and ages, it is the rule'.[107] Rather than categorise this as a wholesale loss of a self that might be seen to pre-exist the identity of the group of football players per se, it can be understood as a *shift* in the performativity towards the group in particular moments, scenes and contexts experienced as peaks and wanes. That is, there are still individual players who either are ethical in their relationality with women or at least can be, but in the context of those particular temporal events of social gathering have limited capacity for ethical relations.

This can perhaps best be seen in the discourses deployed when group members discuss a crime subsequent to the event. In their study of fraternity group rape, Martin and Hummer found through their interviews that 'individual members knew the difference between right and wrong, but fraternity norms that emphasize loyalty, group protection, and secrecy often overrode standards of ethical correctness'.[108] Franklin found that much of group violence is 'committed by individuals who normally obey the law' but that in groups such members 'frequently behave in ways that contradict their individual values',[109] indicating not only the distinction yet interrelatedness of selfhood and group identity, but the ways in which ethics differ between the context of the performative self and the context of the group as subject. Similarly, in a July 2009 case of group violence in Alice Springs, five local young men had been drinking and partying and in the morning, unprovoked, beat indigenous local Kwementyaye Ryder to death and left the body on the road. But in interviews subsequent to the event, perpetrator Glen Swain stated not only his remorse but his bafflement as to how the group violence could have occurred, tearfully stating 'No way, I'd never do that, intentionally do that, to anyone'. What is indicated here is that in the performativity of selfhood, an ethical element is part of the attributes, thoughts and behaviours that ground *his* identity – he could not *normally* conceive of a subjective capacity to harm a vulnerable person and, outside of the context of the performativity of his body within group identity through which the violence materialised, is unable to understand how such behaviour could be a part of his subjectivity. It is thus through the multiplicity of subjectivity and performativities that particular ethics and values which might commonly and reasonably be held by an individual player in some contexts are suspended. In the case of group sexual assault, that suspension occurs in the shift of subjective performance from always-relational but individually constituted identity to the identity of the group and team. Those shifts which occur in the context of homosocial team bonding make possible the scene of group sexual assault as an act in which individual identity is over-ridden and an ethical capacity to recognise the vulnerability of the victims is (temporarily) suspended.

Vulnerability and Ethics

In looking to find both pragmatic and transformative potential to combat homosocially instituted masculine group sexual assault and violence is not to combat the notion of the group nor dismiss localised institutions such as sports teams and their bonds and solidarity as being the site of responsibility itself. As Michael Flood has pointed out, there is enough evidence that it is 'not group membership per se but norms of gender inequality and other bonds that foster and intensify abuse in particular peer cultures that promote violence against women'.[110] Indeed, one does not wish to take the narrow, dichotomous view that men's sports teams are, in themselves, always the site of risk to others, nor to suggest that the bonds between men in sports teams should be undone. In fact, one can argue that in several ways the bonds of solidarity between a team that are necessary for on-field sporting success are healthy, even if the team's group identity is partially forged in off-field behaviours, socialising and partying. Team bonding has significant and proven value for team cohesiveness, sporting success and members' self-esteem,[111] and team sports themselves remain arguably legitimate in their promotion of health, salubrious socialisation and community development.[112]

It is in the distinction between self-identity and group identity as described above where an *ethical* perspective on violence and sexual assault is articulated in individual selfhood outside the group environment: the remorseful 'I would never do that' which both precedes and follows the act when the shift to a more individualised subjectivity occurs. This is not, of course, to reify or naturalise individuality within liberal-humanist claims, for all identity is relational in terms of discursive norms and intersubjective connectedness. Rather, it is to suggest that codes of ethical norms are *currently* better located when the subject is performing identity with a *sense* of singularity as opposed to the bonded sociality of the localised team environment – but there is no foundational reason why this need always be the case. I would like to end this argument by turning to Butler's more recent work in which, drawing on her readings of Levinas, she explores an ethics of non-violence that centres on the capacity to recognise and respond without violence to the vulnerability of the other (e.g., a victim or complainant). I am arguing here that such an ethics is more effective *outside* of the group bonds of the temporal event of team/group sexual behaviour. Acting within an ethical framework or performing one's subjectivity or identity in ethical terms is never guaranteed, but there is some clear evidence that in regard to the sexual relationality between footballers and women, recognising the victim's vulnerability is wholly suspended by the group's subjectivity overriding individual subjectivity in that temporal scene. For Butler, vulnerability itself is common to all human subjects, as it emerges with life itself and is a condition of subjectivity or identity.[113] In the context of our relationality with others, knowing and seeing that another is vulnerable is an ethical responsibility of all subjects, but not an automatic occurrence: it requires a moment of recognition in order to be seen, understood and for the situation of vulnerability to be altered, but such recognition is never guaranteed.[114] This approach to an ethics that can occur in the relationality between men and women in the context of sexual assault is, I am arguing, one pathway towards intervening in the scene of group violence.

From some perspectives, one might assume it would be relatively easy to recognise the vulnerability of a woman during a perpetration of group sexual assault: not necessarily sober, not necessarily fully conscious, on a bed, surrounded by several men. To return to the NRL example which frames much of the contemporary understanding of Australian masculine team sports and the sexual relationality of groups of players with women, it is possible to see how the group suspends the articulation or performance of ethics which might otherwise play out in facing or encounter the subject as other. An interview in the *Four Corners* 2009 documentary on the NRL Cronulla Sharks group sexual assault incident in New Zealand indicates the recognisable signifiers of vulnerability. 'Clare' discussed the event in which two or three players would be performing sexually on the bed with her, while others surrounded and watched:

They never spoke to me; they spoke just amongst themselves, laughing and thinking it was really funny...I thought that I was nothing. I thought that I was worthless, and I thought I was nothing. I think I was in shock. I didn't scream, and they used a lot of, like, mental power over me, and belittled me and made me feel really small, like I was just a little old woman.[115]

In addition to the belittling, it is the failure to address or speak to 'Clare' that indicates the suspension of the capacity to recognise vulnerability, since recognition of the other occurs in the context of an address.[116] This need not be actual speech but an ethical inter-subjective response to the face of the other.[117] In the homosociality of the team's group subjectivity, the performativity of the group's behaviour is directed not by players towards each other but by the *group towards the group itself*, putting aside the ability to address and recognise vulnerability. The fact that player Matthew Johns approached her afterwards in the carpark and apologised to her that other players had come into the room indicates again the ways in which a player, once outside of the context and temporality of the group, is able to make that recognition of vulnerability. In Butler's account, as I will show in greater detail in later chapters, the ways of thinking or framing a subject as dehumanised while attending to the humanity among another group contributes to the situation in which an ethical relationship is disavowed.[118] The inability to recognise a subject as *human enough* is common to the context of group rape among men in homosocially oriented institutions – as Sanday points out, male bonding and sexual dominance privilege the group of men through dehumanisation of women as sexual objects.[119]

Although an NRL example, it provides a useful way of understanding sexual misbehaviour and crime among AFL players, and how these can be understood through ethics. In the context of the group that turns its address unto itself, a discursive apparatus comes into play to reinforce the (non-voluntary) incapacity to recognise the vulnerability of the other, centring on the dual question of vulnerability and consent. The blurring of consent prevents the group from recognising the victim's vulnerability through the assumption that she is sexual available to them (perhaps understood simply through her presence in their space, perhaps by her submission to one player which in the context of bonded group subjectivity that overcomes singularity, means consent to all). As recognition is bestowed on the basis of socially determined criteria that precede an intersubjective encounter,[120] presumptions as to the nature of the victim's availability, stereotypes of women in footballer scenes as predatory[121] and the blurred distinction between consent and coercion in the theatrics of sexual performance[122] prevent the recognition that the woman at the centre of group sex may be vulnerable. It might be noted, however, that in making a claim for an ethical capacity of footballers to respond without violence to the woman as football's other is not to foreground a moral code in which exclusive coupledom should be seen as a superior sexual behaviour over casual sexual encounters.[123] Ethics is not about making such judgments or producing a clear-cut delineation or hierarchy of sexual desires but, instead, a means by which to govern the relationality between partners in a way which produces a disavowal of violence, whether that be forced sex or coercion or forms of injurious speech.

Part of what makes the ethical situation complex within the context of scandals relies on the stereotyping of women involved in a group sexual assault as having been initially consenting but later changing their minds or changing their stories. The assumption that sex is consensual may hide the articulation of vulnerability and, from an ethical perspective, to those involved or witnessing it may well not appear to be an act of violence (which includes the violence of coercion). The group subjectivity fails to recognise the violence of the act as a result of the suspension of the capacity to recognise violence and injury that would be occurring in the encounter from the perspective of the non-grouped subject. But what is common to these cases, and what *should* be recognisable, is the violence of making use of a woman in a vulnerable position. Sexual assault expert Angela Williams, who has provided consultancy to the AFL, made this point in 2009 in discussing masculine team-based group sexual assaults. As it was put in an article in *The Age*,

> The women and girls Dr Williams deals with, brought to her by police investigating whether they are the victims of sex crimes, bear little resemblance to TV victims. Most of the women she examines haven't physically fought back against their attackers. They haven't clawed the skin of their assailant, and they don't have a black eye to support their claims…the men who target them are looking for vulnerability, not ranking them out of 10, she says. Many of them have not cried out or screamed, because they were frightened, or embarrassed, or powerless. Fearing resistance is futile, some position themselves so it won't hurt so much. They shut their eyes and wish it to be over, and they berate themselves: Is this my fault?[124]

This vulnerability is what, under an ethics of non-violence, is expected to be recognised, but the violence occurs not just in the act but in the failure to recognise the vulnerability of the woman being used in this way.

Butler's formulation of a non-violence ethics built on fostering the capacity to recognise vulnerability explores the ways in which the intersubjectivity between the subject and the other occurs as the possible site of recognition, although this tends to be framed within a context of individuality by focusing on the ethical question 'How ought I to treat another?'.[125] As I have suggested above, there is some evidence that footballers are fully capable of that ethical question and the recognition of the vulnerable on an individual level. The group is not like individuals who are able to recognise vulnerability of others through their own vulnerability; rather the group's subjectivity is produced through mutual protection and mutual identification into a subjectivity (in itself) of inviolability signified through the strength of team bonds. But how to impute such an ethics into the scenario of the group, the bond of the team and the social formations which impel the homosociality that, as I have argued, are necessary for on–field team success but are also practiced in off–field environments? At one level, this occurs through broad cultural change since, as Butler points out, we are not dyads on our own, rather the exchange, address and recognition that occurs between subjects is conditioned and mediated by language, convention and norms that are social in character and that 'exceed the perspective of those involved in the exchange'.[126] This suggests that further work on gender relationality is necessary to shift the discursive norms that make a woman appear to be available as an unwitting instrument of team bonding exercises. At the same time, however, intervention can occur through assisting teams in their group subjectivity to recognise vulnerability through a recognition of their *own* susceptibility and risk as something not individual but *shared* among the group or team. Indeed, elite masculine team sportsplayers are in an excellent position to understand vulnerability: they are vulnerable to injury, to injuries which interrupt or end careers, to the shame of defeat in a public spectacle,[127] to media scrutiny of the private and the intimate, to risks of loss when the subjecthood of the group is ineffective and not team-like, among other perils of vulnerability which are, arguably, more extreme than those experienced by other men and women in everyday working and social life. While the specificity of elite-level masculine team sports disavows such vulnerability through a group performance of hypermasculine machismo[128] toughness and bonds of inviolability, there remains the moment of intervention and change through the *shared* vulnerability of the team – if they recognise and identify with their shared vulnerability to injury and loss, thereby making the group, *as a group,* capable of recognising the vulnerability of others from outside football culture (such as these young women) within the context of a vulnerable situation. As a larger task and a later step, developing means by which teams (*as teams* and not as *individual players*) can recognise the vulnerability of others through understanding the shared human condition of vulnerability – in addition to other forms of cultural change – there is currently untapped potential to instil a currently lacking ethics in elite team sports to govern off-field masculine group behaviours beyond the current regimes of risk management and mitigation, and to turn the group homosocial bond into a harmless environment in which the capacity to recognise that a group sexual act may be unethical. I will return to the question of ethics, footballer bodies and injury again in chapter six.

4

Bodies, Pleasures and Compulsions: Drinking, Drugs and Gambling Scandals

Many of the scandals that narrate the relationship between on-field and off-field football behaviours over the past decade have centred on the role and use of drugs, alcohol and gambling. One of the interesting elements as to the ways in which scandals on these three sometimes interrelated topics play out involves the fact that while the media coverage generally relates to off-field issues and behaviours in footballers' social lives, all three are interconnected with on-field health, integrity and ethical issues, including questions of the traditional and ongoing sponsorship of football by alcohol companies, the use of performance-enhancing drugs and the scandalous questions over match-fixing and football gambling by players. Footballer scandals congeal around the three themes of alcohol, drugs and gambling not because there is a public moral outrage at drinking, recreational drug use or betting, not even because footballers might undertake these social and off-field activities in excessive ways. Rather, scandal occurs due to the complex *matrix* of competing and available discourses around sports, health, binge drinking, illicit drugs and addiction. These discourses not only present alternative and sometimes conflicting views, but often shift very quickly when a scandal arises in order to make value judgments that, on the one hand, are about broader, non-football issues such as binge drinking or drug use by younger persons and, on the other hand, operate in complex ways within and against the idea of a connection between sports and bodily health.

An element in scandals that emerges around the specificity of sportsplayers' use of alcohol or drugs or the notion of gambling addiction relates not to their celebrity status, as we are living in a media culture in which stories about singers, actors and reality television celebrities drinking excessively or using drugs are not only banal and repetitive but do not form scandal in a way that invokes institutional statements, public relations activities or government avowals on the need to combat a sports 'problem'. Rather, they emerge because of the residual function of elite-level footballers as 'role models' – a function that has been over-ridden by the shift of footballer identity into a mode of celebrity, but which is persistently invoked within scandal narratives. At the same time, this role model function within the context of alcohol use, drugs or gambling results in scandals that are routinely framed through confession. For example, Western Australian footballer Ben Cousins' documentary *Such is Life: The Troubled Times of Ben Cousins* operates within a broader scandal as an act of *confession* to his use of drugs and his addiction, even though ultimately it is also a *response* to scandal that seeks to mitigate his responsibility in the events that resulted from his use of drugs. Likewise, Australian Rules footballer Brendan Fevola gave an interview in early 2011 on *The Footy Show* in which he confessed to excessive drinking and a gambling habit. The actual phrases used by both were in the rhetoric of scandal:

Ben Cousins: 'I'm a drug addict'.[1]
Brendan Fevola: 'I have a gambling issue and I want to knock it on the head'.[2]

Such confessions are not merely an act of contrite apology to the public or supporters of a football club. Rather, as an element in scandal they are produced within the language of therapy, much like the increasingly common forms of self-help and therapeutic television which ask participants to account for themselves through confession and revelation.[3] Such confessional rhetoric is a response to scandal but it is also a technique for the production of the self,[4] thereby establishing a certain performance of footballer identity as simultaneously repentant and recovering.

In this chapter, I work through each of the three themes of binge drinking, recreational drug use and compulsive gambling, discussing some of the scandals that have emerged around these in recent years, including how they relate to the culture of football, how clubs and league governance bodies utilise public relations statements to disavow any linkage of these with football culture, and how each of these are situated against a broader backdrop of policy and government intervention in what are considered contemporary 'social problems'. There are, however, two areas that can be addressed in understanding the circumstances by which footballers, who are under such heavy surveillance and likelihood of career-damaging penalisation, drink, use drugs and gamble in ways which produce scandal. Firstly, the fact that drinking, drugs and gambling are social activities that are inseparable from the culture of football historically. As Dunning and Waddington have argued, team-based sports took their contemporary form in nineteenth century Britain built on two attitudinal poles, one being the extensive representation of sports participation through a puritanical and stoic perspective that emphasises health and the naturalness of the body, the other being a Dionysian or Epicurean formation that, although both diametrically opposed to the puritanical and generally hidden within the social activities of masculine team sports, emphasises pleasure, partying and excess. Secondly, I would like to show how the pleasures of off-field sociality expressed through drinking, drug use and gambling are not, in fact, separate from the on-field discipline of sportsplayers but can be understood as an extension of the on-field pleasures towards the off-field social environment. In other words, this is to stress that footballers' motivation not only for activities which cause scandal but for playing in the game in the first place are governed by a concept of pleasure that operates as a continuum which constitutes footballer identity across all facets.

Alcohol

Binge Drinking and Scandal

Footballer stories connected with the use of alcohol, excessive drunkenness and group-based binge drinking have been a staple of scandal reporting over the past decade, either as one-off stories that contribute to broader social concerns around the role of alcohol in sporting culture or as spectacle extending out over several days of media and club governance inquiry. Heavy alcohol consumption is an endemic aspect of sociality in Western culture, including in Australia, although it is not uncontested. Connotations of youth, partying, large-group social engagement, self-reward or 'being social' generally are part of drinking culture, and to drink heavily in a social context is regularly deemed to be nothing other than 'heavy sociality'. However, government reports on binge drinking, public discourse on alcohol-fuelled violence, broad critical engagement with the perceptual relationship between masculinity and drinking, and a growing performance of social citizenship that is performed through moderation in alcohol consumption or outright teetotaling is notable in establishing heavy drinking as a point-of-debate in contemporary sociality. The signification of alcohol use in footballer scandals often relates to the intersection between masculine performativity, violence, healthy bodies and disruption of public spaces by footballers, occasionally congealing in news stories about off-field public violence and street fighting, as seen in Brendan Fevola's assault on a barman during a 2006 International Rules tour of Ireland subsequent to a ten-hour drinking binge;[5] indecent or disrespectful behaviour in licensed venues, for example Melbourne's Brent Moloney urinating on a bar in a St Kilda nightclub before being evicted;[6] or public nuisance behaviours, such as the incident in February 2011 in which, during an end-of-season trip the previous year, several Western Bulldogs players harassed motorists and jumped on car bonnets in a Hong Kong street resulting in a video uploaded to YouTube.[7] In all cases, alcohol is an element, although one would want to be careful not to suggest that consumption of alcohol is, in itself, causal of scandal, misbehaviour, unethical treatment of others or events that result in negative reports.

Many of the scandal incidents that centred on former North Melbourne and Adelaide player Wayne Carey, for example, relate to substantial use of alcohol. Known to have been binge drinking regularly since he was sixteen – in 1987, the year he was first recruited by then VFL club North Melbourne – he is said to have been heavily drunk after every match across most of his career.[8] In 1996 he had been drinking with other players for twelve hours, after which he grabbed the breast of a woman passing on the street in Melbourne and allegedly stated, 'Why don't you get a bigger pair of tits'.[9] Scandalous, broadly reported, a civil suit from the complainant was later settled out of court. An ongoing figure of football scandal, Carey was notable for his use of cocaine, for having glassed his girlfriend Kate Neilson in the face,[10] for sleeping with the wife of his close friend and vice captain Anthony Stevens,[11] among many other incidents. Alcohol figures prominently in the scandal reports, and is often framed as related to the cause of the incident. Indeed, Carey himself has referred to alcohol as an alibi. In a 2008 interview with Andrew Denton on *Enough Rope*, he pointed to his unhealthy relationship with alcohol:

> I've always thought that I was a binge drinker and that I'd go and have a drink on a weekend. I never drank during the week, never did a sip of alcohol touch my lips during the week. I was dedicated and disciplined enough to know that you know that was a time that you didn't do it but, if alcoholism is drinking every weekend of every year, to an extent where you know you can't drink any more, then I'm definitely, I'd definitely be in the category of an alcoholic, no doubt about that.[12]

More importantly, however, drinking becomes the defence, explanation and excuse for events in the track record of scandal: 'if I hadn't have had that much to drink and I wasn't in that state, the police wouldn't have been called', and 'it was stupid, it was stupidity. I mean it's something that you wouldn't do if you hadn't had too much to drink'.[13] Both excusing scandal and/or putting it down to use or heavy use of alcohol is problematically simple, as it fails to ask not why scandalous events result from drinking (that much is obvious) but why heavy use of drinking is so closely tied up with the culture and identity of football in the first instance and what that means in terms of the coherent performativity of the figure of the footballer. Indeed, Carey was very much aware of the non-linear causalities between alcohol/drugs and behavioural consequences: 'There's no amount of alcohol or drugs that I blame on any decisions I've made and they're a consequence of decisions I've made. They're not a, it's not a reason, it's not an excuse but it's certainly something that has been present when all of these things have occurred'.[14] That is, binge drinking does not, in itself, bear responsibility for the subsequent problems, but the problems would not be present if it was not for the activity and culture of drinking.

Binge drinking in general has been considered a broad issue for social policy in Australia since the mid-2000s, particularly subsequent to a number of concerns around weekend evening activities in nightclub districts in large cities, alcohol-fuelled violence such as the phenomenon of 'glassings' in bars and clubs, and prompting in 2008 the Australian Commonwealth Government's $20 million anti-binge-drinking campaign as part of its National Binge Drinking Strategy,[15] club lockouts at 2am or 3am in several cities,[16] and the controversial attempts to introduce a tax on flavoured pre-prepared alcohol beverages, also known as 'alcopops'.[17] Indeed, binge drinking in Australia became the object of a moral panic during 2008, with the issue of younger persons' drinking habits described as follows: 'alcohol is out of control, a time bomb, a silent epidemic. Alcohol-fuelled violence is mounting, our cities becoming perilous, our youth in more danger of brain damage and assault'.[18] The panic around binge drinking has continued, with calls from numerous agencies, including the Royal Australasian College of Surgeons, for a ban on 'happy hour' sessions and the revelation that three-quarters of police operations budgets are expended on alcohol-related issues.[19]

The definitions of binge drinking are diverse across different countries: in Australia it is defined as consuming seven or more standard drinks for men and five or more for women on any one day; in the United States the figures are five for men and four for women; while British authors have defined binge drinking more liberally as 'the rapid consumption of large quantities of alcohol'.[20] In Australia, excess drinking has long been defined according to the National Health and Medical Research Council measurement of 'four or more standard drinks in a session'.[21] Binge drinking among masculine-oriented elite-level sports teams in Australia has been noted for some time, with studies on National Rugby League players indicating an extremely high consumption of alcohol per session compared with the overall male Australian population.[22] All team sports including Australian Rules are marked by considerable social drinking, despite the fact that while there may be a greater propensity for team sportsplayers to drink heavily through the sociality of off-field sporting culture, the issue is clearly one which is mirrored by a broader increase in the social use of alcohol.

Presumed high rates of excessive alcohol consumption among Australian Rules football has resulted in some notably high-profile scandals, many of which have impacted on footballers' careers. In February 2006, West Coast Eagles player Ben Cousins was involved in a significant alcohol-related scandal when his car had encountered a random breath test or 'booze bus'. Rather than being tested, he abandoned his car in traffic and ran down a side street, pursued by police. He explained the event in his 2010 documentary *Such is Life: The Troubled Times of Ben Cousins* as follows:

> Getting caught by a booze bus is career-threatening, I just had to take off. And when I took off I wasn't messing around...I couldn't tell you how many houses I jumped through. I was over back fences, I was on top of roofs, and I took off across the river. And I reckon I got really close to being halfway over. The river would have been over a [kilometre] across; it was a long swim. I'd spent you know ten or twelve hours on the drink and whathaveyou, and I started to get pretty tired; I was pretty tired and I thought as important as it is I get away, it's probably not quite as important as not going under.

What Cousins presents here is not only a revelation of the scandal but the extent of the risk of being involved in an alcohol-related scandal, particularly a drink-driving incident, and its potential impact on a football career. Cousins was subsequently stood down as West Coast Eagles captain and required to make a statement at a press conference, saying: 'I understand that through a few errors of judgment I put enormous pressure and scrutiny on the footy club. I do regret having to resign under these circumstances but I do believe it's the best course of action'. However, in the 2010 documentary he did indicate that the resignation as captain was not entirely voluntary and referred to himself as having been 'sacked'. What Cousins' story indicates is that, in part, there are pressures that emerge from being an AFL player that require high-profile footballers to avoid scandal through avoiding being caught or revealed, and that the attempt to evade conviction is considered more significant than avoiding the perceived problem of drinking in the first instance.

In January 2008, Collingwood lost their sponsorship deal with the Transport Accident Commission after it was revealed that player Sharrod Wellingham was charged with a drink-driving offence. Later that year in August, Collingwood players Heath Shaw and Alan Didak were suspended for the remainder of the season for their involvement in a drink-driving incident. Shaw was close to three times over the legal limit for driving and was charged, however both he and Didak lied about the fact that Didak was in the passenger seat at the time. It was understood that Didak's career was at risk with threats of an end to his career if there were any further alcohol incidents after an event in which he was with bikie Christopher Hudson at the time Hudson fired shots out of his car window; Didak had for a time been subject to a contractual total alcohol ban.[23] The scandal was a significant embarrassment for Collingwood who had publicly defended the two players until the truth was revealed. Scandal response in this case thus relies on the longer-running model of denial until that denial would reflect badly on the game and its culture.

Whether or not off-field binge drinking should be considered a matter for clubs and for the AFL has been debated, although clubs and AFL governance routinely condemn the alcohol-related misbehaviour of their players and reinforce this stance through penalties, sanctions and, in extreme cases, sackings. In April 2010 Ben Cousins, who had overcome his drug addiction issues and suspension, having been re-registered and playing then for Richmond, was again suspended for breaching the club's alcohol policies, along with Daniel Connors, Luke McGuane and Dean Polo. The event took place at the Intercontinental Hotel early on a Sunday morning after Richmond's loss to the Sydney Swans;[24] while Connors' suspension for an eight-week period included the charge of 'unsociable behaviour', it is unclear if the other three were necessarily misbehaving or making trouble, or if they were only quietly drinking. At the time of the suspension in April 2010, Richmond chief executive Brendon Gale felt that the club expected better behaviour of their players, claiming that: 'Every player at this club needs to fully understand the responsibility that goes with pulling on the yellow and black jumper'.[25] Given that none of the players were necessarily wearing a Richmond uniform at the time of the incident, that they were not missing a training session or in mid-play, it does again have to be asked whether the penalties for binge drinking during players' downtime are too strong. However, what is clear is that clubs and the AFL more broadly are in the process of cracking down on binge drinking through penalisation not because there is (in their view) anything inherently wrong with team-based drinking, but because players are seen more and more frequently to represent their club across the *whole of their time* as a result of their celebrity status and recognisability, thus allowing for scandal where once none existed.

The Culture of Drinking in Team Sports

In the case of Australian Rules football, claims that binge drinking extends from the culture of the sport are routinely denied, with AFL and stakeholders usually stating that there is not a significant culture of drinking in Australian Rules football. For example, in the aftermath of the suspension of Shaw and Didak over the drink-driving incident, Collingwood's chief executive, Gary Pert, denied there was a drinking culture at Collingwood, and that the behaviour of a couple of players did not indicate a widespread problem: 'Do we have a cultural issue on that? Absolutely not… We have a playing group that lives every day disciplined and focussed on winning a premiership'.[26] An attempt to distance the AFL and clubs from the drinking culture of Australian Rules football occurred in 2009 in a public relations exercise in which eight captains appeared in television commercials as part of the *Just Think* campaign calling for an end to alcohol-fuelled violence which had become a significant issue for the weekend night-life of Melbourne's Central Business District. Targeting not alcohol *per se* but binge consumption, the advertisements were framed by the line, 'We're not saying, don't drink – just think'. They represented some of the injuries that can occur from becoming involved in violence and alcohol-related fighting. Former Essendon captain Matthew Lloyd gave the motivation for involvement in the advertising campaign as follows: 'As leaders within our community we want to make a stand to send a strong message that alcohol-fuelled violence is unacceptable and extremely dangerous'.[27] As with any public relations on a social issue, the purpose is to ensure the 'brand' is maintained or enhanced by the activity, and this was very much one of those media relations, seeking to augment the public profile of Australian Rules football which had been damaged by alcohol-related scandals increasingly over the 1990s and 2000s. This is not to suggest that the intervention is not, in itself, praiseworthy, although one might question the extent to which players representing an institution known for its drinking culture (regardless of individual drinking habits) are effective as community 'leaders' in attitudinal change.

Such attempts to present Australian Rules football as being antithetical to binge drinking culture are, however, in conflict with the widespread social knowledge and public awareness of the ways in which sporting teams and sports culture itself foster binge drinking. As AFL Victoria chief executive Peter Schwab noted in a personal reflection on alcohol and illicit drug use in football, alcohol has for a long time been a major provider of income for sports clubs, always served during and after matches and after training, stating that alcohol has been 'at the core of the club's social life'. He noted that during his time as a player with Hawthorn, he was aware of the significant drinking culture among clubs, with many articulating pride in their drinking sessions and the capacity of individual players to consume alcohol.[28] Beyond the academic claims to a culture of drinking that stems from sports itself, this 'insider' statement is contrary to the public relations and campaign articulations that there is no culture of excess in clubs, indicating instead that the very idea of drinking is inseparable from contemporary football as it has emerged over time.

Within sports research, Dunning and Waddington have powerfully argued that there is a drink-related element to sports as a subculture within an international framework.[29] Exploring this question through the history of masculine team-based sports in the United Kingdom, they demonstrate the existence of a long-standing sport-alcohol nexus which emerges between two ideologies that have characterised sport from the medieval period through its nineteenth century codification in contemporary sporting governance. The first ideological perspective is what they have labelled the Dionysian/Epicurean, meaning a culture of spontaneity, irrationality, rejection of disciplinarity, and indulgence in sensual or hedonistic pleasures. They identify a pleasure-centred strain governing how sport in the on-field and off-field environments has operated historically. In the Dionysian framework, pleasure in both the game and its broader culture of sociality are the central motivators for sport and the means by which sport is defined. Although the Dionysian element shifts increasingly to the submerged and frequently hidden part of sport culture throughout the twentieth century, it is through this element that young men are seen to be socialised into an acceptance of the idea that it is 'manly', not only to play physical contact sports such as football and painful, physically dangerous sports such as cricket, but also to drink beer and to be able to 'hold your ale', that is to drink copious quantities of alcoholic beverages after matches without becoming visibly drunk and losing control.[30] The Dionysian can thus be related to the production of footballer masculine identity, whereby engaging in binge drinking is more than merely a celebratory or social activity but actively produces and reinforces masculinity through risk, competition and achievement in the field of drinking as much as in the field of the game.[31] It is through the Dionysian pole that the culture of excessive or binge drinking emerges as a central and, indeed, 'necessary' cultural aspect of Australian Rules football.

The Puritanical/Stoical framework arises as part of cultural changes occurring during the sixteenth-century Reformation in Europe, increasingly dominating the perception and definition of sport over time through to the nineteenth century. It has its fruition in the discourses of 'rational recreation' in public schools and the increasing social emphasis on health, consolidating in the twentieth century with the rise of physical education as a profession.[32] This framework produces the image of the 'wholesomeness' of the sports celebrity whereby fame is portrayed as reflection of talent, determination and health,[33] and a rejection of passions in favour of rationality and distinction. The puritanical pole thus governs the ongoing production of a public image for

Australian Rules football, with its emphasis on health, integrity and rationality, and is consistently reinforced through the AFL and club public relations machinery in addition to government public and social policy. This submerges but does not replace the Dionysian approach to sports, sociality and pleasure. In this understanding, contemporary masculine team sport is, ultimately, defined by both of these elements, with the wholesome, health-driven puritanical aspect the surface-level and public perception, and the more underground but persistently emerging Dionysian framework governing both the pleasure of play and the social pleasures of being part of a team.

The two poles of the Dionysian and the puritanical become concomitant through a concept of footballer masculinity. Although neither drinking nor binge drinking is, today, an activity that stems from gender as such, there is an element of footballer binge drinking which extends from the performance of a particular type of masculinity on the field to the off-field social environment; a performance of excess that marks masculine footballer identity in both environments. Stewart and Smith, for example, have argued that certain forms of antisocial behaviour both produce and are produced within a hypermasculinity, whereby the 'celebration of heroic deeds in sport also encourages other risky behaviors like excessive alcohol consumption...which reinforce the desire to damage the body to exude masculinity'.[34] Within that framework, placing oneself in the position of being at risk of injury on the field and, likewise, vulnerable to the health risks of excessive drinking are seen as activities which uphold and reinforce hypermasculinity. However, the extent to which binge drinking is understood consciously as a health risk by footballers is not necessarily that clear. Rather, there is a more dominant discourse around excessive alcohol use by footballers that obscures any health concerns in favour of viewing the potential risks of binge drinking in forming evidence for scandal and creating collateral misbehaviour that, too, contributes to narratives of footballer scandal. For example, in an interview on *The Footy Show* in March 2011, Brendan Fevola was asked about his views on his past drinking just subsequent to his release from rehabilitation, and stated the following:

> They said I wasn't an alcoholic, because I hardly ever drunk. But when I drunk I drunk, like I would stay out there all night and wouldn't want to go home, wouldn't want to miss anything. You know, I'd want to be the first one there and the last one to leave. I regret all that and that's my fault. I've gone out and done the wrong thing and now I realise after being in the clinic that it doesn't just affect me, it affected the Carlton footy club, it affected their sponsors, affected the supporters, young kids.

The emphasis, then, is not on *health* but on *role-model image*, an ambassador for the club.

Using Dunning and Waddington's framework of the two discursive poles of sport, it can be argued that scandal involving alcohol emerges not because alcohol is foreign or does not properly belong within football culture, but because the two poles present conflicting discourses about the values of sport. Where footballers' binge drinking and getting into trouble in the social sphere away from the game is narrated through news stories that form scandal, what occurs is the revelation that the puritanical understanding of sport which governing bodies and various stakeholders work so hard to present is not so much merely a facade, but is in persistent conflict with the view of sport held by players themselves. It is not the repetitive, recognisable and often banal stories that come to have meaning for the public, but the fact that the conflict between the two understandings of sport is revealed, albeit only momentarily, in the context of scandal. This is why footballers' excessive drinking specifically comes to be considered scandalous, despite the fact that similar levels of binge drinking occur on weekend nights across Australian cities. That is, footballers are targeted for scandal in this case not because they are celebrities or the event of drinking and drink-related misbehaviour is new, but because they are subject to the conflicting Dionysian and puritanical poles that define their sport and therefore their public identities.

Drugs

Recreational Drugs and Footballer Scandal

There are a number of examples of the improper use of drugs by Australian Rules footballers, including the use of prescription drugs for partying during a breach of curfew by members of St Kilda Football Club while on tour in New Zealand in early 2011,[35] the revelation that six players had tested positive for illicit drugs including cannabis, cocaine and ecstasy during routine tests in 2010, with Hawthorn player Travis Tuck receiving a 'third strike' resulting in a ban and deregistration before a career shift to playing in the Victorian Football League.[36] Wayne Carey was noted for his use of cocaine.[37] The most notable scandal involving the use of illicit recreational drugs by Australian Rules footballers centres on Ben Cousins who had been the subject of rumour over drug use and socialising with alleged criminals for some time, with the drug scandal emerging in 2006 when he was forced to resign from the captaincy of West Coast Eagles. These were followed by stints in a United States rehabilitation clinic during 2007 and, ultimately, his sacking from West Coast after a high profile on-camera arrest. In August 2010, significant information about Cousins' use of recreational drugs was made publicly available in the documentary *Such is Life: The Troubled Times of Ben Cousins* which presented footage of Cousins' partying lifestyle during the 2006-2007 period, interviews with Cousins, his father Bryan (former WAFL Perth and VFL Geelong player), his drug counsellor and other people in his life, focusing primarily on the question not of drug use but of addiction and recovery, as well as the impact of both on Cousins' football career.

Football drug scandals differ significantly from the ways in which spectacle around the use of alcohol or binge drinking among footballers plays out in the media, and this is partly due to the simple fact that illicit drugs are illegal whereas drinking (but not drink-driving) is not illegal. Although popular, the illegality of recreational drugs means that the drug scandals infecting Australian Rules football does not fit within the Dionysian/ puritanical disjuncture in the same way that alcohol scandals do. Further, the Australian Football League enforces a policy on drug use and conducts regular drug testing of players. There are two AFL policies relating to drug use. The first, which was initiated in the 1990s, is the Anti-Doping Code which covers the use of performance-enhancing drugs by players; the second is the Illicit Drug Policy which, introduced in 2005, covers the use of recreational and other non-legal drugs. A 'third strike' failure in drug testing under the latter policy results in a suspension of a player for eighteen weeks (the first failure results in a fine with the second a shorter suspension). However, the extent to which recreational drug use among footballers is treated as a crime as is the case for many non-footballers busted with possession of drugs is a slightly more cloudy issue, with punishments for footballers for these off-field infractions relating to their on-field role, whereas punishments for non-footballers involved in the use of recreational drugs more likely to involve police and state criminal codes. For example, in 2007 it was revealed that a Perth-based police detective had informed West Coast in 2001 that Cousins and other players were known to be using illicit substances[38] and that there existed secretly recorded police tapes of arrangements by players to collect drugs from a dealer who was sentenced the following year for possession with intent to supply.[39] Notable here is the internal club policing of what is arguably a criminal act rather than reporting the act to police, indicating not a culture of secrecy within football but a culture in which 'ownership' of footballer behaviour is assumed by clubs and league authorities.

It is important, of course, to bear in mind the backdrop against which scandals involving illicit or party drugs occurs. A number of Western countries, including Australia, have been conducting what is sometimes still referred to as the 'War on Drugs' – a term coined by United States President Richard Nixon and used regularly in policy announcements, policy adjustments and media reports over the past four decades. The so-called war on drugs established a discourse in which the person who is a user of drugs, whether addicted or not, is positioned to be depicted as criminal, a member of a threatening underclass which is seen to be undermining organised labour, a work ethic and the security of non-drug users.[40] Narrow depictions of drug users also produce the drug user as deviant within a deviance/respectability discourse, usually relying on stereotypes of a person using drugs as being on-edge, a risk to others, deluded, disoriented, disorganised, and living in a world of 'fantasy' produced through a misperceived idea that drugs are inherently hallucinogenic and psychotropic[41] and that the drug user is de-individualised through the regular use of drugs.[42] The discourse of the war on drugs produces this perception of the individual drug user, but also dispatches a risk discourse whereby drugs are seen to be not a risk to the individual user but to society more broadly, and requiring a swift response in increased discipline.[43] Risk, in this sense, needs to be managed by the individual user as the producer of social risk,[44] but at the same time requires that user to be disciplined through governance and punishment mechanisms in order that risk is reduced for others.

In 2005, somewhat prior to the emergence of the drug issue for Ben Cousins and the increased likelihood of scandal, the

Australian Commonwealth Government began a \$12 million television, cinema and newspaper advertising campaign aimed at teenagers to warn against use of party drugs as a new key strategy in the discourse of the war on drugs. The advertisements included a commentary on recreational drugs and sporting prowess with a scene of a teenaged boy who, after smoking marijuana, misses an easy handball in a football game and is confused and upset when criticised by the coach and other players.[45] This increase in advertising on recreational drug abuse put the issue solidly in the public sphere, allowing the perception of drugs and drug use as criminal, dangerous, risky or unwarranted to shift from intravenous drugs such as heroin to party drugs such as amphetamines and ecstasy. Media campaigns about young people and drugs are often, as John Hartley has pointed out, about disseminating a signifier for the need for governability of the young,[46] and these advertisements in several ways shift governmentality over drug use from policing and punishment to an even further individualisation whereby one must reduce the risk of drug use by abstaining or be shunned from the team (representing society). However, the ways in which footballers are governed on recreational drug use is significantly different in that the AFL and individual clubs have a range of mechanisms both to protect and to police. As a result a media scandal involving the use of recreational drugs by an elite-level footballer is one which tends to open questions not about the social formations in which drug use occurs – as is routinely the case during a media panic about drugs and younger persons or party drugs more generally – but about the role and the failure of clubs and the AFL to govern its players 'properly'. And, often obscuring this, for the players to govern themselves.

Media scandals about footballers and drugs, then, are part of a wider moral panic discourse on the use of recreational substances that, as with all media moral panics, depend on a folk devil – in this case, the drug user – seen to be a threat to a fantasy of commonly held values and public security.[47] The footballer drug user, however, becomes simultaneously the folk devil and the folk hero; he is on the one hand a drug-using infiltrator in the supposedly wholesome, public and very Australian institution of Aussie Rules football, but at the same time is that which can be restored to heroic status through a range of narratives around drug use (such as problem friends from outside football culture, personal issues, individual compulsions towards drugs or as someone who can be rehabilitated). Other elements that form the background of footballer drug scandals are the prior concerns about players in other codes and sports internationally. Among the most high profile of cases informing how drug scandals play out is that of Argentinian soccer player Diego Maradona who was suspended from play in the early 1990s for illicit substance uncovered during testing and was ignominiously sent home from the 1994 World Cup in the United States after a positive drug test. In 1996, Maradona appeared on television declaring he had defeated his drug habit, making promises to change his lifestyle and indicating that drug use had led to serious threats to his health.[48]

Anti-Doping and the Natural Body

While we are interested here in recreational drugs that form a substantial part of the party culture of off-field footballer sociality, the use of recreational substances is not entirely separate from the cultural aspects of sports performance-enhancing substances that are used – or, more rightly, prohibited – for the strength and capabilities of players on-field. In attempting to understand footballer drug scandals, it is important to note the fact that the sorts of drugs discussed in scandals about players such as Wayne Carey and Ben Cousins were strictly recreational party drugs, not performance-enhancing drugs – although there may be some question as to the extent to which the use of amphetamines or methamphetamines can enhance performance; methamphetamine use, according to drug addiction expert Professor Rick Rawson, can increase performance either through increased stamina or, over the longer term, assisting in weight loss.[49] Use of performance-enhancing drugs have, until the recent Essendon drug scandal, been more likely to involve individual athletic sports rather than team sport.[50] Use of drugs which enhance performance are, through dominant discourses on sports, understood to undermine the 'authenticity' of sports performance,[51] to damage the longer-term health and welfare of athletes,[52] to impact negatively on sport integrity and a sense of fair play.[53] The AFL's anti-doping policy which polices and penalises for the use of performance-enhancing substances has been more successful in preventing significant use of performance enhancers among football players than in responding to recreational off-field drug scandals. Although the institution is clearly opposed to both, it actively produces a black-and-white distinction between on-field and off-field drugs aligned with performance-enhancing and recreational. As Cousins put it in the documentary: 'I've never taken performance-enhancing drugs. You know, I've never taken drugs game-day, the day before, I've never taken drugs immediately before a game, during a game, it goes against everything I believe in as a sportsman'. In that sense, the issue of drug use in this scandal and other footballer drug scandals is not about the on-field environment but about the location of footballers' social activities within a night-time, club and social culture that has in all other respects embraced drugs as a form of recreation.

The AFL operationalises an anti-doping policy which seeks to prevent the use of performance-enhancing substances that have been registered on the *World Anti Doping Agency* (WADA) Prohibited list. The AFL's policy objective is to ensure that the game is 'conducted upon the basis of athletic prowess and natural levels of fitness and development and not on any pharmacologically enhanced performance' and to protect '[p]layers from using substances which may cause acute or long term harm to their bodies'.[54] The AFL Players Association view is that the use of 'a performance enhancing drug or method to improve athletic performance is cheating'.[55] Such perspectives posit the normative notion of an idealised 'natural' body, which is developed through discipline, training, exercise and food substances that are rationalised as non-chemical. The seriousness of the normative 'natural' body of the sportsplayer is underscored by governmental powers: The Australian Sports Anti-Doping Authority is a federal government agency with legislated powers to investigate and test for the use of performance-enhancing drugs among Australian athletes and visiting international athletes. The 'preferred' representative identity, then, of the footballer is one which is not affected by chemical substances, whether performance enhancing or recreational, but is a body that is stoically produced in its on-field and off-field contexts. Naturally, what constitutes a performance-enhancing substance is not at all clear-cut, despite the WADA list of prohibited drugs – new chemicals are regularly produced and others have effect only in particular quantities which, at times, may not be easily or universally determined.

In early 2013, allegations that players were being given performance-enhancing peptide hormones emerged in an Australian Crime Commission report *Organised Crime and Drugs in Sport,* resulting in both internal and ASADA investigations and a year-long scandal narrative that focused on doping and the corporeal health of Essendon players. The internal report conducted by Ziggy Switkowski was released to the public in May 2013, and detailed the process by which Essendon Football Club's 'High Performance Team' undertook processes to increase the strength of Essendon players initially through a weights and sports medicine program into the probable use of supplements that were not necessarily among those belonging to the legal and mainstream elements of sports pharmacology. As the report states:

the rapid diversification into exotic supplements, sharp increase in frequency of injections, the shift to treatment offsite in alternative medicine clinics, emergence of unfamiliar suppliers, marginalization of traditional medical staff etc. combine to create a disturbing picture of a pharmacologically experimental environment never adequately controlled or challenged or documented within the Club in the period under review.[56]

The primary finding of the report is that while there are concerns related to the health of players in addition to questions (to be handled by ASADA) on the legality of injected supplements programs, poor governance and authority delegation within the club led to competing views, alternative and non-mainstream processes and ultimately a risk environment for footballers that was described in terms of the footballer body. The risk was exacerbated by the failure to fully disclose to players the nature of the drugs injected into their bodies. The initial ASADA report was handed to both the Essendon club board and the AFL legal counsel in August,[57] with the AFL announcing the $2 million penalisation of Essendon (the largest penalisation in Australian sporting history) and the banning of coach James Hird for twelve months.[58] Both public and private concerns emerged, including among the family members of Essendon players, as to the health repercussions of the supplements, including on possible fertility and birth defects – concerns exacerbated by the failure of the club to have detailed records on the source and type of supplements injected.[59]

While this is a scandal relating to an on-field aspect of Australian Rules football, it provides a framework for understanding the relationship between the healthy body, chemical substances and footballer identity. As with the distinction between the oft-submerged Dionysian aspects of football off-field culture and the puritanical and stoic perspective of athletic on-field prowess that emerges in discourses on alcohol consumption and binge drinking, the anti-doping policies and the Essendon supplements scandal point to the broad dominance of the stoic. Indeed, the terminology of the puritanical is significant here, inferring and constituting the notion of a 'pure' footballer body that has its performance capabilities produced through non-chemical means. The drug supplement is positioned as the non-real, invasive and disruptive of the body, thereby constructing the idea of a natural body.[60] In that context, the stoic/puritanical representation of footballers depends on the conceptual possibility of the drug, but distinguishes between the drug that is involved in performance enhancement (thus questioning the purity of the footballer's body on-field) and the drug that is used for recreational pleasure (that sits neatly and less-problematically within the Dionysian pleasure perspective of footballer's off-field sociality).

Party Culture, Youth and Drugs

The substances that are discursively knowable as drugs within the majority of footballer scandals are predominantly recreational drugs such as ecstasy and methamphetamines which, contrary to stereotypes of drug users as out-of-it loners, are highly social in use and can often form part of the regular social activities of a group such as, in these cases, a team. Indeed, senior football writer from *The Age*, Rohan Connolly, stated in an interview in Ben Cousins' *Such is Life* documentary that there had for a long time been 'stories about players seen at nightclubs snorting coke or...dropping tablets or being seen with interesting and colourful characters in the West Australian club scene'. Whether or not recreational drugs carry a lesser status than some other hard-core substances such as heroin or performance-enhancing drugs used in the context of sport is unknowable, although there is certainly no clear-cut or monolithic set of community values that posit recreation drugs as morally wrong on the basis of their illegality – rather there is considerable research and evidence to suggest that communities have notably diverse views on the meanings, use and value of drugs and drug definitions.[61] As recreational drugs that are commonly used in a widespread way by younger persons in the context of nightclub culture, the use of these substances by footballers is very clearly located within the off-field social environment, and one which mirrors the 'partying' environment of younger persons more broadly where we also find the greater use of amphetamines and ecstasy. This does not necessarily mean that their use is not part of the social activity of a team or part of a team, but that it is not ostensibly related with on-field performance, ideals or objectives.

In several ways it is not surprising that footballers would be attracted to the sociality of recreational drugs, given the long-standing role of alcohol in football's off-field cultural activities. Contrary to the idea that there is a clear-cut distinction between alcohol (legal) and recreational drugs (illegal), substances such as ecstasy and amphetamines as found in the culture of contemporary nightclubbing are often better understood as an extension or continuation of drinking. Measham and Brain, for example, refer to a new culture of intoxication that has developed over the past two decades, with a changing use of a range of illicit substances at its core, spurred on first by the development of the underground rave scene, the increased emphasis on dance, and the movement from alcohol to recreational drug use in dance clubs for a significant number of younger persons.[62] As demonstrated in their research, this has resulted in a shift in attitude to recreational drugs whereby they play an increasingly normalised role in social life and their coming to replace alcohol as the core substance in a culture of intoxication.[63] Given the differences in intensity, recovery and hangover, one might speculate that healthy young athletes may well find recreational drugs fit well with the 'work' of being an athlete if recovery is not as painful as an alcohol hangover from an evening of excessive binge drinking. Certainly there is some evidence that involvement in sports has meant a greater likelihood of using substances for social purposes and avoiding those which impact negatively on performance such as tobacco and cannabis,[64] and this attitude to recreational drugs and their place in contemporary culture is reflected in the scant information we have about Australian Rules footballers' use of illicit substances that has emerged through scandal and, particularly, the Cousins documentary.

The Ben Cousins Narrative

The *Such is Life* documentary is itself part of the way in which this drug scandal played out, not because it was revealing scandalous information, nor because it was in any way shocking but because it attempted to reconfigure the relationship between football and drugs into an issue of health and well-being rather than one of individual risk and punishment. It thereby contributed to the overall discourse of recreational drug use by footballers circulating in the public sphere. Sports documentaries themselves are relatively rare and tend to be a niche or sideline form of documentary production as a result of not being perceived as recording or engaging with 'real life' or issues of power and social change that form the subject matter of most documentaries.[65] However, *Such is Life* may be seen as much less a documentary about sports and a sportsperson and more a documentary on a celebrity figure. Certainly, its undertaking is within the normalised discourses of celebrity in that it presents a figure through 'problems and disappointments of everyday life' providing an intimate picture of the private through confession and private revelation in order to present the figure as accessible and knowable to the audience.[66] Promotional advertising in the lead-up to the documentary showed footage of Cousins dancing in his underwear and stating direct-to-camera 'I'm a drug addict', sparking a number of concerns prior to its airing that the film would glamorise the use of illicit drugs.[67]

The documentary itself was presented in two parts in August 2010, with the first part focusing predominantly on Cousins' early career with the West Coast Eagles and the ways in which he managed his on-field success and his off-field drug use. Although interesting and somewhat revealing, the first part was heavily criticised for its failure to present the *reasons* behind Cousins' use of drugs and his subsequent addiction, tending to focus on a surface-level explanation that Cousins used drugs as a 'reward for training harder and longer than anyone else, for being more devoted than anyone else to the game'.[68] While persistently claiming throughout the first part that the use of drugs was a *personal* problem for Cousins, it did leave open questions as to the extent of drug use in Australian Rules football clubs and the AFL more broadly, and whether that played any role in the use of drugs by individual players. While the question of causality was not addressed in the second part either, it narrated the story of Cousins' sacking from West Coast, his deregistration from the AFL, his increased drug use becoming addiction, and the role his father, in particular, played in Cousins' rehabilitation before the 'happy ending' of being re-registered and drafted by Richmond Football Club. The second part was critically received as a positive story about overcoming addiction, although again it was criticised for the failure to reveal how Cousins had avoided ever testing positive for illicit drugs.[69]

Although it presents a specific narrative of drug use through the convention of addiction as an obstacle to be overcome, the documentary simultaneously operates as a mitigation strategy for scandal for Cousins personally, which is different from the usual public relations exercise around footballer scandals which work to protect and enhance the Australian Rules and AFL 'brand' and to ensure the game is not overshadowed by scandals related to drugs, sexual assault and alcohol-fuelled violence.[70] By focusing on the role of Cousins as a footballer and thus 'role model', it produces, through Cousins' confession of his risky behaviour, a narrative of overcoming an obstacle with a final result of becoming not only a better footballer in his return to AFL with Richmond but a better person overall. In that sense it is somewhat contrived from the very beginning, seen in Cousins' to-camera announcement at the start of the first of the two episodes:

> I understand that some of the footage you see in this film is very troubling, and it doesn't always depict me in the best light...but I feel there are some real lessons to be learned here, and I hope some good comes from it...If it helps save one person's life, or helps us better understand addiction, then it will have served its real purpose.

In this way, the perception of Cousins as a potential role model is not one which opens the possibility of the glamorisation of drug use through the wholesale depiction of a party-keen football celebrity. This was, in fact, a fear expressed by a number of parties in the lead-up to the documentary's airing, with the Australian Drug Foundation (ADF) urging Channel Seven and Cousins himself not to air footage of actual drug-taking should it act as a trigger for others to use. As ADF policy manager Geoff Munro put it: 'Our other concern is that Ben has a celebrity status with some people, and a documentary like this might have some people seeing him as "cool". That may encourage some people to emulate his drug use'.[71] The Victorian Association of State Secondary Principals similarly encouraged younger viewers to watch it with their families rather than alone, expressing concerns that reading the documentary or the situation incorrectly could 'glamorise the footballer's troubled life'.[72] However, in contrast with these concerns, Cousins' opening line begins the process of figuring him not as a celebrity role model who could unwittingly encourage drug use but as a person seeking to be a role model in a campaign against drug addiction.

In the footage, the interviews and the documentary's broader narrative, Cousins does not, however, fully come across as a role model and a reformed drug addict. While undoubtedly well-intentioned, there is a particular rhetoric of ill-treatment made in the later interviews that form the crux of Cousins' commentary, and these tend to detract from the confessional narrative of fall and recovery, and rather are represented as complaints that shift some of the drug responsibility onto others who had mistreated him. As Karl Quinn put it:

> Frequently, Cousins seemed to paint himself as a victim of sorts. Someone tipped off the media before the Northbridge arrest. The club didn't warn him they were about to dump him. The players stopped treating him as a leader. Cousins' pain was palpable, but there was precious little sense of him realising he'd long before foregone the right to expect anything else by virtue of his own betrayals.[73]

Others suggested that it would be a legitimate reading of the documentary to see 'Cousins to be an overindulged, unworthy prat who has abused the goodwill of the AFL, his family and his public...'[74] Finally, as Quinn suggested, the documentary is 'less a confessional than a job application, a repositioning of Brand Cousins in the public eye as being worthy of a second (or is that third? or fourth?) chance'.[75] But that is the nature of a documentary in which the subject has been a significant participant in its initiation, the management of its narrative and, according to reports, in not only receiving substantial payment for its airing[76] but having invested in it in both financial terms and a time commitment.[77] If it is about redemption, as claimed, then it is about the redemption of a public image which, as I discussed in the first chapter, is for footballers today a mythical celebrity facade. That does not necessarily mean that there are not positive elements in relating a narrative about drug over-use and addiction, although from the perspective of understanding footballer scandals, it opens some opportunities to think alternatively about these issues in ways probably not intended by the documentary or those who promoted it.

Perhaps the most important act of mitigation encountered in the documentary involves the events just subsequent to former West Coast player Chris Mainwaring's death from a drug overdose. Cousins had been with Mainwaring not long before he died, although there is nothing particularly scandalous about that. He was present at the funeral and clearly upset by the loss of his close friend and mentor. Yet, within a few days, Cousins was taken into police custody in mid-afternoon in Northbridge, led away by police shirtless on camera with footage that was repeated several times in mainstream news over the following weeks. Greg Baum's take on this event in 2007 was to condemn Cousins for the lack of integrity in a drug charge that occurred only days after Mainwaring's death which he said should have been for Cousins 'the sharpest jolt of all'.[78] The writer went on to suggest that Cousins had 'brought shame enough already to his game, his club, his family' and was guilty of 'making a fool of himself'.[79] He stated further that Cousins had, through his selfishness, hurt others and had 'created for West Coast an image of a club addled by drugs, and was recalcitrant about it. It is an awful slur on an overwhelmingly clean majority'.[80] While the commentary is harsh, it can be read as much as a critique about the playing out of the scandal as a criticism of Cousins himself in the sense that the death of a former player highlighted some of the risks involved in being part of a culture of heavy drug use among footballers, but that Cousins was effectively disavowing those risks. However, the documentary acts to provide an alternative narrative on this event designed to eradicate the earlier scandal that was driven through negative perceptions of the player by writers such as Baum. Cousins states in voice-over that he was three or four days into an addiction relapse, effectively caused by his grief and warranting sympathy rather than either condemnation or concern at the ease by which the relapse can occur in such a public way. He complains that the arrest was a stunt organised by police with media involvement, suggesting that he had 'been made aware by "certain people" that something was going to happen eventually. Now it reads like a set-up doesn't it?' His manager Ricky Nixon (himself questioned for use of recreational drugs later in the so-called 'St Kilda Schoolgirl' scandal) defends Cousins, stating the following:

> If my information is correct, Ben was arrested and pulled over and there was a camera already on the other side of the road filming the arrest. Now you as a viewer work it out. If that happened and it is right, then clearly that media organisation was tipped off by the police.

What Nixon and Cousins do in these statements is figure the arrest as a conspired attack on Cousins rather than a response – either by the police, the media, or both, not necessarily wittingly – to the *problem* of drugs within Australian Rules football culture in Western Australia that had clearly played its part in Mainwaring's death. In that way, the documentary serves to reframe this aspect of the scandal in a way which effectively obscures the broader problem of illicit drug use and the larger issue of Cousins' ongoing involvement. Framing Cousins' state as a relapse invokes the concepts of health and illness; suggesting that he was targeted at the point of relapse is designed to invoke sympathy instead of the rage against the 'problem' expressed earlier by Greg Baum.

Responsibility and Individualisation of the Drug Problem

One thing that tends to happen through footballer drug scandals such as that centring on Cousins is that the problem of drugs is wholly individualised. Public discourse as well as theorisation of sportsplayers' drug use has tended to explain the problem in highly individualistic terms, whereby the use of drugs comes down to a rational decision made by an individual player, producing a response in which leagues, clubs and codes initiate policies of penalty and sanction in order to govern against the risks for the team or sport produced by that individual decision.[81] Cousins himself signified it as an individual problem that was separate from his football career, albeit impacting on it. He stated in *Such is Life* that he began using recreational drugs when he was seventeen or eighteen. In his commentary on the documentary, sports writer Tony Jones gave a scathing remark indicating his lack of sympathy for Cousins, stating that Cousins: 'back in his teen years was faced with a choice…to either take drugs or not to',[82] clearly locating the choice within an individualist and rational process of decision-making. However, while Cousins posits the problem as an individualistic one, his persistence in using drugs is blamed not on a *rational decision* but on a *personality attribute*, that being his belief that he is obsessive and compulsive in all facets of his life, work and sports:

> There is no doubt that I am obsessive/compulsive to the way I train. It was bordering on unhealthy at times, I needed to balance that out with something, and very early on, you know, it became drugs…I am an extremist, I do have the ability to hyper-focus on something; the unique thing about my situation was that I was applying that same obsession to football as I was to drugs, I just kept on intensifying it, and I kept on training harder, the longer I did it the better footy I played, the more it reinforced to me that I had a method that was working.

Where this remains an individualised problem, Cousins removes personal responsibility and agency by positing the cause of his drug use and addiction on a claim to having a compulsive personality and extremist nature, thereby ensuring there is no clear rational decision to become a drug user. This individualisation of drug problems is reinforced by Cousins' experience with the AFL subsequent to his deregistration. Although it appears clear that the AFL and West Coast were initially supportive of rehabilitation efforts and prepared to undertake that support within a framework that bonded Cousins' within the league, the event of his arrest in October 2007 resulted in both West Coast and the AFL withdrawing its paternalistic support and leaving the problem of Cousins' persistent relapses as one which was his individual responsibility to manage. West Coast Board Chairman, Mark Barnaba, indicated, as related in *Such is Life* that the decision to sack Cousins within twenty-four hours of the arrest was taken on the basis of 'an accumulation of events'. The AFL bolstered the act of placing full responsibility on Cousins in November with the decision to ban him from football for twelve months. Again, according to the documentary, several sports journalists questioned this ban, asking if Cousins was a sacrificial lamb and a means by which the AFL could assert the significance and weight of their anti-drugs policy.

At the same time, however, the individualisation of drug responsibility and the indication that a player has a personal and private responsibility to manage and overcome such a problem has shifted more recently, as we have seen in the Cousins story, from one in which drug use is perceived as an individual rational decision[83] to one in which it is presented as an individual health issue. Certainly the link with health is important, and it is a considerable advance for AFL stakeholders to draw the question of health into the discourse around drug use. There is some evidence that former male team sportsplayers have suffered considerably in post-sports life as a result of drug use during the time that they played.[84] Nevertheless, drug health concerns are positioned by Australian Rules stakeholders as needing to be managed predominantly by the individual (unlike other health issues such as injuries). For example, Collingwood Football Club president and *AFL Footy Show* host Eddie McGuire, in comparing the scandals around gambling with the issue of drugs in sport, indicated that unethical betting by players on AFL matches is a greater threat to the AFL than the use of illicit drugs: 'The recreational drugs issue is about individual health. Betting is about the health of the game'.[85] McGuire's view, then, is that the use of recreational drugs may impact on Australian Rules football, and may be an issue for football in the sense of capacity and performance, but its use, perhaps even if it were widespread, is not *about* football culture more broadly. He thereby relegates drug use once again to the individual through a sympathetic but ultimately intolerant rhetoric of health concern.

Beyond Individual Responsibility: Drugs, Bodies, Pleasures

There are three ways in which we can re-think the individualisation of drug use in Australian Rules football culture, and each of these emerge from the Cousins drug scandal and the ensuing narrative – that is, alternative views can be 'teased out' if we take a slightly closer look at the role of the individual footballer within Australian Rules culture, if we re-think the place of the footballer's body within the context of the on-field and off-field dichotomy, and finally if we re-think the very meaning of drugs in order to think about how the distinction between the pleasure of the game and the pleasure of drugs might be considerably blurred. In terms of the first, a number of statements emerged in *Such is Life* and the subsequent media discussions about the scandal that have been commonly and anecdotally expressed but rarely discussed in the media and public sphere or in publicity around

AFL policy. In the documentary, Cousins' father Bryan discussed the concerns he had about Ben's fast rise to prominence at West Coast. He stated that Cousins becoming captain at only twenty-two years of age was a mistake, that he directly questioned the club for this decision and that he felt Cousins was 'being built up to see himself as invincible'. In an opinion piece in *The Age* not long after the documentary's screening, Karl Quinn asked if what it revealed was the question: 'Is there something inherently risky in a culture that takes boys and makes them gods without giving them much by way of life skills?'.[86] That is, the lifestyle afforded elite-level footballers is one which allows them to perform as celebrities in the manner of film and television stars, with significant financial resources, social opportunities, free time – a form of notoriety that produces a sense of invulnerability. In 2007, Greg Baum made the point that 'Cousins became a monster of many makings – game, club, city – but most of all, his own. Financially, the game lavished favours on him in a way that has ruined greater men. The city indulged him. West Coast players are royalty in Perth, down to the detail that they are impervious to scandal'[87] Tracee Hutchison described Cousins as: 'A cashed-up big fish in a little pond surrounded by sycophants. Thanks, largely, to his employers: the West Coast Eagles and the AFL'.[88] As another writer put it in discussing both Cousins' and Mainwaring's drug use, 'Perth had given these Eagles the key to the city, handed over their daughters, and created for them an Olympus. They no longer knew whether they were gods or men'.[89] As importantly, such status provides them with access to a very broad range of people who, while not always notorious or celebrities, are part of the party culture in any urban environment. With top players earning salaries of more than $1 million per annum,[90] the financial impediments to illicit and recreational drug use are not there to act as an obstacle to use, nor does access to drugs, dealers and supplies present itself as a barrier to a group who are, then, effectively socialites on the drug scene. With these points in mind, even if drug use were a rational decision, it is not for a celebrity footballer the *same* rational decision as for the average user.

Secondly, it is highly important to remark on the fact that the drug scandals impacting on footballers are exacerbated by the fact that the AFL policy on illicit drug use is about the private lives of footballers when not in a 'working' context. This is, in part, the result of the role and place of the footballer's *body* which, itself, is the point of continuum between on-field performance and off-field sociality. In *Such is Life*, Cousins complained of the requirement to have regular drug tests during 2008 as he was gearing towards the end of his suspension and the possibility of being drafted by Collingwood. The AFL Commission hearing required a hair test before re-registration was possible; senior football journalist Mike Sheahan noted in the documentary Collingwood's involvement of the Victoria Police and the Police Commissioner Christine Nixon as well as the employment of a private investigator to determine the extent of Cousins' off-field use of the prior year may seem extreme, although were about wanting to 'minimise their risk' and may be considered an appropriate action 'under the heading of due diligence'. In his commentary on the day of the Cousins documentary, Drew Petrie made the point that it does remain unusual that footballers should be one of the only groups of people under such considerable routine surveillance as to their private and social undertakings away from the 'workplace' of the sporting field:

> I can understand why some players and athletes occasionally ask: Why us? Why are footballers and athletes subjected to random drug testing when other people – especially those in positions of authority and responsibility such as judges, doctors and teachers – don't have to?…I completely support drug testing for

players, but it does sometimes make you wonder why it is only players and athletes who are tested and so heavily scrutinised. The AFL is not the only industry that has to deal with drug use. It's not uncommon to see stars in the entertainment industry, for example, struggle to deal with these issues...[91]

This does point to the fact that while entertainment celebrities are regularly the centre of drug scandals, the victims of drug overdoses and occasionally subjected to arrest, fines and imprisonment for their possession of illicit substances, they are rarely tested on a regular basis in order to continue working on, say, a film or television series or producing an album.

Why, then, are footballers the subjects of such scrutiny over private (if illegal) substance use that occurs outside the workplace? There are two reasons that, again, allow us to re-think this awkward individualisation of drug use and addiction that has formed such a core element in the discourse of the footballer drug scandal. Firstly, the body of the footballer is governed by the AFL and the team as a product that must, during the season, be able to perform on the field. While the body is regularly trained, disciplined and fostered during the week towards peak performance, maintaining it across the week and out of season involves more than just the official activities of football such as training, use of the gym and playing the game, but ensuring that the maintenance of the body occurs across all facets of its use in everyday life. In several ways, it is treated not dissimilarly from a piece of factory equipment that needs to operate efficiently during working hours but, at night when the factory is shut, is maintained through specified temperatures and perhaps even guarded against sabotage or accident when not in use. Significant salaries are paid for the use of footballers' bodies, for the transfer of the body's *potential* into game wins and a range of other profit-making activities, and in that sense the clubs and the league do protect their investment. The same, of course, might be said for the mind of a lawyer or judge which needs to operate efficiently in court and perhaps therefore the court system – should not the firm or the chambers be ensuring the mind and the brain are well-maintained on weekends by monitoring drug use that might impact a court performance? However, lawyers and judges are not contracted in the same way as footballers and, along with a lower likelihood of celebrity status, have a stronger claim to an ethical protection of privacy in non-working life. Which is not at all to say that footballers should not be accorded the same privacy and agency in non-working aspects of everyday life as judges and lawyers. This articulation, though, is not one which opens a question of 'media invasion' of footballers' private lives but, rather, points to the problem of the institutionalised surveillance of footballers' bodies in *all* contexts of their on-field and off-field lives by the AFL machinery.

At the same time, the protection of the investment in the body occurs potentially through an understanding that the introduction of drugs into that body is not necessarily purely an individual decision nor something which happens external to football culture itself, despite the ways in which the public relations around Cousins' drug use and his suspension can be read as an attempt by the West Coast Eagles and the AFL to externalise and individualise drug usage. Indeed, it was reported in 2010 that Robert Clemenger, a close friend of Chris Mainwaring and later Ben Cousins, was fully aware of the extent to which drug culture existed within West Coast Eagles and other Australian Rules football teams. Clemenger:

> knew from Mainwaring that Cousins' excesses were 'no better or worse than anyone in the Eagles. They all knew. It's a joke. That's the hypocritical part of the AFL, and the press. They got the big guy in Cousins, but he is just the twig on the branch of a massive tree'.[92]

When asked if Ben Cousins had introduced drugs into the culture of the Eagles, the response was: 'Of course not. Cousins was inducted by the Eagles'.[93] While this is one version in a scandal in which it is difficult to uncover a 'truth' given the mix of narratives occurring through media, commentary and the documentary itself, it is an indication of the relationship between drug use and the culture of the football club that precedes Cousins' corporeal encounter with that environment. It might be remembered that Cousins indicated in *Such is Life* that he began taking drugs aged seventeen or eighteen; he had been involved with the Eagles from the age of sixteen and, through his family and his own early prowess, had been part of Australian Rules football culture all his life. While we are unlikely ever to know the true extent of off-field recreation drug use among footballers either before the testing regime or subsequently, it is important to see that recreational drug use is, as I have argued, an *extension* of a culture of intoxication, which is something endemic to football culture through the Dionysian sociality of alcohol use and binge drinking among team members off-field. Indeed, if there *is* a drug culture within Australian Rules football, it is only because that is a modernisation or update of the culture of intoxication that was formerly dominated by booze. Thus if the AFL and individual clubs are keen on deploying an illicit drugs policy and testing regime to ensure the maintenance of the body during off-field and down-time activities in preparation for peak game performance, then part of that investment is a mitigation for the drug culture that exists within football, even if that is always located in the off-field sociality of football life. It is about protecting the investment in the footballers' bodies from themselves.

A third and final way in which we can approach footballer drug scandals differently is by thinking through how the body operates as a site of pleasure within a continuum across the on-field environment of the football match and the off-field environment of sociality and drug use. Sporting culture is often discussed in terms of work: indeed stoical hard-work, discipline, mastery and achievement[94] and thereby antithetical to off-field activities such as drinking and using drugs. The on-field work and off-field life are often viewed as diametrically opposed. What is left out of this picture, of course, is the fact that on-field performance, however tough, has its own pleasures. In some interviews undertaken by Gard and Merrill with younger sportsplayers, they found that although players tend to discuss the 'pain' involved in play – often in positive ways related to masculinity, toughness and sports identities – there was a tacit communication of the *pleasures* of play in relation to contact sports that focuses on the role of the body on the field.[95] The act of participating in sports may thus involve pain, injury, vulnerability and hard labour, but it is only attractive because it has its pleasures through play, through competitiveness or, from a neurochemical perspective, the release of adrenalin and dopamine in the activity of playing. Indeed, in their promotional guidelines for junior development for football clubs, the AFL indicates the role of pleasure for younger persons as a motivator for participation in Australian Rules football, whereby the shared:

> fast pace of the game and the opportunity to play skilfully culminate in fun for players. The pace of the game engages players' attention, adrenaline is produced in close competition and success is experienced through skilful play.[96]

In other words, pleasure is the purpose behind participation in sport, but for football it is not merely the pleasure of the body in movement but the sociality of the game which, of course, extends *off* the field and into the social activities of teams and clubs in both official and unofficial social situations. In being in proximity to each other, footballers experience and seek ways to further pleasure, and this includes the choices of activities that are undertaken in a shared environment off the field.

When one puts pleasure into the context of risk-oriented, sometimes violent, contact sports, one must also draw out the question of pleasure in the use of recreational drugs. Drugs are used by footballers and non-footballers alike because of the ways in which they invoke and/or extend pleasure, often in the context of sociality. Yet 'authorised' discourses, such as that of the 'war on drugs' and preventative messages, routinely obscure *pleasure* in favour of risk, the pain of addiction or negative social impact. In looking at the ways in which discourse positions drugs, Foucault was highly critical of what he referred to as a puritanism that made such substances an object for which we are interpellated to be either 'for' or 'against'. He indicated instead that, by the 1970s, drugs had very much become an integral part of contemporary culture related to the production of 'very intense pleasure'.[97] By showing how the discourse of drugs has persistently exalted the ideal of 'the normal, rational, conscientious, and well-adjusted individual',[98] he asks that we relocate the site of drugs and pleasure to the body in sociality. This contrasts significantly with a number of psychoanalytic and pedestrian approaches to the use of drugs which see their effect as being purely within the non-embodied psychic space that, through their use as an intoxicant, is shut off from the non-psychic space of an outside world.[99] Likewise, in examining the rhetoric of drug addiction, philosopher Jacques Derrida pointed to the ways in which even uttering the signifier 'drug' invokes a prescriptive or normative 'diction' that presents value judgments around the health, security, productivity and orderly functioning of social institutions.[100] For Derrida, this rhetoric is deployed to reject the drug user because he is *understood* to 'cut himself off from the world, in exile from reality, far from objective reality and the real life of the city and the community; that he escapes into a world of simulacrum and fiction'.[101] In doing so, this normative discourse similarly locates drugs away from the perception of the body and the production of embodied pleasure, obscuring through a moralism what the drug user and the cultural theorist both know: that the drug offers access to an embodied affective pleasure bypassing the rational, reasonable and cognitive.[102] Within his deconstructionist approach, Derrida teased out the ways in which the concept of drugs is located at the interface of an undecidability between poison and antidote[103] in addition to a range of other conceptual oppositions such as nature/culture, nature/convention and public/private – all of which become disrupted and blurred when we take a closer look at the notion of drugs and the diction of addiction.[104] Through deconstruction and the critique of this rhetoric it thus becomes possible to return '[p]leasure and play' to the notion of drug use,[105] and to reject the idea of the drug as an interiorising force that disrupts a notion of the 'natural' ('drug-free') normality of the body.[106] This is instead to see that drugs are part of the pleasure of sociality without necessarily making a statement on value.

Following this, we can state that the revelation of the use of recreational drugs by footballers becomes scandal as a result of the *mutuality* of the dominant discourses governing drugs (supposed loss of rationality, normativity, work, coherence) and sports (gaining and maintaining health, fitness, functioning bodies), whereby a moral outrage at the incompatibility of the two is produced and circulates in the public sphere, exacerbated beyond any moral outrage over the use of recreational drugs in general, even if by large groups of younger persons (just as long as they are not elite athletes). The celebrity status of Australian Rules footballers, of course, intensifies the scrutiny in combination with the anti-drugs mitigation strategies of the sporting governance agencies such as the AFL. However, Derrida's approach, when taken into consideration with the pleasures of sports, operates as one which demonstrates very clearly *why* footballers might use recreational drugs and answers the persistent question asked in the aftermath of *Such is Life* as to why Cousins was using drugs in the first instance.

The attractiveness of drug use for footballers is not because drugs (unreality, irrationality) are diametrically opposed to football (health, reality, naturalness), but because *both* operate within a *continuum* of pleasure from on-field activities to off-field sociality and back again. This is a continuum in which the motivator for both sport and shared, if sometimes illegal, social activities is the experience of pleasure across a range of forms. Cousins indicates this himself in the documentary, despite his persistent use of the sport-equals-work rhetoric. In discussing his obsessiveness with both football/training and drug use as a personality attribute that allowed his on-field success but drove his downfall into addiction, we can read through the articulation of bodies and pleasures that what drove both was a compulsion towards pleasure on-field and pleasure – enhanced through drug use – in his off-field activities. Both are social, shared, bodily pleasures that extend from one site to another, effectively producing the drug-using footballer while simultaneously making the footballer both vulnerable to being read through scandal in ways others are not. The mutuality between the on-field and off-field pleasures is, of course, disavowed in official discourses in favour of the health, puritanical and stoical discourses of on-field play and the relegation of drugs from pleasure to negativity.

Gambling

Gambling, Football and Scandal

I would like to turn to the third and final form of off-field footballer scandal that, as with alcohol and drugs, has a tendency to be seen as an activity of compulsiveness, fixatedness or addiction: gambling. As with drug use, it has its on-field and off-field components. Where there are concerns about the use of performance-enhancing drugs effecting on-field bodily capacity operating in mutual juxtaposition to off-field illicit, recreational substance use, gambling scandals are similarly located in a framework in which there are ethical and integrity concerns around the betting on matches by players and family members (relating to the official and the on-field elements of Australian Rules football) and the obsessive act of gambling outside of football itself (relating to the sometimes compulsive or unhealthy off-field activities of Australian Rules footballers).

Scandals around betting on matches and match-fixing are relatively recent in Australian Rules football, although they were occurring internationally in cricket somewhat earlier. Certainly they have been one of the current 'big items' on the football integrity agenda from the mid-2000s, resulting in the development of an anti-gambling policy that prevents any AFL footballer, AFL stakeholder or club official from betting on football. In June 2011, former *Age* and *Herald Sun* editor Bruce Guthrie bemoaned the rise of betting on AFL football by the general population, stating that it was affecting the ways in which spectators watch and appreciate the game, prophetically noting that a gambling integrity scandal within the AFL would impact significantly on the game.[107] Fears of the ensuing problems were not because of a lack of effort within the AFL and clubs to ensure integrity and ethical behaviours in regard to gambling and insider information. A network of information that aims to catch players who breach the AFL anti-gambling rules were set up after a number of AFL players had been discovered placing bets on games. The AFL's rules relating to the use of insider information state, 'A person must not disclose or provide any information, advice or opinion to any other person about the teams playing in any match'.[108] The rules protect against unfair betting by players and significant others on the basis of information that would ordinarily not be disclosed to the public prior to a match. In late May, Commonwealth and state government agencies met and agreed on the need to curb promotion of live betting during games of football and cricket;

this was a discussion that occurred in the wider context of current debates on the reform of poker machines and plans to legislate for mandatory pre-commitments to machine-based gaming.[109]

In 2013, the federal Australian Gillard government sought to intervene in the growth of Australia's gambling culture by restricting gambling advertising and banning the promotion of live odds during radio and television broadcast of sporting events. Prime Minister Julia Gillard stated that: 'Families have become increasingly frustrated about the penetration of live odds into sporting coverage, and worried that their son or daughter is now talking about the game, not through the prism of what's happening on the field but through the prism of the associated betting'.[110] Importantly, this policy points to the awkward relationship between gambling and sport – the relationship is old, but has strengthened over the past few years particularly in team-based sports that have a national and community focus, and there is a clear need to untangle the connection between betting and sport that presents sport activity as one based on participation through gambling.

Such anti-gambling policies, however, have not yet been effective in preventing football scandals related to betting, both directly on the game and as a potentially problematic recreational activity for its players in their off-field social lives. In July 2011, Collingwood captain Nick Maxwell was sanctioned and player Heath Shaw suspended for eight matches and fined $20,000 after he and a friend both bet $10 on Maxwell kicking the first goal in a game against Adelaide in which Shaw had known Maxwell would start the match in the forward line. Maxwell himself was fined $5,000 after revealing that three of his family members also placed bets.[111] The bust occurred through part of an information-sharing arrangement between bookmakers and the AFL.[112] Commentators described the incident not as a lapse in integrity or an act of corruption 'but just a moment of stupidity'.[113] The incident that operated as scandal across several days in July 2011 later prompted the AFL Players Association to note that there was a need to increase the effectiveness of education among footballers on confidential inside information, with AFLPA general manager Ian Prendergast stating that the 'future and the livelihood of our members really relies on the integrity of the competition and robust rules around things like gambling being actively enforced'.[114] However, other commentators felt that although the bets themselves were relatively small, the issue was a markedly large one, with Greg Baum referring to it as 'insider trading, precisely' that risked the 'unravelling of the game's integrity'.[115] Importantly, however, Baum felt that the harshness of the AFL's penalties against the two players was 'because it knows (though will never admit) the problem is partly of its own making',[116] which indicates again the role of neoliberal governance system of sport in establishing – unwittingly – the conditions through which integrity is put at stake and scandal emerges.

Brendan Fevola and Compulsive Gambling

Scandal around gambling has been more intense when related to non-AFL betting by current and former AFL players. A number of players have been reported as 'problem gamblers' in their off-field world, including after retirement. Daryn Cresswell, who played with the Sydney Swans 1992–2003, is such an example, having become bankrupt through gambling and related fraud in 2009 and ultimately sentenced to prison.[117] The desire for high-level and risky gambling among both current and former players points to the substantial element of competitiveness that becomes part of the coherent performativity of footballer identity, in some cases leading to serious problems later in life. The most prominent figure in football scandals related to non-official or match-related gambling is Brendan Fevola, who was known to have a problem with gambling on poker games and horse racing from the time he left Carlton and joined the Brisbane Lions in 2010. It emerged that Fevola was struggling financially, owing between $100,000 and $300,000 to bookmakers for horse racing debts.[118] Among the concerns raised subsequent to the revelation of Fevola's gambling habit were that AFL chief executive Demetriou and Michael Voss, coach of the Brisbane Lions, had been aware of the problem from as early as 2009, allegedly without offering or recommending help, support or assistance of the sort players with alcohol and drug problems initially receive.[119] Fevola had already been the centre of significant scandal, particularly in September 2009 when his heavily intoxicated behaviour at the Brownlow Medal Count resulted in his sacking from *The Footy Show*[120] and ultimately also his being traded by Carlton to Brisbane in October that year.[121] The gambling issues came to the forefront during 2010, his only season with the Brisbane Lions, although these were overshadowed by the Lara Bingle incident in March and later the allegation he had indecently exposed himself to a woman in September.[122] He was sacked in February 2011 after multiple contract breaches that were not detailed by Brisbane management[123] although it is known that the breaches included two alcohol-related incidents while previously in China during an exhibition match.[124] Importantly, his gambling problem was not widely cited as contributing to his sacking although in subsequent press and interviews it was revealed to be an ongoing issue during that period.

In March 2011, immediately after 65 days in a mental health clinic, Fevola appeared on *The Footy Show* in a candid pre-recorded interview for which he received payment.[125] In the interview, Fevola discussed a suicide attempt, his significant drinking – 'all my troubles come down to alcohol' – and the gambling debts which had resulted for a period in having to use the entirety of his pay to cover his liabilities. He confessed to having a gambling addiction, particularly noting the ways in which gambling losses impacted on other parts of his life: 'I just block it away; but that's the build up with all the tension, then you have a blow up and do something stupid'. The interview brought significant additional viewers to that *Footy Show* edition and was noted broadly in news and opinion pieces as a substantial confession and apology by Fevola, thereby mitigating some of the concerns that were raised in the light of his ongoing scandalous off-field behaviours. However, scandal did also emerge as a result, not from the interview itself which was easily read as honest, unscripted, uncontrived and clearly not a public relations exercise. Rather it came from the revelation on both *The Footy Show* discussions and the news media the following day that immediately after recording the interview Fevola was not only seen playing poker at the Crown Casino in Melbourne, but had to be removed by a Responsible Gaming Officer.[126] This resulted in some further *Footy Show* discussion as to the nature of Fevola's gambling addiction, and whether or not playing poker constituted an addiction in regard to his known compulsive betting on horses. Questions were asked as to the extent he could be considered both accountable and responsible, the effectiveness and indeed reality of his rehabilitation and the significance of relapses during programs to overcome an addiction.

However, what some of the ensuing debates have done is open questions about the extent to which gambling *is* an addiction in the same form as an addiction to illicit recreational drugs. Compared with alcohol and other recreational substances, there is no physical material that is 'taken into' the body that intensifies the release of dopamine thus permitting 'unnaturally' intense pleasure. That is, as Derrida puts it, not an external foreign substance that is typically regarded through the '*interiorizing* violence of an injection, inhalation or ingestion' that being an act that 'is condemned by a society based on work and on the subject answerable as subject'.[127] This is a question which has been debated in scientific literature since the early 1980s. Concerns have been raised as to whether obsessive but non-drug related behaviours such as exercise, gambling, sex, computer games, internet use or even knitting is problematic if discussed as an addiction, not only because of the lack of a foreign substance having an impact on neurological chemistry but because it creates additional stigma for the person suffering from that behaviour through the rhetoric of addiction and the term's connotations of drug use and illegality. That does not mean, however, that obsessive gambling is not a problem requiring treatment, only that there has been an 'unscientific' application of the term addiction to a number of other behaviours that did not originally fall under the terminology's meaning. Rather, there is 'pathological gambling', which Carlton Erickson has described as being characterised:

> by persistent and recurrent maladaptive patterns of gambling behavior, and it leads to impaired functioning, reduced quality of life, and high rates of bankruptcy, divorce, and incarceration. However, this disorder lacks some of the key characteristics of chemical dependence. For example, there is as yet no strong scientific evidence for a direct involvement of the mesolimbic dopamine system in gambling-related problems, as there is with cocaine, heroin, and alcohol dependence.[128]

For Erickson, gambling problems have been found to be relatively transitory, and the compulsive behaviour does not always follow a chronic and persistent course but is a behaviour from which the subject can recover without formal treatment and without necessarily the need for abstinence that marks the treatment of most drug-related dependences.[129] What this implies in the case of Fevola and his lapse into playing poker within hours of his *Footy Show* confession is that a lot of presumptions were being made on his gambling obsession through the *discourse* of addiction, and these mirror a drug dependence and series of lapses of the sort seen with Ben Cousins' narrative of use and addiction. The reason they become debatable concerns, of course, extends from the formation of scandal around these issues. Although Fevola's off-field behaviour is open to scandal as a result of a relatively broad range of misdemeanours that have acquired significant media and public attention, his gambling issues become more forcibly related to the discourse of problematic addiction through the feigned 'moral outrage' that is central to scandal as a form of communication. This is not, again, to suggest that his gambling is not a problem for either himself, his family, his team or the league more broadly, but that the way in which his gambling came to be seen as addictive was exacerbated by scandal.

Moreover, the tendency of the AFL and other Australian Rules stakeholders to relegate problematic behaviour to an individual health problem requiring care, rehabilitation or support (until such a time as the problem is either resolved or becomes too damaging for the league) is another reason why the notion of Fevola's gambling as an addiction emerges through the scandal and the public relations responses. By using the rhetoric of addiction, it initially is seen as a health rather than a behavioural issue, but one which is located in the individual and not through that players' role within the team-based culture of Australian Rules. Once again, we find that a close look at the scandal reveals some of the tensions between the individualisation of a problem that can, of course, only ever be cultural, and the role of football culture itself in either introducing the problem or exacerbating it. In his *Footy Show* interview, for example, Fevola discussed drinking and gambling scandals through the rhetoric of individualisation and personal responsibility which has become the familiar public line in the majority of scandals related to Australian Rules football.

However, once again it is important to bring the culture of Australian Rules football back into the equation, and this was something noted more recently by those who have been affected by Fevola's off-field misbehaviours. For example, Fevola's former wife, Alex, made a public statement about the role of the AFL in taking Brendan and 'creating a monster'.[130] Her view was that footballers in both the official circles and off-field social world are subject to different rules, stating that this is 'the culture that needs to be changed'. She noted that 'Fevola stopped growing up the day he was drafted to the AFL in his final year of high school'.[131] Importantly, this contributes to the discourse of scandal around Fevola's gambling (and other behaviours) through the fact that the culture of Australian Rules football not only gave a false sense of protection from scandal but also established the situation in which some footballers' off-field actions are not only unreasoned but tend to be irrational and improper; not the behaviour of a role model, an adult or a reasonable person; in her formation, playing football stunted Fevola's growth of reason and sensibility. All subjects are produced through an array of cultural conditions, but what tends to emerge in the Fevola gambling case is the fact that he is not merely the 'bad apple' in the league but a person with significant problems, including gambling, that result from an identity formed as a *product* of AFL culture. That is not to suggest that he was necessarily introduced to gambling solely within Australian Rules football, but that the ways in which football culture shapes his identity, actions and capacity for value judgments opens the possibilities of problematic behaviours that regularly result in scandal.

Conclusion

It might be noted that Ben Cousins and Brendan Fevola were not sacked from their respective clubs for their addictive behaviours but, in both cases, for what was publicly stated to be an accumulation of problems. However, that does not indicate that compulsive or excessive behaviours related to alcohol, drugs and gambling that result in scandal are not at the core of the sackings; rather it points to the fact that suspending, sacking or deregistering a player is a response to scandal where that scandal has become so exacerbated it is likely to impact on the club, the league and the integrity of the game in both its on-field and social capacities. One element that might be noted, however, is that subsequent to the end of their formal football careers, both Cousins and Fevola have unfortunately ended up as 'tragic' figures. For Cousins, despite his return to AFL success with Richmond and the narrative of drug rehabilitation given in his *Such is Life* documentary, drug controversy and alleged addiction has continued long after his last game. Reports alleged that he was continuing to battle drug-related problems according to eyewitnesses who had encountered him in public,[132] was arrested and charged for possession of supply-quantities of methylamphetamine in March 2012,[133] and implicated in a suspicious fight with other men in a park in August 2013.[134] In 2013 Brendan Fevola was declared bankrupt over debts that allegedly were incurred as a longer-term result of his gambling problems. In both cases, scandal narratives shift from a tone of reported outrage to one of tragedy in which former players' ongoing problems subsequent to their retirement from elite football are related not purely as an invasive misbehaviour but as a problematic result of their former elite status. The culture of football and its on-field and off-field construction of footballer identity is thus implicated in the longer-term effects and, sometimes, criminal behavioural outcomes of former players.

The three 'fields' of scandal addressed in this chapter are binge drinking, drug addiction and gambling, and all three have been considered serious issues for Australian Rules football. However, as I have indicated, all three are not purely off-field activities occurring in the spare time of footballers but explicitly *extend* from the culture of football. The distinction between the puritanical and health-driven discourse that props up the league's integrity and promotional capacity and the submerged but ever-present

Dionysian culture of pleasure and partying as the driver and motivator of both on-field play and off-field playfulness is central to how the situations that cause scandals in these three areas emerge, yet this remains to be explored in a serious, deliberative and reflective way by clubs and league governance organisations. This is not to suggest that there is anything sinister or insidious by the way in which clubs respond to issues related to binge drinking, drug use or compulsive betting, but that to properly address these issues requires looking at the ways in which they are situated within a *continuum of pleasure* from the on-field to the off-field in order to develop an ethical and preventative response that protects players not from the outside or from their social lives but from the risks that emerge from being footballers per se.

5

Undoing Exclusions:
Footballer Sexuality, Homosociality,
Homophobia and Homoeroticism

In 2010, the Australian Football League (AFL) and the AFL Players Association (AFLPA) began participating in a highly publicised anti-homophobia campaign, referred to as 'Inclusion and Diversity', which responded to a range of comments during the year on the rate and experience of homophobia by lesbian and gay (LGBT or, to use an academic umbrella-term, 'queer'[1]) players in a range of sports. The campaign was highly publicised, involved a number of high-profile players and included publicity shots of players holding up hand-written placards with comments about inclusiveness in Australian Rules football. However, this public relations exercise became scandalous subsequent to footballer Jason Akermanis writing an article for the *Herald Sun* which argued that queer players should remain in the closet for their own safety and for the protection of the team. He made a number of comments about the fact that team players would not be comfortable engaging in homoerotic playfulness in the locker room should there be a known queer person present. This caused something of a public uproar, with a number of commentators and opinion writers arguing against Akermanis' statement and accusing him of being deliberately controversial and thoughtlessly creating scandal.[2] Akermanis defended himself by stating that the newspaper had added words to his column that were not his own but, subsequent to the paper's denial, admitted the full article was written only by himself.[3]

The controversy was not helped by AFL chief executive Andrew Demetriou's comment stating that both the column and the scandal that was erupting out of it were the result of an unnecessary 'media circus' and a 'distraction to what we call our great game football'. As he stated further: 'For the last 24 hours we've been talking gays and closets. It's an unnecessary distraction'.[4] While Demetriou was correct to point out that controversies and scandals distract from the core profile of the game itself, the fact that he depicted it as a minor, irrelevant issue indicates the problem and the ways in which the AFL publicity machine reproduces and reinforces the core culture that makes the football sporting environment unattractive to queer players. Held together by masculine homosocial bonds that rely on heteronormativity and the exclusion of women, queerness and otherness results in many of the scandals I have so far been discussing; such media crises relate significantly to the ways in which non-heterosexuality and non-normative masculinities are signified as purely external to Australian Rules football despite half-hearted campaigns towards inclusion of diversity.

Australian Rules football, organised through the AFL, is an institution that is not different from other masculine-oriented institutions founded on homosociality. The concept of homosociality is derived from the sociological term that identifies relationships (non-sexual and non-erotic) between persons of the same gender. Usually discussing men, it is argued that in certain contexts homosociality is the primary constitutive arrangement of relationships, social life, working life and subsequent meanings that are built on that same-gender sociality. As with the military,[5] certain blue-collar workplaces, and other men-only organisations, sports teams are built primarily around gender performance which involves the exclusion not only of the opposite gender but of those who are *seen* to compromise gender norms. This is the source of homophobia, heterosexism and heteronormativity in Australian Rules football, and there is a very strong argument that it is football's homosociality and hypermasculine culture – so out of step with broader contemporary articulations of the masculine – that needs to be addressed in ways which go beyond safe inclusivity and diversity public relations campaigns. Gay sportsplayers who remain closeted continue to baffle a public that has increasingly tolerated non-heterosexuality among celebrities. However, coming out as a gay male sportsplayer is notably difficult and complex given the expected performances of masculinity that are difficult to disrupt without upsetting the public impression of the sport itself or attracting hostile criticism. As Ian Thorpe made clear when he came out in an interview in 2014 after years of speculation about his sexuality, the compounding of denials – that began when he was at the more vulnerable age of sixteen – make it more difficult to come out even when the stigma of non-heterosexuality has lessened.[6] High-profile sportsplayers and celebrities who attempt to make themselves inviolable by denying their non-heterosexuality have effectively made themselves more vulnerable to the pressures of criticism, speculation, accusation and rumour. It is, perhaps, important to therefore pay attention to the fact that if it has been difficult for a masculine solo sportsplayer such as a swimmer to 'muddy' the public image of his masculine heroic prowess with non-heterosexuality, then for a team sportsplayer such as a footballer whose on-field success depends on the unified performance of group masculinity, coming out is made more difficult and less desirable, for the player, the team and the public. At the same time, claims have been made that Australian Rules football, like other masculine-oriented institutions, contains an element of homoerotic behaviour. Comments by Akermanis argued that the presence of queer players would be detrimental to the *existing* homoeroticism of the locker room. Such claims that the sport is homoerotic extend from the field, to the showers to post-match social events, as well as to claims that footballer group sex and sexual assault are themselves the result of a desire by male players to engage each other sexually rather than the woman involved. Here, however, I argue that such claims to homoeroticism are not very useful in overturning the anti-queer environment of Australian Rules football, as they are often a (mis) reading of other forms of transgression and carnivalesque play that is one of the mechanisms of team bonding. That is, to claim that masculine bonding through activities that may include nudity or sexualised behaviour is homoerotic is overly simplistic, and there may be some value in thinking such ideas through a more complex approach to sex, sexuality, desire and eroticism beyond arbitrary distinction of 'hetero' and 'homo'. I will begin this chapter with a run-down of the AFL's 2010 'Inclusion and Diversity' campaign in the context of contemporary understandings of heterosexism and queer marginalisation or exclusion before exploring the issue of homoeroticism. I would like to end by briefly discussing some of the ways in which Australian Rules football can take up the question of what constitutes norms of masculinity, sexuality and eroticism outside of the 'too safe' public relations campaigns of the AFL in order not only to present a queer-accepting environment but to overcome some of the more problematic elements of the homosocial bonds that govern contemporary football culture. Scandals relating to homophobic comments and remarks in football have increased over the past few years in line with a growing acceptance of diverse sexualities, and the scandals themselves are important in communicating the fact that Australian Rules culture needs to catch up with other contemporary spheres in relation to the treatment of gendered and sexual others.

Come Out to Play, and Don't: Homophobia and Australian Rules Football

Significant research has indicated that masculine-based team sports, whether elite, community or amateur, are based on an institutional culture that reproduces forms of masculinity, disavowing the participation of non-heterosexual players and potentially marginalising non-disclosing queer players through rhetoric or violence.[7] However, more recent studies have pointed out that it has become easier in both Europe and the United States for queer athletes not only to participate in masculine team sports, but to disclose their sexuality publicly without reprisals.[8] Despite the reduction in outright homophobia, the increasing visibility of queer persons in media,[9] and the implementation of anti-discrimination policies that protect non-heterosexual persons, there are currently no Australian Rules football players in AFL teams who are known publicly to be gay. National Rugby League star Ian Roberts disclosed he was gay in 1995, but of the elite masculine team sports in Australia, he is the only one. When Ian Roberts came out, there was no significant impact on the ways in which the sport or athletes more generally were perceived, but there were some quite significant shifts in the perception of gay men, not always entirely positive. The fact that the AFL and other elite-level football leagues in Australia have not subsequently had an out gay top-tier player in the twenty years since Roberts indicates that the contemporary cultural environment of football continues to be one which is not open to queer sexualities.

The public perception of Australian Rules football as a homo-phobic institution is thus not surprising. It is not entirely due to the lack of openly gay players, but to the awareness of the forms of player masculinity and related activities that dominate in media and public profiling. This is much more about a public imagination of football culture than specific examples of homophobic abuse or violence which, in general, are rare. For example, during a verbal spat at the Etihad Stadium in April 2010 between Collingwood coach Mick Malthouse and St Kilda player Stephen Milne, which resulted in Malthouse being fined for offensive language, Milne was reported to have questioned the sexuality of Collingwood assistant Paul Licuria. This resulted in news reports on the incident, with AFL football operations general manager Adrian Anderson stating publicly his concern that 'Milne used language towards Licuria that was homophobic and unacceptable'.[10] This, however, is a rare example of outright homophobic abuse or verbal injury related to sexuality in Australian Rules scandal reporting; rather, the perception that Australian Rules is homophobic results more from the combination of the lack of openly gay players, the forms of hypermasculinity that are understood to exclude queerness, and the public perception of the heterosexual exclusivity of masculine team sports in both on-field and off-field formations.

A campaign combating homophobia begun in 2010 by the AFL to change its image, and the response to the campaign made in a newspaper article by Brownlow Medallist and former Western Bulldogs and Brisbane Lions player Jason Akermanis resulted in the campaign backfiring significantly and a scandal for the public image of Australian Rules football with regard to sexuality and acceptance of non-heterosexual players. The background to the campaign began with comments by AFL chief executive Andrew Demetriou in 2009 stating that homophobia was unacceptable in football.[11] Not long afterwards, Eddie McGuire gave an interview to the gay periodical *DNA* in March 2010 in which he stated that he knew there were queer players among the AFL teams:

I've had my suspicions and there are a couple in particular that I've known quite well and they've nodded to me and I've winked to them, but they didn't want to take that next step in making it public...if they wanted to go forward and do something, I would be in a good position to offer them a haven to express themselves.[12]

Although probably motivated by well-meaning acceptance of non-heterosexuality, the somewhat patronising statement of McGuire's ability to offer a sanctuary for queer footballers to come out, and his protection of secrecy through metaphorical winks and nods did grate with members of the queer community in Australia, and certainly did not help to frame the upcoming campaign in a positive, well-articulated and accepting tone from the beginning. The 'Inclusion and Diversity' campaign had, itself, a relatively long lead-up with significant public information about who would be involved, including some major names in Australian Rules football such as Neil Balme, Joel Selwood, Jimmy Bartel and Adam Goodes. These and other players and coaches were photographed holding handwritten signs which called for acceptance and understanding of queer persons.[13] It was noted in the lead-up to the campaign that it was not at any stage a response to a crisis or scandal, unlike the campaigns against racism in football and the respect for women campaign.[14] The public relations strategy was designed to coincide with the International Day Against Homophobia (IDAHO), which has usually been an acknowledged day in May each year.

The anti-homophobia campaign coincided with the release of the report *Come Out to Play: The Sports Experience of Lesbian, Gay, Bisexual and Transgender (LGBT) People in Victoria,* which was produced by the Institute of Sport, Exercise and Active Living (ISEAL) and the School of Sport and Exercise at Victoria University in Melbourne. The authors, which included significant academics researching in sport and sexuality-related health such as Carolyn Symons, Melissa Sbaraglia, Lynne Hillier and Anne Mitchell, pointed out that while sporting activities from elite team sports to community, junior and school events play a significant role in Australian society, for the most part they remain a site in which queer Australians are 'largely silent and invisible'.[15] The report, which involved a little over three hundred participants surveyed about their experiences as non-heterosexuals participating in sport, ultimately concluded that while there were codes and teams which were highly accepting of non-heterosexual persons and had strong policies to protect non-heterosexual persons from discrimination or abuse, there were also significant sporting environments in which verbal harassment of non-heterosexuality was experienced, and a significant number of clubs which were considered unwelcoming. Perhaps most alarming for the AFL was the finding that among the sports queer men wished to play but in which they felt they would not be welcome due to their sexualities, forty-five per cent named Australian Rules football, with a little over seventeen per cent stating rugby and ten per cent soccer[16] – that is, *all* masculine team-based sports with Australian Rules topping the list. The release of the report in 2010 likewise did not underpin a successful AFL anti-homophobia campaign, with newspaper opinion pieces discussing some of the more startling findings in the context of the campaign.

However, the most significant response to these reports came from Jason Akermanis whose article 'Stay in the Closet' appeared in the *Herald Sun* on 29 May. Akermanis began by pointing out that he *would* be supportive of a queer player coming out if not for the fact that 'the world of AFL footy is not ready for it', concerned that the news of a player coming out 'could break the fabric of a club'. Much of his concern centred not on what impact the act of a gay player coming out would have on that player, but on the culture of football both within the team and the league more broadly.[17] He wrote that 'In an athletic environment the rules are different from the cultural rules for men' and suggested that the locker room would be an uncomfortable place for players showering if a known gay man was present, stating that he too has been uncomfortable in the past when a queer person was present.[18] The article became scandalous over the following weeks as a number of responses were made, particularly in the press. Queer activist Gary Burns threatened to lodge a complaint with the Victorian Equal Opportunity and Human Rights Commission, suggesting that Akermanis' rant only served to exacerbate homophobia and encourage both stereotyping and prejudice.[19]

While Akermanis' article and the controversy that followed were central to the failure of – and dismal response to – the AFL's anti-homophobia campaign, there were inherent problems in the ways in which the campaign itself was conceived. The failure of the campaign and the poor publicity around it can be attributed to other elements related to the ways in which it was organised and the rhetoric and discourse deployed in its public relations strategy. Problematically, for example, the AFL Players' Association made a claim that 'footballers know how it feels to suffer negative stereotyping and want to help another group of maligned individuals'.[20] This statement was, of course, a significant public relations error in terms of gaining queer support for the AFL, given that it is relatively obvious to most Australians that Aussie Rules footballers are not maligned in the way queer persons have been, they do not have genuine experience of discrimination or shame in the same way over extended periods of time, and instead enjoy occasional national-heroic status, significant income and celebrity notoriety. Part of the problem with the campaign was the way it addressed homophobia as an issue. Rather than articulating a policy to combat sexuality-based discrimination, harassment, marginalisation or exclusion, it operated as a very 'safe' public relations exercise, focusing on the term 'diversity' in the campaign itself and the term 'homophobia' predominantly in the publicity preceding and surrounding the campaign. The 'safeness' in using the term 'diversity' is apparent in the images of footballers, coaches and others holding placards and the terminology written by hand on the vast majority of those placards. Of twenty-one placards, only one used a term for sexual identity, reading 'Black, white, gay or straight, it's about diversity mate!' (held in publicity photographs by Drew Petrie and also by Matthew Pavlich); one placard used the term homophobia, which was Ted Richard's 'Stand up against homophobia'. The remainder make some very generic statements about inclusion and diversity without actually addressing sexuality (or, indeed, race or any other typically excluded category of identity) in any way or articulating who it is who *ought* to be included or accepted in football, leaving it for the surrounding publicity to interpret sexuality as the focus of the campaign. For example, placards read: 'Everyone deserves a sporting chance;' 'You can't shake hands with clenched fists;' 'Freedom of choice;' 'When the sun rises it rises for everyone'.

At the same time, the use of the term homophobia in the publicity preceding the campaign itself was somewhat out of step with contemporary research and public attitudes towards issues impacting on non-heterosexual persons. *Homophobia* is usually defined as an irrational fear and/or hatred of gay and lesbian persons, resulting in hostility and unjust discrimination.[21] Homophobia is a regulatory mechanism that produces and values the idea of homosexuality[22] and it is one which has proven to be significantly resilient in the face of campaigns and policies that seek to combat homophobia.[23] However, as Gerald Walton has pointed out, the problem with the idea of homophobia is that it suggests an *individualised* pathology, whereby it produces the image of an individual person with an irrational phobia of homosexuals, ignoring the ways in which discrimination, marginalisation, silencing or bullying are produced through widespread social and cultural factors rather than just the poor attitudes of individuals.[24] A more recent concept that is used to understand the ways in which non-heterosexual persons are marginalised in broader society as well as in specific cultural groupings and institutions such as football teams is *heterosexism*, which draws attention to the sense of entitlement and privileged received by heterosexual persons on the sole basis of a claim to heterosexuality, resulting in the denigration, stigmatisation or exclusion of non-heterosexual persons.[25] Even more useful a concept is that of *heteronormativity* which points to the ways in which heterosexuality is culturally produced as normal while non-heterosexuality might remain tolerated but not quite ever as *legitimate* as heterosexuality.[26] That is to say, homophobia can often be the source of abusive remarks and insults[27] and bullying.[28] However, in an environment in which queer persons are increasingly tolerated but not necessarily fully accepted,[29] or protected only through policies and legislation rather than social codes of welcome, heterosexism and heteronormativity are the more important targets for changing the ways in which queer persons are excluded. Claims to tolerance tend not only to be patronising but also somewhat fruitless; likewise claims to banning homophobia. Neither of these actually changes the cultural environment and institutional mechanisms that make it possible to marginalise a queer person (e.g., refusing to disclose sexuality, feeling excluded) or to make a queer person feel that she or he will not be accepted (e.g., avoiding playing particular sports because of an expectation of not being accepted). Homophobia was, as Eve Sedgwick once pointed out, a necessary power mechanism on which the structure of patriarchy and hence hegemonic masculinity depended.[30] However, with the shifts in perceptions of non-heterosexual persons and increasing tolerance, homophobic abuse, discrimination, insult and bullying as punishments for transgressions of heterosexuality are no longer as prevalent as they once were, for it is now the more subtle heteronormativity which upholds masculine dominance and masculine institutionalised cultures. The tacit insidiousness of heteronormativity is, of course, more difficult to combat and stem than the more obvious forms of homophobia through direct insult, violence and exclusion.

While no one would necessarily expect a public relations campaign to utilise complex rhetoric such as homonormativity, the use of homophobia as the term accompanying the safe discourse of the placards was inadequate in addressing how discrimination, marginalisation, and exclusion of non-heterosexual persons occurs and is maintained by the culture of Australian Rules football itself. By opposing homophobia through safe rhetoric about diversity and inclusion, yet failing to acknowledge the role the culture of contemporary masculine team sports plays in producing and upholding anti-queer sentiment produces a cynical view of the possibility of change. In the case of football culture, greater public awareness of non-heterosexual persons over the past twenty years, in addition to a greater capacity to recognise queer persons through means other than just sissiness, effeminacy or other older stereotypes but through a range of other signifiers that do not question masculinity (think Ian Roberts) creates the opportunity for new forms of anti-queer sentiment. This is not a new shift, but one which Dennis Altman rightly pointed out occurred during the 1970s and 1980s in wider North American society in which queer persons became increasingly recognisable through the Gay Liberation movement which, in turn, created the situation for new vehicles of discrimination.[31] Thus the onus was on the AFL, if serious about combating heterosexism and queer exclusion, to undertake a campaign that avoids utilising rhetoric that reinforces a normal/abnormal dichotomy through which queerness is marginalised. If players are unable even to use the words gay or queer or homophobia or heterosexism in the written placards, then it is clear that such forms of heterosexism not only persist in the culture but are reinforced through the campaign itself.

While lesbian/gay sexualities might be tolerated, celebrated, made spectacle or increasingly experienced as 'common', they remain a construct built on *differentiation* from a norm by virtue of being marginal, less-common, the so-called 'ten per cent', external to expectation or spectacle. Michael Warner has recently put this in the framework of the contemporary cultural imagination of statistical and demographic social organisation, whereby subjectivities are revealed in 'their lawfulness by standard distribution; the norms and averages of population' whereby one experiences shame in the degree of *deviance* from this imagined 'distributional norm'.[32] This is to suggest that queer sexuality no longer operates in contemporary culture within the disciplinary and institutional separation of the normal from the abnormal, the dichotomies that align normal and heterosexual and legitimate against abnormal and queer and sinful/criminal/other. Rather, it draws attention to the importance of contemporary biopolitics as a technology of power that makes populations and multitudes its object through statistical measurements of ratios, rates, forecasts and estimates.[33] For Foucault, norms circulate between the disciplinary mechanisms of power that, through institutions surveil and normalise individual bodies, and through biopolitical mechanisms which seek to regulate larger bodies or groups of people through the regularisation of processes of life and living.[34] Where disciplinary power mechanisms distinguish between the normal and the abnormal, the regulatory functions of biopolitical power technologies plot the normal and the abnormal along 'different curves of normality' whereby certain distributions are considered to be 'more normal than the others, or at any rate more favorable than the others'.[35] What this means for sexuality is that, in some contexts including the contemporary neoliberal formations of governance through which contemporary dominant social attitudes towards masculinity and sexuality are produced, the strictures of the hetero/homo binary *do not* map to a normal/abnormal set of mutually exclusive categories. Rather, it is a matter of proximity and distance from a mythical norm. Heterosexuality is discursively articulated as normative, and non-normative sexual identities such as queerness are non-normative by nature not of *opposition* or *abnormality* but of not being as *distributionally proximate* as heterosexuality from that which is sometimes considered the norm. Ultimately, the anti-homophobia campaign relied on an older cultural model that places queerness within the dichotomies of insider/outsider, normal/abnormal, belonging/excluded, whereas the experience of queer persons in contemporary society is more complex and operates along that distributional curve within the framework of normativities produced within neoliberalism. For example, outness, extent of gender performance conformity or the willingness to remain closeted when required are all related to the reality of queer people in terms of the *extent* of distance from the normative, rather than the idea of a wholesale exclusion of all queer persons as abnormal per se. Effectively, this demonstrates not only the extent to which the campaign was out of step with contemporary pro-queer political and social concerns but, through the continued exclusion, marginalisation and, for Akermanis, silencing of queer persons, the extent to which Australian Rules football culture is no longer representative of dominant masculine cultures in wider society but, ultimately, a residue of a past cultural formation of maleness that depends on queer exclusion to reproduce itself as masculine.

Footballers and Homoeroticism

In his 2010 article that caused such a fracas around non-heterosexual players in Australian Rules football, Jason Akermanis gave a reason why the presence of queer players would be disruptive to the team – the impact it would have on the *existing homoeroticism* of the locker room. As he put it: 'Locker room nudity and homoerotic activities are normal inside footy clubs'.[36] He added to this when later questioned on the Nine Network about his comments, stating that a queer player would not only be uncomfortable around straight players, but that straight players would not be comfortable engaging in homoerotic activities with a gay man in the room:

> the homoeroticism around football clubs…what workplace would you be able to see twenty men nude all the time if you wanted to? When you're slapping blokes on the bum and just having a bit of fun, what would that do to a man in there when you actually work out, "Oh wait a second, wait a second. I don't know if I can handle that guy".[37]

At one level, it appears somewhat ironic that Akermanis suggests queer players should not disclose their sexuality because it might disrupt the very queerness of contemporary football culture. At a slightly deeper level, he is unwittingly pointing to the ways in which homophobia serves as a mechanism that protects not only the homosociality of the football team (the male-male bonding, that is, which is so essential to strong team performance) but makes the claim that such homosociality persistently slips towards the homoerotic.

Akermanis is not, of course, the first to point to the homoeroticism of masculine team sports and similar male-male bonded environments. Indeed, team sports have frequently been *read* as highly charged homoerotic environments,[38] regardless of the real or imagined activities that take place both on-field and off-field. Many commentators have remarked on the ways in which the on-field expression of men hugging after scoring a goal, of the mutual male-male affection, and of fit bodies fighting, struggling and sometimes wrestling on-field can be viewed as homoerotic. In his book about the very queer ways in which masculinity is performed in contemporary society, commentator Mark Simpson pointed to the ways in which the physical, toned, worked-out body of the footballer draws attention to the very sites that are typically coded as queer:

the swollen gluteus maximus and quadriceps are the strong, sturdy, vigilant "goalkeepers" of his rectum. But as ever, the disavowal contains within it the seeds of his failure: the overdeveloped legs and arses of footballers have the effect of drawing the spectator's eye to them, so that the male rectum…becomes the unacknowledged centre of attention.[39]

In the context of the post-match environment, the football team is also frequently coded as homoerotic, with the circulation of stories and imaginings of fit young men showering together, naked together, playing up in the celebration subsequent to winning a game. A countless number of gay male porn videos have relied on the theme of footballers, hot and horny, in the locker room needing to get off with someone and no easily available woman around, leaving the two or more players (or sometimes a whole team) to get off with each other instead. Such stories and themes and readings are, of course, fictional – whatever actually happens in the locker room is not the same as the steamy scene of a gay porn in which ostensibly straight young men are suddenly penetrating each other with gay expertise and sex accessories to hand.

Spaces such as the locker room are not authentically or naturally 'straight' spaces[40] which can be invaded, transformed or disrupted by the presence of a queer person. Rather, they are actively *produced* and *heterosexualised* in the first place. In launching the scandal around queer men in Australian Rules football, Akermanis actively worked to reinforce the heterosexualisation of the space of the locker room and, by corollary, the entire culture of Australian Rules, but ultimately points to the ways in which such heterosexual space is unstable and contingent and always has been. In her study of sporting bodies and shame, cultural theorist Elspeth Probyn has likewise pointed to the idea of the locker room as the frequently imagined site of either denied or enacted homoeroticism, the place where naked bodies parade 'in intimate anonymity'.[41] Showing how this is a culturally constructed conception of the locker room, Probyn draws attention to its contingency and the instability of the space as either heterosexual space or the site of homoeroticism. That is, if the locker room is to be, today, the site of homoeroticism, it is not a matter of whether or not any homoerotic or homosexual activities take place there, but relates primarily to the fact that the locker room – like most public bathroom or toilet facilities – is gender restricted albeit a space which operates as the site of intimacy and nakedness. Thirty or forty years ago, it would have been remarkably difficult to imagine the locker room or men's showers as a site of homoeroticism or, for that matter, *any* sexuality or eroticism. What has changed is not the ways in which people in the room behave, but the fact that the nakedness, the banter, the playfulness of group showering is increasingly coded as both erotic and sexual in a way that had not occurred previously. Indeed, there are only a few sites and spaces in contemporary Western culture where two or more persons (of any gender) can be naked together without a coding of sexuality. These include being within a power relationship that involves an authority figure gazing at the naked subject such as parent/ child at bath time, doctor/patient during a consultation or police officer/prisoner during a strip search. Other sites not built on a specific, institutionalised power relationship include those which are bounded off from other public places, such as the locker room, the nude beach, the nude club – all places where bodies can be naked and be gazed at by others who are also usually naked but without the overtones of sexuality and eroticism.

However the past twenty or so years have seen an increasing sexualisation of all forms of nakedness and this contributes to the ways in which the post-match locker room is perceived as the site of homoeroticism and the venue for the fear of the gaze of the homosexual. Today, the parent/child bath experience is likewise fearfully policed as one which might involve the sexualisation of the child (particularly when the trace of that very common scene – the all-pervasive bath-time photograph – results somewhat ludicrously in arrests of parents for the production of child pornography, and that has occurred frequently in recent decades, usually without conviction) and such that the locker room is increasingly thought of as a site of sexuality and eroticism, regardless of the genders, sexual identities and desires of the persons present.[42] The increasing sexualisation of nakedness is one of the reasons why younger persons, including in school, are apparently no longer showering after sports and physical education classes, in contrast to several decades ago in which a greater number of same-sex activities were undertaken naked for pragmatic reasons, including group showering and casual swimming.[43] Group streaking is also part of this activity, although for less pragmatic reasons and more for the act of bonding. In 2009, there was a minor scandal in Queensland when five police officers streaked naked through Brisbane traffic, and were subsequently stood down from their jobs.[44] In commenting on the scandal, Michael Flood indicated that the activity is more about male bonding than sexuality, although he did also state that the activity *is* homoerotic.[45] This is an example of the *sexualised reading* of nudity and nakedness that might occur for reasons of transgression, bonding, sociality as being erotic in some form or another. Such a reading of naked male bodies together as homoerotic is, ultimately, an *interpretation* by the spectator, the participant, witnesses or other who have read or heard about it. Such a reading, however, is conditional – all persons make such judgments on the basis of their own knowledge frameworks, available discourses or what Tony Bennett refers to as 'reading formations' meaning the pre-existing knowledge and know-how through which all readers 'activate meanings'. In other words, no text, event or activity *has* a meaning; the meaning is produced, sometimes diversely, in the act of reading, witnessing or interpreting.[46] Thus no particular meaning is correct or intended or, in the case of naked bodies, signifies in the same way for everyone or is erotic for everyone. The argument here is that the spectator, witness or person who hears about these activities might *read* such naked male antics as erotic and homoerotic, but there is no inherent reason why groups of male bodies without clothes on is in any way sexual at all (traditionally it is not).

In his attempt to claim the space of the locker room as simultaneously heterosexual but homoerotic, and in the broader 'worry' about the eroticisation of football teams showering, Akermanis reinforces the sexualisation of players' bodies in that cultural space. Gay porn videos that draw on the theme of the homoeroticism of the locker room scene do likewise, actively re-coding naked bodies that gaze upon each other (and ultimately engage each other sexually) as sexualised and erotic; again, this is not necessarily to produce this scene as a homosexual one, but as homoerotic, since the narrative of much gay pornography is not gay men having sex, but straight men having gay sex. The eroticisation of footballers themselves is reinforced by what Mark Simpson has dubbed *spornography* – the phenomenon of high-level, elite celebrity sportsplayers, both men and women, appearing nude, semi-nude and usually sexualised in charity calendars and promotional materials.[47] By arguing that the space is marked by homoeroticism, fear of the homosexual gaze in that space is produced, as if homosexuals are drawn to that site or, even, drawn to playing football for access to that site. Thus the claim to homoeroticism by Akermanis is, in itself, heterosexist rather than supportive of non-normative sexuality.

Claims that football teams' mutual activities are homoerotic extend beyond the space of the field and the post-match locker room, but into the off-field activities of footballers, including those activities that have frequently been the site of scandal. For example, a British ITV documentary show, *Generation Xcess*, presented a story in 2007 about the drunken antics of an amateur rugby club,

Sandbach, based in Cheshire. The program's premise is that young persons in their twenties represent an out-of-control culture of excess, particularly in terms of drinking and partying. This excess was depicted in the out-on-the-town behaviour of members of the Sandbach team whereby drunkenness allowed homosocial masculine bonding to slip into homoerotic play, touching, mutual masturbation – all while in a series of pubs and clubs. The documentary shows members of the team on their night out subsequent to winning an away game, beginning their drinking early, engaging in bar-jumping in their preferred pub, and moving quickly to a scenario in which the drunk captain congratulates his team members with intense snogging in front of the other patrons of the bar. As one player stated in an interview after the night: 'We're all pretty much comfortable with our bodies, our sexuality; you know, what's it matter if there's a bit of male-to-male contact throughout the night?' As the night goes on, the filmed footage shows the young men on the dance floor removing their shirts and pants and showing off toned bodies to each other and to nearby women. Some men remove the clothes of each other, and there is some flashing of genitalia. That is followed by some men suckling the nipples of others, some naked arse slapping and then touching and grabbing at each other's exposed penises. The team as a group were shown the video footage later when sober, and were neither phased nor uncomfortable about the touching or kissing; rather, it was treated as a joke, a laugh, a bit of fun, and bit of masculine team bonding. The team captain, Tim Oakes, stated: 'It's obvious we're not gay, but we have a laugh, it's just one more for the list for that night'. Not surprisingly, no women were picked up during the night, although it would seem clear that this was not because of an unwillingness to engage with women, but because the drunken behaviour that became more and more excessive, and included a fair amount of vomiting, was not necessarily much of a turn-on for women out that night.

Again, all of this team-based off-field behaviour *can* be *read*
as homoerotic, and certainly there are dozens of comments on
online blogs that make such a reading. Yet it was not erotic and
certainly not *homo*erotic for the players involved. An alternative
here is to step away from the fixation on the homoerotic, the
erotic and the sexual – and questions of 'true' sexual desire
or nonsense about drunkenness allowing true feelings to be
revealed – and to consider instead the context in which this
touching, playing and kissing among the members of the team
actually operates. The evening out is subsequent to a win, so it
is an evening of celebration of a success and thus falls into the
category of the carnivalesque – a celebratory temporal moment
and space framed-off from the norms, values and legitimacies of
everyday culture. Carnival frequently involves the transgression
of sexual and erotic norms and these need not be necessarily for
the pleasure of sexuality but for the pleasure of transgression itself.
That is, they transgress discipline and boundaries as a temporary
refusal of authorised sacredness and aesthetic norms,[48] which is
not about a desire towards the pleasures of erotic engagement but
festive refusal of the shutting down of such erotic engagement. As
Richard Parker notes:

> The polymorphous pleasures of erotic ideology become the
> normal rather than the transgression of the established order, and
> the fullest possibilities of sexual life take concrete form in the
> play of human bodies.[49]

Such festivities have been part of culture for a very long time, going
back at least to the drunken debauchery of Roman Bacchanalian
festivals, but evidenced in everything from mardi gras festivals to
European carnivals to groups of people out on a Saturday night.
In that sense, it is important to recognise that any reading of the
football team members' behaviour in touching, playing, feeling,

kissing and getting naked in a celebratory context is not necessarily *about* erotics and sexuality, nor is it about sublimated homosexuality, nor is it necessarily about desire towards a gender. Indeed, to read the act of one player spanking the naked arse of another, or one player grabbing the penis of another as homoerotic is to bring the entire activity down to sexuality and to the idea that sexuality is defined only by the gender (and genitals) of participants. Rather, there is no reason why any touch between men is necessarily about desire or is necessarily erotic, and when it is an act of transgression or irony or play it is neither (even if it will be read by spectators and others as such). Rather, it is a transgression that is taken up and utilised as mechanism for homosocial bonding, the off-field play that occurs as part of that necessary binding of a team which takes place not on the field but in all of the spaces and times of the off-field engagement of team sociality. In that sense, the program's title of 'Generation Xcess' is the more accurate indicator of what occurs here – behaviour in *excess of norms,* transgressions that are utilised for team bonding not inherently grounded in any form or homoeroticism or sexuality.

In chapter three, I discussed the ways in which the scandals around football teams' group sexual assault of women can be understood through a notion of group identity that suspends any ethical impulse to recognise, protect and respond to the vulnerable. This activity, too, has at times been read through a notion of homoeroticism and, indeed, an idea of repressed homosexuality; thus significantly worthy of returning to that topic in the context of discussions around homophobia and homoeroticism in contemporary Australian Rules football culture. Such an idea that group sexuality is inherently and intensely homoerotic is, in fact, a relatively old idea. A 1959 article by social psychologist W. H. Blanchard suggested that homoeroticism is a core *causal* component in group sexual assault. Blanchard analysed a number of groups of young men who had been charged with group sexual assault or attempted group rape to determine the dynamics among the perpetrators. He argued that:

> [t]he erotized adulation of one boy for another is perhaps the primary factor in the unconscious homosexual feeling of adolescents. The idea of 'sharing the girl among us fellows' congregating around a common sexual object, and being sexually stimulated together as a group certainly have their homosexual implications.[50]

He reasoned that the eroticism of a group rape scenario and the sexual feelings it invoked both in the act and in group-based discussions among the perpetrators afterwards was 'largely a relationship between the boys rather than between any of the boys and the girl involved'.[51] In her study of fraternity gang rape, which is situated within a similar masculine context of homosocial bonding that is found in football team culture, Peggy Sanday pointed to the homoeroticism of the act of gang rape – known in fraternity culture as 'pulling train' – in asking why, since the sexual act is staged by men for other men, if the woman is even necessary, and concluding that the presence of the woman in this act is a mechanism to prevent the reading of the scene as a homosexual act.[52]

Where Blanchard and Sanday point to the idea of a submerged desire to participate in homoerotic activities, however, what they do is make a homoerotic reading of an activity that may well be *erotic* in nature (although how erotic a group sexual assault or rape can be is, of course, debatable) but is not necessarily for the perpetrators either a conscious or a submerged desire to participate in the homoerotic by, for example, sharing the woman or performing sexually in front of each other. Other scholars have, in fact, disputed the idea that gang rape is homoerotic, pointing out instead that it is much less about the presence of *any* sexual desire and much more about the male bonding of the group through power and domination; the gaze and spectatorship of team members becomes then a dramatic site in which participants evaluate their own and each other's sexual prowess as an *effect* of masculinity and hypermasculinity.[53] A team of men together sexually assaulting a drunk, intimidated or unconscious young woman, and this being entirely about the relationship of sociality among the masculine group,[54] may well be *erotic* for the players involved and they may well get off on the shared experience and the sexual performance under the gaze of their fellow team members, but this does not necessarily make it *homo*erotic, because that 'getting off' is not necessarily about the *gender* of the team but the *team as a team*.

Thus, the relationality that occurs is homosocial but is negotiated and acted out through acts which may appear to some, including some players such as Akermanis, as being homoerotic. But to presume that either homosociality or hypermasculinity is the site of repressed or secretly desired homosexuality is, then, usually a reading that is far removed from the behaviours when understood in context. Beyond the carnivalesque activities that may be available to be seen as homoerotic, there is the reinforcement of the erotic through intimacy. Despite the hypermasculine nature of elite team sports and the hypermasculine, muscled bodies of those involved, team sports do offer opportunities for intimacy and emotional expression that do not necessarily occur as easily outside of that environment.[55] Furthermore, it is important to bear in mind that elite, AFL footballers are also celebrities, and thus operate within contemporary celebrity culture. That means that, at the surface or the visual at least, there is a softening of masculine imagery that is somewhat at odds with the traditional image of the footballer as working class hero. This softer masculinity, that is sometimes referred to as metrosexuality, is defined by straightness, but an emphasis on grooming and hairstyles, fashionable clothing and accessories, high-level aesthetic tastes – that is, an archetype that has certain previously articulated gay sensibilities while being straight, produced and defined by consumer magazines and taken up early by sports celebrities such as David Beckham, among others. This is, of course, a shift in hegemonic masculinity away from the visuality of the hypermasculine towards an identity more amenable to the purchase of marketable grooming products and fashion and other elements of lifestyle, and it is most readily taken up by celebrity sportsmen who, naturally, are more likely to be photographed, displayed in a range of magazines and invited to the sorts of social events that require a higher-level aesthetic appeal. This too, then, plays into the various shifts in homosociality that have opened a number of questions about the state of masculinity in football, the sexuality and erotics of footballers and the role and place of non-heterosexual players.

Although homoeroticism has been *read* in the spectatorship or activities of footballers in the context of the game, the post-game showers, the post-win social activities and partying and in the context of sexual assault, I am arguing that these are simply readings that are not necessarily the intentions of the footballers involved. It is also wrong to assume that footballers are *really* enacting homoeroticism but are unaware of it – this is to fully remove agency from the activities of team members. Rather, what is important is to consider that, on the one hand, activities that may be read as homoerotic by some may well be understood as absolutely non-sexual and non-erotic by others (including the players) and that, on the other hand, it is the cultural context of the homosociality of football that makes possible such readings. While Akermanis made a claim to the homoeroticism of the locker room, and indeed justified it and normalised it as an activity of heterosexuals in a sporting team context, the shared group subjectivity of transgression, carnival and play is a more nuanced way of thinking about that scene and the ways in which football homosociality occurs. In other words, it is not highly productive to claim homosociality slips into homoeroticism in the ways in which we perceive and attempt to make meanings around football culture, and that includes in the attempts to understand why homosociality operates through the exclusion of homosexuality.

Beyond Hetero/Homo and Homophobia

To move beyond the homophobia that marks Australian Rules football thereby requires more than (a) a public relations campaign that argues for the acceptability of queer players in the team; and (b) reading and articulation of footballers' behaviour in the field, the showers and in off-field social and group activities as being homoerotic. Ultimately, the homoeroticism of football culture is a *reading* of behaviours, events, activities, bodies and spaces that is relatively unproductive in attempting to make football a more inclusive space. The reading is legitimate – anything is available to be read in diverse ways, and if either theorists, Jason Akermanis, spectators or players wish to see homoeroticism in the on–field and off-field activities of masculine team sports, that is absolutely fine. However, looking at it from a deeper, theoretical and contextual perspective which destabilises the distinction between hetero-eroticism and homoeroticism is more productive in that it opens the space to being read as erotic without value judgments as to 'proper' forms of gendered and sexual eroticism. In other words, not expressing heterosexual *or* homosexual desire, but eroticism in general. In that sense, it is possible to suggest that there is some value in Akermanis' own reading of football culture as homoerotic in that it draws attention – in combination with cultural theory – to the ways in which masculine homosocial cultures such as Australian Rules football actively produce, maintain and reinforce the distinctions on which exclusions are based: hetero/homo eroticism, hetero/homo sexual identities. That is to say that a careful engagement with the instability of football culture as either homoerotic or otherwise erotic needs to be undertaken in order that homoeroticism does not serve as the excuse by which to reject queer persons from participation in the homosociality of contemporary football.

The same technique used to critique football homoeroticism can be applied to the question of the appropriateness of queer players in football teams. Akermanis' scandalous attempt to protect an ideal of homoerotic play in the locker room by banishing or invisibilising queer players was not only unproductive but ignored the inherent problem – the reproduction of a masculine homosocial culture that (a) requires the repudiation of the homosexual as one mechanism by which to maintain that homosociality as an 'in-group' form of team bonding, and (b) allows some slippage between the homosocial and the homoerotic in the readings and perceptions of behaviours around players' bodies in the space of the field, the locker room and off-field activities. As an institution, Australian Rules football is much like other masculine institutions such as the military in that it is founded on homosociality and the valuation of the masculine ideal,[56] and it is *this*, rather than specific acts or behaviours of individual footballers that needs to be addressed in order to shift away from the risk of homophobia and the marginalisation of non-heterosexual players.

With the exception of group sexual assault, the homosocial carnivalesque activities that I have mentioned above are mostly harmless forms of team bonding in off-field environments – which is not to say at all that they are *always* ethical or safe. If useful for the formation of group identity and team bonding of the sort that leads to team success, then is it necessary that queer players be marginalised in order to maintain the masculine hegemony of the homosociality of the team? If such activities are not, as I have been arguing, best thought of as homoerotic, then why can a queer player not participate? Is it because the presence of one whose desires are coded as same-sex re-establishes the carnivalesque eroticism as homoeroticism? Is it that the activities that are seemingly homoerotic cannot occur due to players' discomfort at the idea that the present homosexual might actually be getting off on it – that is, not participating due to the transgression but due to desire for same-sex erotic behaviour?

One of the ways, then, in which we can overcome the impasse around the acceptability of queer players in football teams is to undo the distinction between heteroeroticism and homoeroticism – the seeds of which are already sown by masculine homosocial cultural environments such as football teams – and thereby to undo the value distinction, stereotypes and presumptions around heterosexual and homosexual players. The framework for this is already, in fact, available in the form of queer theory. Different from queer studies, queer theory is a set of post-structuralist theories deployed in the fields of gender and sexuality. Queer theory takes to task the commonly presumed idea that the *only* ways in which sexuality, eroticism and sexual identity is through gendered objects of attraction and desire – that is, from one gender to another as the *base line* of all eroticism. Since the early 1990s, queer theory has criticised the self-evident, common logic of the 'naturalness' of the binary opposition of heterosexuality and homosexuality and the idea that sexual and gender identities are innate, fixed and unproblematic. Eve Sedgwick critiqued the hetero/homo binary, pointing out that while it is the dominant means by which sexuality is categorised in contemporary Western culture, there are alternative sexualities, desires and erotics that do not fit neatly in the same-sex attraction or opposite-sex attraction and, in some cases, may not be about the gender of the persons involved at all.[57] The very idea of heterosexual identity or homosexual identity is, rather, historical, discursively produced but has come to appear natural and timeless. Other queer theorists have furthered this critique, indicating that other ways of thinking about or categorising sexuality are suppressed and made silent by the monolithic nature of the hetero/homo binary.[58] For Sedgwick, what a post-structuralist, culturalist approach to sexuality points to, then, is that there is no foundational, logical, biological or ethical reason why sexuality should be shackled to gendered objects of attraction, that there are ways to think about, critique and perform erotic desire that are different from the contemporary cultural imperative of sexual-beings dichotomised as heterosexual and homosexual. She suggests that certain

> dimensions of sexuality, however, distinguish object-choice quite differently (e.g., human/animal, adult/child, singular/plural, autoerotic/alloerotic) or are not even about object choice (e.g., orgasmic/nonorgasmic, noncommercial/commercial, using bodies only/using manufactured objects, in private/in public, spontaneous/scripted.)[59]

There are also discernible trajectories generally not encompassed in dialogue on sexuality. Gender – *any* concept of gender – might be discharged entirely from a trajectory of erotic desire. Time, space, place, the disunified body, or, as Elizabeth Grosz hints, body parts that are not usually constituted as libidinal or gendered zones,[60] may well be the codes or factors which constitute the naming of a sexual act and the codes that make sexual desire intelligible. In other words, there are a range of possible logics that can organise sexual thinking, and *gender* is only *commonly* considered the primary factor in (sexual, emotional) attraction because it is the result of deployments of disciplinary power. Forms of sexual fluidity and configurations of sexual subjecthood that are not dependent on gender-based trajectories of desire arise at the margins of contemporary culture, but they depend for cultural intelligibility, stability and identity on the sociality of a recognisable logic.

None of that, of course, is to suggest that homosexual and heterosexual identities are not real or meaningful to people, only that they are historically produced, relatively recent identities and not grounded in some *natural* essence or innateness. The fact that queer theory points out that there are alternative ways of categorising sexuality, eroticism and desire means that it is possible to undo the ways in which contemporary culture structures the values given to sexualities and sexual identities – the legitimation of heterosexuality and the less-legitimate-but-tolerated non-heterosexualities or, in the case of football culture, the exclusion of non-heterosexuality as the means by which masculine team bonding is upheld. The key to doing this is not just to acknowledge the contingency of gender-based trajectories of desire, but to understand that the homosociality of contemporary team sports provides the discourse which structures those values within the context of football culture. Focusing on undoing the power of homosociality is not about undoing the gender distinctions in sport, since the gender-based league categorisations are very likely to be around for longer than many of us may wish. However, it is to attempt to undo the *valuation* of gender in sport in order to make it possible that the *gender which one desires* becomes meaningless – that is, to make any distinction between heterosexual and homosexual valueless and irrelevant.

Again, these are activities that are already being undertaken outside of football culture, in ways that are sometimes unexpected but could easily occur within the football environments in ways which can transform the hypermasculine, machismo or aggressive maleness that emerges as the performance of team homosociality.[61] Indeed, Eric Anderson and colleagues recently studied the practices and behaviours of intimacy among university-aged young men, which included games of sustained kissing related to homosocial bonding as well as other acts of genuine intimacy between men, such as greeting kisses, hugging, holding. His primary finding was that across these behaviours, the acts were stripped of all sexual connotations.[62] This implies that gender becomes at least partly eradicated from activities that, for a much longer period during the twentieth century, were highly gendered (the kiss, the hug) in terms of authorised and unauthorised, proper and improper behaviours for men. In the same way, the behaviours among masculine sports teams on-field, in the locker room and in off-field sociality are stripped of the erotic even, as I maintain, they are available to be *read* through the erotic or even as the homoerotic.

What is important is to see the pivotal, central and monolithic role of homosociality in structuring masculine team sports, and the exclusion through homophobic discourses of the apparently 'true representative' of the homoerotic – the homosexual. Homosociality requires the repudiation of the homosexual in order to prevent there being any kind of relationship between the homosocial and the homosexual – that is, in order to avoid the masculine team bonding, its male-to-male intimacy, its play, its forms of transgression and its in-group and out-group dynamics from being sexualised. It is not just homosocial bonds which insist on the repudiation and exclusion of queer players and queerness in general. Rather, there is a hyper-homosociality about team sports in particular which is, in general, out of step with contemporary forms of hegemonic masculinity found more readily among younger persons, white-collar workplaces and urban environments. As the *Come Out to Play* report indicated, the marked hyper-homosociality operates to uphold an older model of masculinity, rather than *actually* targeting specific queer players through homophobic rhetoric:

> In the same way that women's gender can be called into question
> if they play sport well, men had their gender and heterosexuality
> called into question when they played badly or as a way to spur
> them on to a better performance. By definition, men who play

badly cannot be heterosexual men – they must be sissies, girls, or they must be gay.[63]

That is, what is needed for a shift in football culture is not a question of whether or not queer players will be tolerated, nor is it a question of how particular forms of team bonding occur. Rather, it requires that the culture of Australian Rules football reflect contemporary attitudes towards masculinity more readily – at least the ones which have shifted away from older, dominant and hegemonic masculinities that depended on homosocial sensibilities and the repudiation of otherness. It is to take the 'hyper' out of hypermasculinity, and that requires a cultural shift and a shift in group relationality more than any individual change in attitude towards queerness.

Conclusion

Although scandal reporting is often banal, sometimes boring and occasionally very damaging to those who are unwittingly and undeservedly dragged into reports, it can also serve a useful purpose in opening up ways of thinking about a situation or an issue. The Akermanis homophobia scandal was valuable in pointing to the ongoing exclusion of non-heterosexual persons in Australian Rules football, to the cultural environment that has, through language and disposition regularly vilified non-heterosexual desire, and to the very fact that sexuality, eroticism, desire and gender identity are in fact highly complex in the context of football as an institution. The Akermanis scandal created the environment for ongoing debate and public discourse on the topic of sexuality, diversity, homophobia and team sports in Australia. Former Hawthorn Football Club president and former Victoria premier Jeff Kennett bemoaned the idea of Australian Rules being over-involved in campaigning against homophobia as it is already committed to championing other social causes. As he put it: 'It's almost foisted upon [the AFL] because of broader expectations and the simple wonderment of what the AFL represents. The AFL will never be perfect, [but] we're putting on to them responsibilities that they were never expected to perform'.[64] He nevertheless lobbied Andrew Demetriou to promote anti-homophobia through a themed match. While resistance to addressing homophobia in football may be given the alibi that the AFL already deals with a number of social issues, there was a considerable push during 2012 toward continuing the discussion, much of this resulting particularly from the Akermanis scandal. Openly gay footballer for Yarra Glen, Jason Ball, began a petition on Change.org and ran a campaign calling for a Gay Pride match, and dozens of footballers, coaches and stakeholders from community clubs spoke out about their experiences and witnessing of homophobia in football culture.[65] Elite players Daniel Jackson (Richmond) and Brock McLean (Carlton) both marched in Melbourne's 2013 annual Pride March, aiming 'to make the game more inclusive and a safer place for gay men'.[66] In May 2013, North Melbourne captain Andrew Swallow, Brownlow medallist Jobe Watson, Collingwood players Scott Pendlebury and Luke Ball, among others, made a public pledge to avoid using homophobia language and anti-queer verbal abuse, acknowledging that such terms are injurious and work to cement the exclusion of non-heterosexual persons from football.[67] These are all substantial advancements that would not have (yet) occurred had it not been for the scandalous remarks of Akermanis and the public outrage over their thoughtlessness and injurious effect. The extent to which the AFL governance and publicity machinery can genuinely embrace the topic of homophobia as an ethical issue is unclear. Although it was widely stated in December 2012 that the AFL was considering a themed Gay Pride match between Sydney and Hawthorn in the 2013 season, it was announced in May 2013 that it would need to be postponed due to 'scheduling and fixture issues'.[68]

Nevertheless, the way in which the Akermanis commentary opens up the social possibility of critiquing the very notion of homophobia and sexuality in football is substantial in advancing the capabilities of the AFL to participate in ethical inclusiveness. By framing the issue of sexuality, homophobia and homoeroticism through a considered rethinking of the ways in which masculine homosociality underscores contemporary football culture is a considerably more advanced means than an anti-homophobia campaign or than attempts to equate non-heteronormative sexualities with the apparent homoeroticism of masculine team sports. But in doing so, it is important not merely to attack the bonds of the team, given their centrality to sporting success. Rather, what is needed is having players speaking publicly about the very structure of the team bond, allowing it to appear in the public sphere in more complex ways, and thereby opening the discussion in a manner which has, to date, been shut down by the narrow, safe and carefully controlled public relations mechanisms of the AFL that, whether knowingly or unwittingly, reproduces the same problem again and again. In other words, it is not to speak out and say, yes we are inclusive and would like to include non-heterosexual players as they can today be tolerated, but to undo the heteronormativity that marks exclusion of non-heterosexuality by having the most significant stakeholders in Australian Rules football – the players – spearhead this activism by asking and articulating the question: what is *normal* for *normative masculinity* anyway?

6

Vulnerable Bodies:
Footballer Identity, Vulnerability and
Ethics towards Cultural Change

Across the previous five chapters, I have addressed a number of football scandals as they have played out during the past few years in media and online environments: sex scandals, binge drinking and drug use, gambling and homophobia, among others. While often damaging to the public perception of footballers, clubs and stakeholders, as well as to others who become wrapped up within the discourse of the scandals, they have also been useful in opening up possibilities to rethink masculine team-based sports culture from the perspectives of identity, bodies and ethics. Not all scandals are the individual fault of players and, as I have argued, there are many occasions in which a scandal is merely the revelation of private, normative behaviour that is an excuse to create a narrative of moral outrage *as if* footballers ought be held to a higher standard than others. However, there are also many cases, as I have similarly argued, in which scandalous behaviour of footballers, individual clubs, and the broader culture of football in general involves unethical behaviour or incidents in which violence and injury are inflicted on others. At times, this has included sexual violence in a physical sense, but also the violence of injurious speech, such as insults or denigration of others by players, clubs and league governance bodies, sometimes in media and frequently in scandals that centre on examples of homophobia, sexism and racism.

In this conclusive chapter, I would like to return to some of the issues brought up at the end of chapter three on group sexual assault around the possibility of an ethics of non-violence that might govern how footballers as a group relate to women. There, I argued that, as a result of the close bonds of footballers necessary for on-field success, the off-field environment can involve similar bonds that produce a group subjectivity in which the ability to recognise the vulnerability of others is suspended. Here, I would like to expand on some of the ways in which a more 'ethical footballer' can be produced through scandal in order to prevent the harmful events that sometimes cause scandal. To do this is to suggest that scandals have provided an opportunity for us to reconsider the *role* of the footballer (and other team-based masculine sportsplayers) in that players are well-placed to be understood as ambassadors of ethical behaviour. This is not as easy, of course, as suggesting that players make a few speeches or endorse a public campaign on social issues. Rather, it involves embracing some complex forms of the philosophy of ethics that effectively transform and put permanently into question the notion of a 'footballer identity'. Much of the ethical framework I will discuss here is drawn from the recent work of theorist Judith Butler who posits an ethics of non-violence that can emerge when subjects recognise the bodily vulnerability and precariousness of life common to all of humanity. That is, to recognise one's own vulnerability and to recognise the vulnerability of the other, such that an encounter of non-violence is produced through responsibility. The argument here is that the problematic encounters between footballers and others in the off-field environment that lead to scandal can be transformed into encounters which recognise commonality and which involve being *for the other* rather than objectifying, utilising, violating or in some way injuring the other.

Scandal is the result of the fact that, in some situations, footballers do indeed act ethically, non-violently and with dignified responsibility towards others but, in some specific contexts such as in relating to women in a partying environment, such an ethical response is foreclosed by cultural norms of hypermasculine behaviour and attitude. Scandals occur not because *either* ethical behaviour *or* non-ethical behaviour is seen as normative among footballers, but because *neither* is normative, opening up the possibility for journalistic and social outrage over certain behaviours and events that play out in the off-field environment, sometimes justifiably and sometimes not. This approach is highly important for considering the utility of football scandals as a means by which we can point to the possibility of – and necessity for – change and transformation of Australian Rules football culture into an environment marked by ethical relations and responsibility.

I will use here the Australian example of the Lara Bingle photograph scandal and the response by the AFL to her claims as a way of pointing to some of the gaps in football culture that would be well-served by the development of ethical relations. The Bingle scandal was a somewhat banal but informative case: a photograph of her showering and taken without consent was distributed among footballers, eventually published in the magazine *Woman's Day*, and resulted in Bingle taking legal action against Brendan Fevola. However, the element of the scandal that created concern was the way in which the AFL responded to her claims. The argument here is that not only the taking of the photograph and its distribution for the amusement or gratification of others was a form of violence towards Bingle, but the response of the AFL was similarly violent and injurious; hence a claim here for an ethical response which would not only reduce scandal but work to transform scandalous events and behaviours into more positive situations. I will work through this example to demonstrate *why* an ethics of non-violence is called for in football culture before discussing firstly how Judith Butler's ethical position might work in the context of football, secondly the common impediments and ways of thinking or framing, such as dehumanisation or objectification, that routinely prevent an ethical relationship from occurring. I will then show how footballers are in a prime position to respond to an ethics built on recognising the vulnerability of others given the ways in which footballers, more than many others, experience the precariousness and vulnerability of the body through the likelihood of on-field injury.

An Ethics of Non-Violence

Why should the off-field behaviour of Australian Rules footballers be bound by an ethics of non-violence? If footballer scandals are not the results of individuals but of the culture in which those individuals are produced and through which the identity 'footballer' is given meaning, coherence and intelligibility, then how do we ask that footballers behave in ethical ways? This is a difficult question, but it is not one that is answerable through an idea of developing policies that prescribe particular behaviours, whether for the on-field game and training environments, or in the off-field social world. Such prescriptions, while sometimes useful in pointing to behaviours that would be unacceptable to a broader, contemporary Australian society or by drawing attention to behaviours which may be harmful to others, is not the best means by which an ethics can be developed. Rather, ethics is produced through a critical understanding of the complexity of identity, how subjects are constituted and through a reflexive approach performing those identities – in both individual and group contexts – through the relationality of our selves to others. Within this framework, an ethics of non-violence, although never guaranteed, is possible as a tool for attitudinal change, a goal for behaviour in relationality and an outcome that is both desirable and necessary.

In using the terms violence and non-violence, I am not referring to specific acts of physical violence which, in the off-field environment, do occur but are relatively rare. Rather, I am referring to a broad range of violences in a very generalised way; violences which impact on bystanders, non-footballers and others who may become involved in the fringes of football culture. These violences include the objectification of women; the marginalisation of non-heterosexuals through homophobia and exclusion; and the impact, risk and inconvenience to family members and bystanders of footballers' propensity for binge drinking, use of recreational drugs and compulsive gambling. In other words, violences that do not necessarily involve hitting, rape or abuse, but acts that – whether deliberate or unwittingly – *injure* those who are on the margins of contemporary Australian Rules football culture; that is, injuries which are not restricted only to the physical. These injuries are the result of actions, attitudes and behaviours which form the core theme of modern footballer off-field scandals, so an ethical approach becomes not only a response but can provide a range of ways in which scandal can be avoided.

I will give an example as to how these injurious violences can occur as a result of contemporary football culture by looking briefly at the Lara Bingle case. In December 2006, it became public gossip that fashion model and celebrity Bingle was involved with Carlton player Brendan Fevola, resulting in a breakdown in Fevola's marriage with his wife Alex. Bingle claimed that she was unaware Fevola was married,[1] a point which was contradicted by former Hawthorn, Sydney and Collingwood player, Dermott

Brereton, several years later when he claimed he had informed Bingle in 2006 prior to their first meeting that Fevola was married. This subsequently was denied by Bingle's agent Max Markson who reiterated Bingle was unaware of Fevola's personal life and knew little of AFL footballers and surrounding gossip.[2] The relationship between Fevola and Bingle was rumoured to have lasted only a small number of weeks; although she claimed publicly there was no affair, Alex Fevola's parents released details of telephone messages apparently left by Bingle on Fevola's phone.[3] In early 2010, a nude photograph depicting Bingle in the shower was published in gossip magazine *Woman's Day*. It was claimed that the photograph had been taken by Fevola during their brief affair and distributed over a period of years among AFL footballers and a number of Australian cricketers – Bingle's then fiancé was Australian cricket vice-captain Michael Clarke.[4] The image showed Bingle in the shower, clearly alarmed or annoyed that a photograph was being taken without her consent, as she attempted to cover herself. AFL football operations manager, Adrian Anderson, announced that Fevola would be questioned about the image, while Bingle began legal proceedings against Fevola. As the scandal unfolded, it was revealed that Bingle was paid $200,000 for an interview with the same magazine *Woman's Day* to discuss the nude photograph scandal.[5] Fevola initially denied taking the image and Brisbane Lions coach Michael Voss supported Fevola's claim to innocence.[6]

There were a number of public statements about the capturing and distribution of the image of Bingle in the shower during the days following the initiation of the scandal. Then Deputy Prime Minister Julia Gillard commented that the act of Fevola taking the photograph without consent was 'the wrong thing to do'. As she put it:

> For someone to take a photograph of someone else…which obviously may show them in a compromising circumstance and

then disseminate it without their consent is the wrong thing to do…it's wrong. It shouldn't happen. If it has happened then obviously the person responsible should take all steps necessary to apologise and make good the damage they've done.[7]

Adrian Anderson similarly stated that: 'We find unacceptable any behaviour of taking a photo of a woman without her consent and circulating that, it's completely unacceptable from an AFL point of view'.[8] AFL chief executive Andrew Demetriou responded to the scandal by stating that the AFL 'educate all of our clubs about taking photographs and distributing without people's consent'.[9] In interviewing Brendan Fevola for Channel Seven's *Sunday Night*, Peter FitzSimons caused Fevola to storm out abusively after asking about the Bingle image scandal. FitzSimons discussed his views on the Bingle scandal in an opinion piece about the interview that appeared in *The Age*, stating:

> When I said that what he did was "visual rape" – on the grounds that taking the photo of his then lover in the shower was done without her consent and by her own account she felt "violated" – the atmosphere did indeed get a little ugly. But what the hell?[10]

So we already have a culturally recognisable concern around the capturing and distribution of such images without consent, represented by the words of the then Deputy Prime Minister, a policy position by the AFL censuring such action and claiming that it does not meet the expectations of Australian Rules clubs and footballers on the basis of AFL-sponsored education campaigns on the very issue, as well as claims by further commentators and journalists that the act perpetrated by Fevola was a form of violent violation.

The fact that the image was distributed and passed around among footballers is, then, an act of violence against Lara Bingle.

It is a deed of injurious violence for three reasons: firstly, because it uses an image of Bingle taken without her consent for the amusement or gratification of a number of sportsplayers, thereby turning Bingle into an object – an act of objectification. Secondly, the distribution of the image transfers control of her public reputation from her and places it into the hands of others – something which, in some ways, might be understandable at one level given the controversy that has followed Bingle through her many relationships with high-profile sportsmen as well as her ongoing commitment to fame and publicity; at another level, however, the particular type of image and her state of undress are a somewhat different genre from the texts that resulted from her role as a bikini model. Finally, it is violent because it fails to recognise the vulnerability of Lara Bingle as a subject in the act of distributing the image. This is the kind of vulnerability which is, in Judith Butler's formulation, common to all human beings, but it is represented quite pointedly by the vulnerability of Bingle as a young woman in a state of undress. The vulnerability shown in the non-posed image is, indeed, that which is consumed by the footballers and, ultimately, by the readers of *Woman's Day* and the audiences of the subsequent scandal. In this way, the unthinking or uncaring – and very much unethical – act of Fevola and other players is to do injury and violence to Bingle.

Additionally, an act of violence was perpetrated on Bingle by the AFL itself. According to reports, the AFL sought to interview Lara Bingle on the matter of the photograph, despite the fact she had stated she would begin legal proceedings through the more public institution of the courts. The AFL claimed after her persistent refusal to be interviewed that her lawyers were being uncooperative, and Demetriou accused Bingle and her team of being 'quick to get into the media and say all sorts of things and even tee off at the AFL' but that her co-operation with the AFL's internal investigation was nevertheless necessary.[11] Ultimately, the right of Bingle to choose to pursue a matter of this nature through the recognised public institutions is denied in favour of the AFL's process of acting to resolve a scandalous issue independently, secretly and internally, denigrating Bingle and denying her the same level of subject recognition any citizen ordinarily has. According to Bingle's lawyers, the AFL persistently and publicly demanded that she attend the AFL for interview and that the interview be tape-recorded; later complaining that Bingle and her lawyers were not co-operating by refusing to participate in the AFL's internal investigation. In a media release, Bingle's lawyers stated that it was 'completely insensitive and oppressive for the AFL to pursue her in this manner at this time'.[12] In demanding she undergo what the lawyers referred to as 'interrogation' by the AFL, and then publicly announcing that she had refused while insisting they wanted to 'keep the public informed that Lara Bingle was not co-operating' is a further act of violence perpetrated against Bingle. While there are certainly some questions over why she would agree to make public her views in a paid interview with the very magazine which published the photograph in the first instance, it does remain that there is an ethical question over the AFL's pursuit of her to participate in resolving the matter through their own processes and to publicise her response to that demand rather than, as the lawyers stated, to 'leave her alone to deal with the damage that has been done by people who should have known better and treat her (and women in general) with dignity and respect'.[13]

Sports journalist Caroline Wilson likewise objected to the AFL's behaviour towards Bingle, seeing it as an act of violence that was motivated by the idea that she was 'fair game because of her dubious scruples and connections' and lack of credibility. Wilson pointed to the AFL's hypocrisy by noting that on the same day it was questioning Fevola, it was presented with $400,000 from the Commonwealth Government for the AFL's Respect for Women campaign.[14] Ultimately, Wilson points to the violence of the vilification of Bingle, showing how the old approach of virgin/ vamp comes in to play to discredit the woman involved in a scandal, and reminding the public that the initial violence – the fact that 'Fevola photographed Bingle in a highly embarrassing moment and, on all available evidence, then proceeded to send the picture to his mates' – is repeated in the failure of the AFL to maintain its 'responsibility to finish what it started which was an investigation into an act of violation by a footballer against a woman'.[15] The act of violation is a violence towards one rendered vulnerable, and this violence is thus repeated in the further injury of denial and the refusal of respect for her claims to be heard. This thus requires and demands an ethical response which works to avoid the violence of objectification and denial, but is instead built on the making of a response – that is, a response through responsibility.

Ethics, Recognition and Responsibility

Across several works, including her *Precarious Life*[16] and *Frames of War*,[17] Judith Butler develops an ethics of non-violence that is grounded in recognising the vulnerability of the other. Butler here conceived of the human subject as predicated on a primary vulnerability to and dependence on others, meaning that all our identities are built on our relationality with others. This is marked by the fact we are all vulnerable to the violence of others and always from the very beginning of our lives we are dependent on others for physical support, whether that be society's protection, parents feeding us, schools educating us, governments ensuring shelter or the emotional nourishment and support of friends and family. Effectively, Butler re-reads and expands on the earlier philosophic work of Emmanuel Levinas who proposed an ethical position through the notion that one has a *responsibility* to others ('the other') that emerges in an act of encounter and recognition of the other's face – again, a commonality among human beings. This is not, for either Levinas or Butler, a simple injunction to *behave* in a particular way. Rather, it produces a quandary, a requirement persistently to question ones' actions and a situation that produces the subject anew in the encounter with the others. What the encounter with the face of the other describes is a 'struggle over the claim of nonviolence without any judgment about how the struggle finally ends'.[18] In other words, it does not resolve the ethical problem it raises, but opens the *possibility* for subjects to recognise the vulnerability of others through understanding it in terms of their own vulnerability and thereby initiating a struggle one must undertake with one's own violence.[19] As Levinasian scholar Alphonso Lingis put it, 'The face of the other is a surface of suffering, upon which her sensitivity and susceptibility and her vulnerability and mortality are exposed to me'.[20] This exposure, when recognised, refigures us, and calls on us to respond to that face only ever in a non–violent way. Within this framework, then, there is an ethics that situates itself within a basic human capability of recognising the common, sometimes variable vulnerability of others. For Lingis, this is beyond the effective recognition of kinship or sameness or brotherhood of individuals, but an ethical relationship of responsibility and non–violence that can occur among those who appear to have nothing in common, since what is after all tacitly in common is the community of people, not just our teammates, nationals, kin-folk or social class.[21] That is, the one thing to which we are always vulnerable. Importantly, what this opens up is the possibility of an ethical relationship between people who are or appear to be wildly different or distinct. In the case of the ethics of off–field footballer activities, this can be the difference between the team players and women encountered, between the footballer and the non–sporting homosexual, between the team out for a night of drinking and the bystanders in the street.

Ethics thus occurs always in a relationship between persons: as Butler puts it: 'Ethics is not a calculation, but something that follows from being addressed and addressable in sustainable ways'.[22] In his reading of Levinas' formulation of ethics, philosopher Jacques Derrida likewise interrogated and expanded the notion of the relationship between the self and other in the encounter, and the responsibility one has to the 'face' of the other as the site of communication and commonality.[23] For Derrida, the encounter is grounded in the possibility – not always guaranteed – of a 'duty of hospitality' that 'opens the way of the humanity of the human in general'.[24] Without going into the complexity of Derrida's deconstruction of hospitality and the relationship between host and guest, what is pointed out is the way in which this form of ethics involves a responsibility by being a *self* who is directed unconditionally *for the other* as opposed to being concerned about what the other can do for me.[25] This is important for the ways in which footballers are defined as an identity enacted or performed through a range of intelligible, coherent or recognisable performances and behaviours in both the on-field and off-field environments. In this context, then, the most ethical subject is the hero who risks everything to save a person whom he or she does not even know and in a scenario in which he or she will not benefit from saving that person. (This is a somewhat different notion of hero from the footballer as local or national hero, but thoroughly rewarded for on-field success – the two types don't need to be mutually exclusive, however). If, for Levinas, it is the encounter with the humanity of the face of the other and if, for Derrida, the possibility and impossibility of hospitality towards the other is an element of ethics, then what Butler asks as part of her revision and expansion of these perspectives is the significant question as to whose face will be counted as human.[26] That is, if this is the means by which we can build an ethics that recognises the vulnerability of the other and responds without violence responsibly is built, then we need to ask what are the mechanisms by which certain norms and frames prompt an ethical response to some but not to all? When do these become suspended or impossible? And how does that change? In the context of Australian Rules football, then, it is important to ask what it is about football culture that impels an ethical response of non-violence to others in some contexts, but not in others, leading as we have seen to scandal.

An ethical position differs from that of a *policy* governing footballers' behaviour. For example, the AFL's *Respect & Responsibility* initiative, while a very valuable contribution towards opening up the possibility of interrogating the ways in which football culture sponsors a set of attitudes and behaviours towards women as football's 'external other', it does not promote an ethical relationship but, rather, presents a set of commands that reflect back only on the footballers themselves, their careers, their options, the restrictions that would come through penalisation, and so on. For example, the AFL's *Respect & Responsibility* policy[27] contains an executive summary by chief executive Andrew Demetriou which states the position of the ALF and AFL clubs is that 'we find any form of violence towards women abhorrent and we support moves by government and other community-based organisations to eliminate violence or the potential for violence'. The practical implementation of this policy is to undertake education programs, public education campaigns as well as to implement 'rules to require compliance by everyone bound by the rules without diminishing in any way the ultimate responsibility of every individual to behave in an appropriate manner in accordance with the laws of the land'. What this means, effectively, is that a set of rules operates as an injunction under the imperatives that govern players' and stakeholders' 'Conduct Unbecoming', but ensures that criminal accountability is held by individuals rather than the organisation itself. In terms of adapting player behaviour, there are three levels in the policy. The first addresses a situation in which a court or tribunal has found liability for a sexual assault, including a conviction, a guilty plea by a player, a committal for trial by a magistrate's court or a payment made to a victim to avoid costs and inconvenience of litigation. For breaches of this nature, the AFL states it will respond with sanctions which can include termination or delisting, financial penalties, standing down, suspension for a period, or restricted duties of representation.

Secondly, an improper, inappropriate, unfair or unreasonable response by an official or player to an allegation of sexual assault includes a failure to report an allegation of sexual assault made against a player or official to the AFL, a failure to reasonably co-operate with a police investigation, 'inappropriate comments in the media in relation to an allegation of sexual assault', vilification of the complainant publicly, or making a payment to a victim to avoid court proceedings. These likewise have a number of stated sanctions with AFL responses including fines and suspension from play or representational duties. It is noted that an apology for misbehaviour will be part of determining the level of sanction imposed, and that this element of the code 'can be invoked when a complaint of sexual assault is made either to a club or the AFL, the police or in the media and throughout the process of investigation'. It is notable that for this policy to come into effect a complaint to the police is only *one* option, the other two being a public/media allegation or a complaint directly to a club or the AFL. Whether such a policy can operate effectively to produce a cultural change when it does not require a police complaint in the form most other persons (excluding those in positions of authority or governance over a complainant, for example a doctor or nurse) are bound by is a matter of some controversy, contributing in this case to the ways in which the Bingle case played out, with her expectation of being able to pursue her claims through courts while the AFL expected that the claims would be pursued and addressed within the institution itself. There is, of course, a question as to the extent to which their response to her choices might form 'inappropriate comment' and thereby itself not be compliant with the policy.

Thirdly, the policy prescribes that any behaviour associated with an alleged sexual assault placing women at risk is 'Conduct Unbecoming' and can include responses designed for 'reducing and managing possible future harm to women' without being punitive. This can include warning, coaching, mentoring, training and development, increased supervision, counselling, retraining, personal development, performance enhancement agreements or a prescribed apology to the people affected. It is noted that any from this range of responses can be invoked at any time, and this includes a scenario in which an alleged incident is being investigated, in which police or the Director of Public Prosecutions has decided not to take further action in the case of a complaint, or when 'there is no publicly available evidence of related conduct'. Where policy governing or sanctioning behaviour is problematic, then, is in the fact that it does not compel a subject (or institution) to be transformed in the ethical encounter but, rather, allows that subject (or institution) to protect its own interests by avoiding behaviours or actions that would result in sanction.

Alternative to policy is an ethics of non-violence. To put this in the context of Australian Rules football culture, then, is to ask that footballers recognise the vulnerability of others and respond by being unconditionally *for the other*. At both an individual and an institutional level, using the example of the Lara Bingle scandal, it would be to understand Lara Bingle initially as the other, the outside, the WAG and to act in a way which is non-violent towards her by, firstly, not taking a photograph without consent; secondly, not distributing that photograph in a violent act which exacerbates the first violence; and finally respecting her attempts to resolve the issue in a manner and pace on which she has herself decided. It is, then, to be *for* Lara Bingle, to be a footballer and a football organisation that is oriented *towards* her not in 'respect' and 'responsibility' alone governing behaviour and attitude, but in a manner that responds to her vulnerability by opening the question of *how to be* (a footballer) and *how to be* (a footballer in a particular way). Why, then, does the *Respect & Responsibility* policy, as an instrument designed to avoid and/ or manage scandal, not cover this? Aside from the fact that it operates as an institutional 'law', which is not the same as an ethics, the policy does not seek to change the subjectivity of 'Australian Rules footballer' in the way that an encounter with the other that requires an ethical and non-violent response does. It includes education of players, officials and other stakeholders, but the identity 'footballer' remains intact as the recipient of that education rather than the participant in an encounter or moment of encounter that requires ethics.

At the same time, an ethics built on responding to the vulnerability of the other must emphasise the perspective of recognition. This is something which the *Respect & Responsibility* policy lacks, whereby 'the other' in the case of alleged sexual assault remains relegated to otherness or labelled as 'victim' rather than being the subject to whom the AFL, clubs and involved footballers must recognise through response (being *for* the other). Recognition, which is a central albeit debated tenet in much philosophy, politics and theories of justice, requires more than a recognition as complainant by public institutions and through the procedures of private organisations.[28] Rather, it depends on a recognition in terms of status which, for theorist of justice Nancy Fraser, means 'parity of participation in social life'.[29] In Butler's formulation, it is at a moment of fundamental vulnerability that recognition becomes necessary, possible and self-conscious, and this form of recognition is a reciprocal state of being *for the* other or *given over to* the other.[30] It is not a collapse of the self into that of the other, but a communicative process through which one understands oneself to be reflected in the other and vice versa; not a literal moment of seeing and being seen but a communicative form by which one is transformed through engaging with the other.[31] For Butler, as Estelle Ferrarese points out, such 'recognition' is not merely an outcome of an ethics but can be seen to operate across the three levels of inaugurating an ethical relationship, being a tool of ethics and, at the same time, being the result of an ethical way of being.[32] It is the starting point because the act of recognition is an act of recognising also the self – identity is produced, changes, transforms or is renewed in an ethical act of recognition, it is a positive and transformative site of identity disturbance.[33] It is a tool towards ethics, because the act of recognition of the other's humanity is a condition for responding ethically to his or her vulnerability. And it is an ethical goal in itself, for recognition is asked for and demanded by the other.[34]

This means, in very simplistic and practical terms, the ethical demand on footballers and football culture is to acknowledge the ways in which the encounter with the other – the encounter with Lara Bingle, as other, who makes the claim or complaint of a violence done unto her – begins with recognising her subjectivity through recognising the subjectivity of footballers and football organisations; secondly providing an environment in which the recognition of a person such as Lara Bingle occurs through taking account of her vulnerability and thereby providing an equitable space in which she can address her claim, not simply recognising her through an identity position such as woman, wronged woman, celebrity, gold-digger or various other stereotypes. Finally recognising that Bingle has made a claim is an ethical goal, since 'not responding to this expectation, and closing off such a possibility constitutes as much a violation of moral obligation as not holding back a gesture of physical destruction of the other'.[35] The *Respect & Responsibility* policy, then, presents some useful guidelines on player behaviour, but – as with any such policy that depends on guidelines and sanctions – fails to include an element of recognition that would locate the 'wrong' in social relations rather than individual accountability or individual psychology or individual attitude or individual lack of knowledge of 'appropriate' behaviour.

Frames and the Efficacy of Norms and Ethics

Addressing the claim of Bingle and answering the problem of the violence that Australian Rules football culture does unto the other in various ways requires, then, an approach built on the recognition of the other as subject, as vulnerable and as one to whom the individual, club or organisation must *respond* in non-violence and non-objectification, and in which there is an understanding of the inter-relationality and cultural norms that allow the problem to arise in the first instance. In *Frames of War*, Butler further develops her ethics of vulnerability and recognition of the other by questioning some of the power regimes that unfairly and inequitably operate to make some subjects appear worthy and others as less-than-worthy of being recognised. Maintaining that humans are vulnerable and shifting this further into the realm of embodiment, whereby all human, living bodies are to be understood as precarious,[36] she makes the important point that some subjects are understood as more worthy of being understood as a human life than others; a human life for whom we would protect against violences and injuries, not only physical but otherwise. This is despite her injunction that the 'precarity of life imposes an obligation upon us' not only to be responsible to the other, but to be responsive.[37] Interrogating this through the scene of war, she asks what it is which makes other lives capable of being killed, and how it is that one country will mourn its own, while failing to grieve for the 'other' lives lost on the other side. One *must* act towards recognising the other in a non-violent way, for Butler, because our very selves are built not on an individual, inherent identity, but on the relationality and the mutual dependence between our selves and the lives other lives. In exploring this relationality further, Butler takes the earlier ethical work to task, shifting from the question of recognition, which is too problematically characterised as an act or practice or scene between subject, towards the idea of 'recognisability' which characterises instead the 'general conditions that prepare or shape a subject for recognition'.[38] This allows us to ask, then, what it is that prevents Bingle from being seen as a subject worthy of response and recognition from the perspective of Fevola, footballers and the AFL; to ask what it is that prevents as being understood as worthy of a response which does not do violence to her. This is an important question, as relying on the idea that subjects will recognise the vulnerability of the other must not fall into a complacent assumption that ethics will somehow naturally or automatically come to the fore.

Through opening ethics onto the field of recognisability,[39] Butler presents a number of ways in which we can understand what *prevents* that ethical relationship of responsibility. First among these is the question of norms and normativity. Norms, she points out 'allocate recognition differentially',[40] due to the fact that all subjects are constituted through norms which produce but also 'shift the terms through which subjects are recognised'.[41] Butler asks, significantly, what are the schemas of intelligibility that condition and produce norms of recognisability,[42] according some lives as worthy of a non-violent response and others as not. She indicates that norms are enacted and conditioned through visual and narrative frames,[43] meaning that the discourses that govern which lives will be regarded as *human enough* to be recognised as worthy of an ethical and non-violent response operate through the ways in which various persons, subjectivities and lives are framed.[44] Norms are given culturally,[45] but it is through the methods by which subjects are framed that norms take hold of subjects and present precarity and responsibility differentially across different lives:

We cannot easily recognize life outside the frames in which it is given, and those frames not only structure how we come to know and identify life but constitute sustaining conditions for those very lives. Conditions have to be sustained, which means that they exist not as static entities, but as reproducible social institutions and relations.[46]

In the case of the Bingle scandal, frameworks of normativity produced a response by the AFL and by players towards her that lacked responsiveness, denied recognisability as precarious, vulnerable and therefore dehumanised Bingle. In taking, without consent, a photograph of her in a state of some vulnerability, distributing it for laughs and entertainment among players over the course of several years, and then – at the institutional level – refusing a responsible autonomy in how she is able to respond to the scandal denies her humanity in a wholly unethical way. This can be seen through what we routinely refer to as objectification, treating Bingle as only an instrument for the gratification of those within football culture and denying her a sense of ownership over the narrative of the scandal. To objectify a person in this manner is to treat them as less-than-human and, importantly, it is to fail the ethical requirement to be *for the other*, to be responsible to her as a subject, no matter how much trouble the scandal is causing. In pointing to the ways in which Bingle is framed, it is possible to see that this is not an individual's responsibility in the pedestrian sense of accountability. That is, while one might expect Fevola to have *known better* than to take a photograph of his lover in the shower without permission, to have *felt* the wrongness of distributing it to other players and, along with the AFL in general, to have *understood* that Bingle required ethically a response that did not do further violence to her, the failure to have achieved an ethical position that treated her as human, precarious, vulnerable and worthy is not the fault of an individual but the ways in which discourses frame her as woman, as a particular type of woman, as non-footballer, as *object*.

Rather than using this account of ethics as a means by which liberal norms of 'placing blame' on those who fail to recognise the precarity of the other can be enacted, it is important to think through how these frames not only deny the vulnerability of the other and disavow responsiveness to the other, but how they produce certain forms of ignorance about the dignity, humanity and vulnerability of others. Normative frameworks, as Butler indicates, can mandate ignorance about a subject,[47] meaning that ignorance becomes not a trait of a person, a claim to their being uneducated or under-educated or dim-witted, but a *cultural product* whereby the capacity to see the humanness, precarity and vulnerability of the other is suspended. Ignorance is not a 'lack of knowledge', although we often speak of ignorance in this way, assuming that a person who might be labelled ignorant has simply not read up on a topic, or encountered and learned some important piece of information or routine way of living. Ignorance, rather, is something that is 'actively produced and maintained' by cultural forces, power arrangements and disciplinary techniques.[48] In several ways, the inability of players, clubs and the AFL to see Bingle as human and deserving of response and responsibility during the photograph scandal is not the result of deliberate maliciousness but of the ways in which she is framed in the context of the scandal as, on the one hand, non-precarious and non-worthy and, on the other, through an ignorance of her needs or dignity or the effect of distributing the photograph. In that sense, part of the ethical problem resulting in behaviours that cause or relate to scandal, harm, violence or failing to recognise the precarity of others is the fact that, within a nexus of institutions, expectations, and roles, footballer identity is produced as one which conterminously produces *certain kinds of ignorance* that suspend the possibility of seeing the frames and framework that make the other appear less human, less worthy of respect, less worthy of response and responsibility.

Thus, where campaigns for education that form the backbone of much AFL policy such as the *Respect & Responsibility* initiative are important in drawing attention to the issue of respect (in this case for women), they may not necessarily meet the challenge of producing an ethical response. That is because such educational seminars, workshops and individual and group activities are themselves framed within a particular set of notions of both ignorance and learning, whereby it is begun from the assumption that the recipients of such education are ignorant of the 'truth' and, through workshopping scenarios, will come to know through learning. As stated, yes, very important and the overall effect of such campaigns is, of course, unknowable, so they should not be dismissed. But where they can be expanded is in ensuring there is an inclusion of learning the capacity for critical investigation of the frames and discourses which, say, make a woman or certain types of women appear to be available to be objectified, or where a non-heterosexual person appears to be less worthy of respect, or where a bystander caught up in street-level team bonding or celebratory misbehaviour is not a matter for consideration and responsibility.

Ignorance is produced actively, but culturally. In this case ignorance of the framing mechanisms that prevent being *for* the other (being for Bingle; responding with responsiveness to Bingle) is produced to uphold, reinforce and reproduce over time the existing concept of Australian Rules football culture. In attempting to foster a more ethical Australian Rules footballer, it is thus a matter for cultural change that encourages the critique of the frames of normativity which produce ways of seeing the other – the outside, the non-footballer, women, non-heterosexuals, bystanders, and so on – in such a way that recognises the shared precariousness and vulnerability common, as Butler indicates, to humanity in general and that demands an ethical relationship. Critiquing the frames that make some subjects appear worthy and others less so is the means by which subjects become recognisable and therefore worthy of a response and responsibility. As Butler puts it:

> When those frames that govern the relative and differential recognizability of lives come apart, as part of the very mechanism of their circulation – it becomes possible to apprehend something about what or who is living but has not been generally 'recognised' as a life.[49]

Such an ethical perspective aids in locating the problem not in footballers' individual decisions, thus sharing accountability across the culture and its governance bodies, which is not to say that we do away altogether with making footballers (like others) accountable for their actions, for example, in the scenario of a sexual assault or injurious form of speech such as an insult or other forms of violence. However, the injustice that extends not just from the act, but through the scandals, particularly in cases in which the wronged party is denied the capacity to participate in the discussion, is also a matter of redistribution of the power to speak authoritatively on the events and narrative of a scandal – something which occurred unwittingly in the case of the 'St Kilda Schoolgirl' scandal, but something which Lara Bingle was denied.

Injury and Precarious Bodies

Understanding one's own precariousness is a means by which the frames which obscure vulnerability and ethical relations with others are put into question, thereby opening up the possibility of ethics. As Butler argues:

> precariousness as a generalized condition relies on a conception of the body as fundamentally dependent on, and condition by, a sustained and sustainable world; responsiveness – and thus,

ultimately, responsibility – is located in the affective responses to a sustaining and impinging world. Because such affective responses are invariably mediated, they call upon and enact certain interpretive frames; they can also call into question the taken-for-granted character of those frames, and in that way provide the affective conditions for social critique'.[50]

In chapter three, I argued that footballers are in a particularly powerful position to recognise their own precariousness and vulnerability, and therefore that of others outside of football culture who too often are impacted by off-field misbehaviours. In expanding on this point, it is important to bear in mind that the precariousness of humanity, in Butler's account, is grounded in the body. For Butler, precarity is found at the site of the body for which it is impossible to eliminate the possibilities of illness, injury or accident – these are, as she puts it, 'built into the very conception of bodily life considered both finite and precarious, implying the body is always given over to modes of sociality and environment that limit its individual autonomy'.[51] That is, while even the concept of the body is produced through cultural knowledges, coming to materialise as a particular type of recognisable body,[52] the body as something inseparable from concepts of life and living is always marked by the implication of its own mortality.[53] The body is always produced socially and depends on sociality for its continuation in life, therefore it is the site of a shared, common vulnerability[54] and thus a means by which an ethical relationship can be forged.

More than just the shared vulnerability, precarity and precariousness, however, marks the body of the footballer. Footballers are, in many ways, more susceptible to their own vulnerability to injury than are others. By that, I mean the precariousness and risk the footballer body undergoes in the on-field environment is significant, visual, reported upon, mediated and forms the bulk of sports news during the middle of the week and the pre-game lead-up commentary. It is thus a particularly notable type of vulnerability which, I am arguing, if handled well, can shift or disrupt the frames by which football culture is made ignorant of the violences perpetrated in the off-field environment on others. Injury, of course, is not core to an ethics of vulnerability. As Butler points out, it is *one thing* that can happen to a vulnerable body, but that vulnerability occurs as one 'comes up against the outside world' in an 'unwilled proximity to others and circumstances beyond one's control'.[55] Injury does not *make* a body vulnerable, but is one mode of impact on the body and the self that is vulnerability's *effect*. In that sense, then, it draws attention in a specific way for footballers (and, undoubtedly, other players of contact sports) to the precariousness of the body that is a common, albeit *differentiated*, element of being human in a world of sociality.

Australian Rules football is particularly notable for being a site of on-field injury, and the game has been identified as the sport most associated with admissions to hospital due to injury.[56] Facing and managing injury is both publicly and privately an integral element of contemporary footballer identity. A study by health insurance company Medibank Private found that Australian Rules was the most injury-prone sport with the risk of injury being the result of the game's 'speed and full body contact nature of the sport and the constant physical competition for the ball'.[57] Injuries sustained during play typically result in significant media commentary, and spates of injury reporting result in parental concerns about the safety of the game for younger persons.[58] This is despite recent improvements in elite-level AFL games, with an ongoing lowering of the rate of injury and the implementation of an injury surveillance system since 1992 that collects and monitors information about injuries sustained by AFL players.[59] Indeed, despite stereotypes and reputations, Australian Rules has been considered by many to be a tougher, more injury-prone game than Rugby League.[60] Although the elite-level game has a lower likelihood of injury than that found in community and amateur football due to higher levels of fitness, training and greater access to medical knowledge,[61] junior football is increasingly marked by on-field violent clashes,[62] and injury at all levels remains a central concern of the sport itself, thus providing a nodal point which can highlight the precariousness of play and the vulnerability of the body in this scene. At the same time, media stories of the relationship between play, vulnerability and injury have further emphasised the precariousness of the body in the on-field site of the game, and this can include the ongoing physical impact of relatively minor injuries sustained over a longer period of time as a player. For example, former Demons player Daniel Bell has sought compensation from Melbourne Football Club for the impact of a number of concussions sustained during a career of sixty-six games. At only twenty-five years, Bell has been diagnosed by a neuropsychologist with significant cognitive function disabilities, impacting on short-term memory to the point that he would 'sometimes forget his position' on the field. The impact is, according to reports, something which extends to his capacity to play football again at any level, with warnings given that a further concussion could increase the chance of his developing dementia in later life.[63] Additionally, recent research has also linked on-field concussions with an increased likelihood of developing Alzheimer's disease[64] and other brain injuries.[65] Rule changes made during 2011 aimed at further protecting AFL players from injury were criticised, although Andrew Demetriou did point to the necessity of taking action against player tackles that improperly target the vulnerable body-point of the head on the basis that the 'head is sacrosanct' and that this 'is the most physically brutal game'.[66]

On-field injury is not the only marker of vulnerability found in Australian Rules football culture. Recent reports have indicated a surprisingly high level of pressure-related burn-out among coaches and assistant coaches, and the overuse of substances such as caffeine and sleeping pills in order to manage all-night match reviews.[67] Players' careers have been interrupted as a result of off-field physical violence, which is not necessarily always the result of players' own actions. For example, WAFL player Luke Adams was in critical condition for several days after becoming involved in a street brawl in Perth's nightclub district, Northbridge, on a weekend night in May 2011. Head injuries resulted from a single-punch assault, and it was not clear through the reports if Adams' notoriety as a footballer was the cause of his being hit, or if his own sense of physical *in*vulnerability led him to intervene in the brawl.[68] The fact that he was with another player does reopen the questions I asked in earlier chapters about group-based identity and the suspension of ethics. In this case, group identity can lead to a greater disavowal of one's own bodily precarity. Regardless, however, as to the cause of the brawl, that he ended up on life-support does once again highlight the specific precariousness of life and the vulnerability of the body within Australian Rules football culture, whether on or off the field.

With all these examples of physical (and other) injury that emphasises the precariousness and vulnerability of the footballer body what is it, then, that prevents the ethical relationship that, in Butler's formulation, might emerge by embracing the commonality of vulnerability and prompting its recognition in the relationships forged by footballers with external others? The fact remains that while injury plays an absolutely central role in the discourse around playing the game (and off-field play), injury is *not* a marker of the footballer's identity. Rather, we have yet another situation that falls under Butler's perception of the frame: the ways in which the embodied subjectivity of footballer identity is coded through a hypermasculinity that requires, for the very intelligibility and coherence of that identity, a disavowal of vulnerability. Injury, then becomes not a signifier of the deeper precariousness of the footballer body but, instead, a symbol of masculinity. This can be understood if we look more closely at some of the ways in which the discourse around injury and pain plays out. In their study of younger players at school, Gard and Meyenn found that the themes of physical injury and pain were central to dialogue about the experience of play, but were also the stated concepts through which boys established a sense of masculinity in relation to their bodies.[69] These young men's discourse on injury risk in sport involved the 'claim that it is "natural" for males to engage in these activities and that tolerating pain is an important part of "becoming a man"'.[70] Such fortitude in regard to injury and pain is not limited to the young in a desire to shore up the constitution of a footballer identity as hypermasculine, but includes former footballers living with osteoarthritis (OA) that had a causal association with their playing career. According to Turner and colleagues, despite considerable post-career pain and disruption to work, social and leisure activities, ex-footballers interviewed in their study generally adopted a 'stoical attitude towards their situation and considered that OA was something that just had to be endured and ultimately accepted as "a price worth paying"'.[71] By restricting the articulation of emotion and utilising a rhetoric of stoicism to avoid drawing attention to vulnerability, a particular cultural model of masculinity is upheld.[72] In commenting on the claim that rules designed to reduce injury in Australian Rules games has made football 'soft', Tim Lane points out a number of historical cases of toughness that can be read as a disavowal of vulnerability and precarity of the body, including the story of Bob Chitty who played for Footscray and Carlton during the period of the Second World War. After a workplace accident severed his finger, he insisted on playing the following weekend against medical advice, found the guard he was wearing was interfering and continued to play with this significant injury exposed.[73] While such stories have become part of Australian Rules folklore in which former players gain a heroic status for their masculine denial of vulnerability, what they effectively demonstrate is that a particular way of framing injury and pain not only produces masculinity, but presents the masculine self as invulnerable and inviolable.

It is thus the case that Australian Rules football culture (along with other sports) reproduces over time a performance of masculine stoicism which disguises or disavows the vulnerability of footballer bodies and, contrary to the wishes expressed here, a denial of the possibility of ethics. Where the masculinity of footballers is produced through a performance of hypermasculine 'toughness', injury becomes separated from vulnerability in a way which is not found necessarily among the broader population of men. On the one hand, this thereby makes it difficult for footballers to recognise other, differentiated forms of vulnerability in their encounters with others (the other) and, on the other hand, maintains and reproduces a culture in which it is difficult to communicate to younger up-and-coming players how their own future health is vulnerable, seen particularly in the decreased likelihood of the use of helmets or other bodily protections as young players move into their mid-teens.[74] This is exacerbated by the competitive nature of the game whereby, according to a study, an 'intense motivation to win' has been linked with increased injuries in the earlier weeks of a playing season.[75] However, despite the extent to which injuries form a central element in the discourse not only of the game but of the meaning of 'footballer identity', it is through a nexus of identity factors such as performance, masculinity, heroism, commitment and pride that frames the concept of injury and separates it from the capacity to bear witness to the fact that such identities, all identities, are formed in the commonality of vulnerability and the precariousness of embodied life.

By looking to alternative ways in which football culture can conceive of footballers' embodied identity – that is, by foregrounding the precariousness and vulnerability of footballers' bodies to injury rather than performing selfhood through masculine posturing of *invulnerability* – it is possible to overcome the framed ignorance of the vulnerability of the other. Gilson highlights the importance of overcoming such posturing when she states:

> ignorance of vulnerability must be understood through an analysis of the practices and habits that propagate invulnerability. Since vulnerability and invulnerability are matters not just of being but also of knowledge and ignorance, they must be addressed along these lines and must be understood not as general properties but as states that have diverse contexts, differential meanings, and disparate conditions of creation.[76]

That means, then, that in transforming football culture into a site which recognises vulnerability, it is necessary to re-figure footballers' knowledge of selfhood and identity from one of hypermasculinity to one which undertakes to recognise one's own vulnerability as a particular form that is different from – but always related to – other types of precariousness, such as that of a woman in a group sexual encounter, a bystander in a bar during a drinking session, family members who might be affected by the over-use of recreational drugs, non-heterosexuals or men who do not conform to outdated hypermasculine standards being subject to insult or other forms of verbal or physical injury. Footballers' ignorance of vulnerability – of the fundamental vulnerability that is shared as a common trait – and thereby the inability to recognise the vulnerability of the other, thus occurs through the formation of footballer subjectivity as hypermasculine with its performative traits of being invulnerable (or, at least, disavowing vulnerability) as a central part of footballer identity. Such ignorance, then, is not a personal failing and it is certainly not to suggest that footballers are somehow not intelligent, but that their subjectivation *as* footballers within contemporary Australian Rules culture governs the framework which prevents the capacity to recognise the vulnerability and precariousness of the other.

Towards an Ethical Brand of Football

Ultimately, to overcome the sorts of off-field behaviours that regularly result in scandal, damage to reputations and the reputation of the game and, most importantly, risk harm or forms of violence to others, football culture needs to be transformed from one which disavows vulnerability through stoical masculine responses to injury in order that players are able to recognise their own vulnerability and thus open the possibility of recognising the vulnerability of others by coming to understand the commonality of the precariousness of bodies, subjects and lives. I am not, of course, speaking of individual footballers here, many of whom demonstrate this already and many of whom do relate to others ethically, non-violently and with respectful responsiveness and care. Rather, this is about the forms of footballer identity that are cultivated by clubs, institutions, governance organisations and the broader culture of contemporary Australian Rules. When we recall the fact that identities are performed according to particular norms and practices that give that identity coherence and intelligibility, it is simultaneously important to remember that 'footballer identity' is also performed in ways which are intelligible and through practices, behaviours and attitudes which precede the footballer himself and emerge through the culture of football. At the same time, all identities or subjectivities/selfhoods are always constituted in a process, and are open to change, transformation and moments of 'disturbance' that are generated in the encounters with others in a world of sociality and relationality.[77] This means there is no inherent, endemic reason why Australian Rules footballers *must* perform an identity according to hypermasculine strictures, stoicism and the disavowal of precarity, rewriting injury as a badge of honour rather than a signifier of vulnerability; there is thus no inherent, endemic reason why football institutions should not be in a position, through the critique of the frames that make such identities intelligible and sensible, to relate in encounters with others through an ethics of non-violence based on the recognition of shared precariousness of embodied life.

Indeed, part of the argument here is that if football culture can be transformed such that hypermasculinity – so out of step now with broader attitudes to gender – can be marginalised from the practices and performances of 'footballer identity', then footballers are well positioned to recognise vulnerability, to become ethical subjects *par excellence*, ambassadors of ethics. Through celebrity, national heroism and notoriety, a new form of masculinity (non-hyper) and a new form of ethics (non-violent and non-objectifying) can be role modelled for a more ethical society. This is a radically optimistic, virtually utopian and highly idealistic statement, of course, as no cultural transformation can be designed and impelled in advance and no transformation is guaranteed to have an outcome that could be considered ethical. Nevertheless, if footballers are to continue to play the role of role model, then there is an opportunity for communicative practices which draw attention to the inherent vulnerability and precariousness which marks all subjects including their own, and this is something that can be achieved by re-figuring the risks of injury in ways which are not framed by masculine stoicism. In doing so, this is about producing the footballer's identity as one which is being *for the other*, where the other is the non-footballer, the bystander, the outsider – not the fellow subject who is within the commonality of the game, the club stakeholder, the league management or even necessarily the fans and spectators.

In the third chapter, I pointed to some of the ways in which we can understand the mechanisms by which an ethics of non-violence and recognition of the vulnerability of women to sexual assault and harassment is frequently suspended in the temporal site of footballer group or team identity; that is, where a group of footballers are acting together or in concert in a sexual encounter with a woman or several women. Because team bonding is so absolutely essential to successful performance in the game, and because that bonding involves the development of group affinities in off-field social and sexual environments, this complicates the matter of transforming football culture into a site marked by an ethics of non-violence through a reframing of injury to point to vulnerability. As a group in which individual subjecthood is temporarily suspended, a certain heightened sense of invulnerability comes into play – this is what, in many group scenarios, makes a gang crime possible, a riot possible, a rape possible, whereby consequences of a crime or misdemeanour may be known and understood but the subjectivity of 'group-ness' provides the sense of imperviousness to those implications. Ultimately, this is one element in developing a transformative ethics of football culture in which the sanction and penalty must be constantly imputed, such that group identity can continue (and off-field group activities can continue, including consensual sexual activities, drinking and other forms of 'partying'), but whereby it is important to target not the *individual subject* but the *group* with an understanding of vulnerability such that it is possible – again, not for individuals but for the group – to recognise the vulnerability of those outsiders who may be wrapped into those off-field scenes with the group.

In other words, a reframing of group behaviour away from the group as a *collection of individuals* who may be sanctioned, penalised or charged with a crime and instead looking to develop ways in which an entire *team* is no longer deemed impervious or invulnerable (perhaps by the suspension of entire teams from the game in the sorts of circumstances I described in chapter three) would be a starting point. At the same time, as these activities are part of a continuum from the on-field identity to the many sites of off-field (mis)behaviour, it is important to develop ways in which a team can remain bonded, committed to a win and committed to longer-term success *without* the need for producing the team as a community of imperviousness and the wholesale suspension of subjecthood. Rather, to see the team as a network of subjects who are bound by relationality to each (a commonality) and relationality to everyone else outside football (where the commonalities, such as vulnerability, need to be teased out to be recognised), and understanding that the network of selves operates differently in different sites from the on-field to the off-field, we are some of the way towards producing the group and its identity *through* an ethical perspective.

As indicated in the first chapter, some of the ways in which scandalous or unethical behaviours can be addressed is through a transformative deconstruction of the recognisable and standard narratives that govern how footballers, club and leagues behave and respond to others who claim injury or wrongdoing against them. What was demonstrated was the effectiveness of Kim Duthie's persistent use of traditional and digital media to maintain public attention on herself as complainant, rather than have her public image and identity framed by the more standard narratives that emerge through the Australian Rules institutions' public relations machinery. The AFL and others attempted to make great use of the rhetoric of vulnerability to argue that Duthie was unstable, in need of help and that therefore her claims were not justifiable or worthy of attention or response. However, within a different context of vulnerability, Duthie was able to invoke her own vulnerability in order to maintain her demand for a non-violent and non-injurious relationship with the Australian Rules football social world; that is, a relationship in which she would *not* be sexually used by players and stakeholders and then cast aside or ostracised. At the same time, however, her actions in distributing the nude and sexualised images of St Kilda players demonstrates the very vulnerability of football celebrities to scandal — a particularly increasing vulnerability in the context of a digital communications environment. Likewise, Ricky Nixon's own vulnerability became apparent as his involvement in the scandal cost him firstly his reputation, his licence to operate as a player agent and finally his business. What the run of the entire scandal demonstrated is the *mutuality* of vulnerability on all sides. Likewise, the Bingle scandal pointed to the vulnerability of Fevola as much as to her own; so too has Ben Cousins' drug scandals in regard to his family and other outsiders, or Wayne Carey's behaviours in regard to his teammate, his teammate's wife. However, by looking to the all-pervasive relationality that governs all subjects here, the opportunity to transform scandal into an ethics led from within Australian Rules culture was opened but sadly missed.

Former Australian Treasurer Peter Costello may have well asked why footballers should be visiting schools, as they are neither philanthropists nor good role models, but paid players[78]. However, we might turn this question around and ask, Why not re-figure footballer identity as philanthropic and as good role models in order that their visits to schools have a better outcome? This is perhaps the right kind of question the AFL and individual clubs should be asking in their roles in organising such off-field events for footballers. To put the question another way, How might footballers present and communicate an ethics of non-violence through a communicative re-thinking of what it means *to be* a footballer? If, by re-figuring Australian Rules football culture in such a way that vulnerability rather than masculinity is foregrounded, then we might be some of the way towards not only reducing the incredible likelihood of footballer scandals and the damage they cause to the game, the team, the players and the fans, but also turn the role of the footballer in the off-field world into an ethical ambassador and an ambassador for ethics. No one is suggesting, of course, that such transformation would not be incredibly difficult work involving significant reflexivity, the critique of subjectivity and the critical investigation of the full range of values that are core to football culture. But, given the scandals, the crimes and the precariousness of both footballers and those others who come into contact with the world of football, it is necessary work and, in several respects, recent scandals help point the way.

NOTES

Notes to the Introduction: Football Scandal, Identity and Ethics

1   C. Wilson, 'Signs of Ricky Nixon's unravelling apparent for years', *The Age*, 20 February 2011, accessed 20 February 2011, <http://www.theage.com.au/afl/afl-news/>.

2   C. Wilson, 'Nixon should be kicked out, not handballed', *The Age*, 25 February 2011, accessed 25 February 2011, <http://www.theage.com.au/afl/afl-news/>.

3   D. Silkstone, 'Saints ban four for six weeks', *The Age*, 1 February 2011, accessed 1 February 2011, <http://www.theage.com.au/afl/afl-news/>.

4   M. Levy, 'Details emerge of girl at centre of AFL nude pic scandal', *The Age*, 21 December 2011, accessed 21 December 2010, <http://www.theage.com.au/afl/afl-news>.

5   J. Akermanis, 'Stay in the closet, Jason Akermanis tells homosexuals', *Herald Sun*, 20 May 2010, accessed 29 May 2010, <www.heraldsun.com.au/sport/>.

6   S. Robbins, 'Will Cousins' final confession lead to redemption?' *The Age*, 5 August 2010, accessed 18 July 2011, <http://www.theage.com.au/sport/blogs/sally-stands-up>.

7   E. Hunt, 'Stephen Milne case should have gone on – ex-cop', *Herald Sun*, 21 June 2010, accessed 14 August 2011, <http://www.adelaidenow.com.au/sport/afl/>.

8   E. Trosby, 'Public relations, football and the management of player transgressions in Australia', *Public Communication Review*, vol. 1, no. 2, 2010, pp. 49–66; L. M. Mawson, 'Sportswomanship: the cultural acceptance of sport for women versus the accommodation of cultured women in sport', in L. K. Fuller (ed), *Sport, Rhetoric and Gender: Historical Perspectives and Media Representations*. Palgrave Macmillan, New York, pp. 1930; J. J. Paterson, 'Disciplining athletes for off-field indiscretions: a comparative review of the Australian Football League and the National Football League's personal conduct policies', *Australian and New Zealand Sports Law Journal*, vol. 4, no. 1, 2009, p. 106.

9   L. Albergo, 'Gambling investigation', *Australian Football Association of North America*, 18 February 2007, accessed 29 August 2011, <http://www.afana.com/drupal5/news/2007/02/18/>.

10   J. M. Connor & and J. Mazanov, 'The inevitability of scandal: lessons for sponsors and administrators,' *International Journal of Sports Marketing & Sponsorship*, vol. 11, no. 3, 2010, p. 214.

11   Connor & Mazanov, 'Inevitability of scandal', p. 214.

12   J. Steele, 'Scandals great and small', *Hofstra Law Review*, vol. 36, no. 2, 2007, p. 505.

13   J. Coakley, C. Hallinan, S. Jackson & P. Mewett, *Sports in Society: Issues and Controversies in Australia and New Zealand*, McGraw–Hill Australia, New South Wales, 2009.

14   L. Chalip, 'Toward a distinctive sport management discipline', *Journal of Sport Management,* vol. 20, no. 1, 2006, pp. 1–21.

15   J. Boxill (ed) *Sports Ethics: An Anthology*, Blackwell, Oxford and Melbourne, 2003, p. 153.

16   D. H. Zakus, J. Skinner & A. Edwards, 'Social capital in Australian sport', *Sport in Society*, vol. 12, no. 7, 2009, p. 994.

17   M. Green & B. Houlihan, 'Governmentality, modernization, and the "disciplining" of national sporting organizations: athletics in Australia and the United Kingdom', *Sociology of Sport Journal*, vol. 23, no. 1, 2006, p. 56.

18   A. Lowe, 'Former St Kilda player Lovett raped woman while she slept, court hears', *The Age*, 11 August 2010, accessed 12 August 2010, <http://www.theage.com.au/victoria/>.

19   The Age, 'Bingle sues Fevola over nude photo', *The Age*, 2 March 2010, accessed 21 June 2011, <http://www.theage.com.au/breaking-news-national/>.

20   L. Rickard, 'West Coast player fined, suspended for disparaging remarks over Demon player's mother', *The Age*, 16 August 2011, accessed 16 August 2011, <http://www.theage.com.au/afl/afl-news/>.

21   B. Guthrie, 'Footy needs to clean up its act off the field', *The Age,* 21 August 2011, accessed 23 August 2011, <http://www.theage.com.au/opinion/politics/>.

22   J. Pierik, 'Partying claims dog Suns' Ablett', *The Age*, 18 April 2011, accessed 18 April 2011, <http://www.theage.com.au/afl/afl-news/>.

23   J. Pierik & M. Beck, 'I hit rock bottom: Fevola bares his soul', *The Age*, 11 March 2011, accessed 11 March 2011, <http://www.theage.com.au/afl/afl-news/>.

24   A. Lowe, 'Lovett charged with second count of rape', *The Age*, 7 May 2010, accessed 7 May 2010, <http://www.theage.com.au/afl/afl-news/>.

25   C. Hickey & P. Kelly, 'Preparing to *not* be a footballer: higher education and professional sport', *Sport, Education and Society*, vol. 13, no. 4, 2008, p. 479.

26   G. Clanton, 'The sport star: modern sport and the cultural economy of sporting celebrity', *Contemporary Sociology: A Journal of Reviews,* vol. 36, no. 1, 2007, p. 49; C. Rojek, 'Sports celebrity and the civilizing process', *Sport in Society*, vol. 9, no. 4, 2006, pp. 683–684.

27   Paterson, 'Disciplining athletes', p. 143.

28 E. Dunning & I. Waddington, 'Sport as a drug and drugs in sport: some exploratory comments', *International Review for the Sociology of Sport,* vol. 38, no. 3, 2003, p. 356.

29 J. Butler, *Gender Trouble: Feminism and the Subversion of Identity,* Routledge, London & New York, 1990, pp. 16, 18.

30 J. Butler, *Bodies That Matter: On The Discursive Limits of 'Sex',* Routledge, London & New York, 1993, p. 2.

31 P. Hanlon, 'Dogs on notice over Hong Kong prank', *The Age,* 8 February 2011, accessed 8 February 2011, <http://www.theage.com.au/afl/afl-news/>.

32 Hickey & Kelly, 'Preparing to *not* be a footballer'.

33 A. Lowe, 'Charges dropped in pack rape case', *The Age,* 8 July 2010, accessed 8 July 2010, <http://www.theage.com.au/national/>.

34 P. Munro, 'Nixon faces sex scandal inquiry', *The Age,* 20 February 2011, accessed 20 February 2011, <http://www.theage.com.au/afl/afl-news/>.

35 C. Webb & M. Levy, 'Photo-scandal teen tackles Saints at new HQ', *The Age,* 11 January 2011, accessed 26 March 2011, <http://www.theage.com.au/afl/afl-news/>.

36 T. Clarke, 'Cousins banned after drinking binge', *The Age,* 12 April 2010, accessed 13 April 2010, <http://www.theage.com.au/afl/afl-news/>.

37 A. Lowe, 'Rape trial told Lovett felt entitled', *The Age,* 21 July 2011, accessed 21 July 2011, <http://www.theage.com.au/victoria/>.

38 R. Devlin & T. Sheahan, 'Brendan Fevola sacked by Brisbane Lions for "mulitple" contract breaches', *Perth Now,* 21 February 2011, accessed 21 July 2011, <http://www.perthnow.com.au/sport/>.

39 Connor & Mazanon, 'The inevitability of scandal', pp. 216–217.

40 J. Butler, *Precarious Life,* Verso, London, 2004; J. Butler, *Frames of War: When is Life Grievable?* Verso, London & New York, 2009.

41 Dunning & Waddington, 'Sport as a drug and drugs in sport'.

Notes to Chapter 1: The 'St Kilda Schoolgirl'

1 D. Waterhouse-Watson, *Athletes, Sexual Assault, and 'Trials by Media',* Routledge, London & New York, p. 4.

2 F. Attwood, 'Sexed up: theorizing the sexualization of culture', *Sexualities,* vol. 9, no. 1, 2006, pp. 78–79.

3 J. Gamson, 'Jessica Hahn, media whore: sex scandals and female publicity', *Critical Studies in Media Communication,* vol. 18, no. 2, 2001, pp. 157–173.

4 C. Wilson & S. Lane, 'Saints players in the clear after schoolgirl sex investigation', *The Age,* 27 May 2010, accessed 27 May 2010, <http://www.theage.com.au/afl/afl-news/>.

5 S. Spits, 'Nixon demands apology over St Kilda schoolgirl sex claim', *The Age,* 27 May 2010, accessed 29 May 2010, <http://www.theage.com.au/afl/afl-news/>.

6 M. Hawthorne, 'Players emailed "Saints girl" pic', *The Age,* 29 May 2010, accessed 29 May 2010, <http://www.theage.com.au/victoria/>.

7 Hawthorne, 'Players emailed "Saints girl" pic'.

8   Hawthorne, 'Players emailed "Saints girl" pic'.

9   M. Levy, 'Demetriou blasts St Kilda Schoolgirl email forwarders', *The Age*, 4 June 2010, accessed 4 June 2010, <http://www.theage.com.au/afl/afl-news/>.

10   S. Spits, 'Saints take action over explicit photograph', *The Age*, 20 December 2010, accessed 20 December 2010, < http://www.theage.com.au/afl/afl-news/>.

11   P. Millar & R. Sexton, 'Naked Saints go viral', *The Age*, 21 December 2010, accessed 21 December 2010, <http://www.theage.com.au/afl/afl-news/>.

12   D. Prestipino, 'Saints schoolgirl silenced by Facebook over nude photos', *Perth Now*, 21 December 2010, accessed 21 December 2010, <http://www.perthnow. com.au/news/>.

13   W. Brodie, 'Naked photos pierce the "bubble"', *The Age*, 21 December 2010, accessed 21 December 2010, <http://www.theage.com.au/afl/afl-news/>.

14   B. Butler & P. Millar, 'Teen denies asking $20,000 for photo', *The Age*, 22 December 2010, accessed 22 December 2010, <http://www.theage.com.au/ afl/afl-news/>.

15   J. Pierik & G. Gannon, 'Nude-pic teenager strikes deal with Saints', *The Age*, 22 January 2011, accessed 22 January 2011, <http://www.theage.com.au/afl/ afl-news/>.

16   P. Costello, 'Hard to be charitable about sports stars' philanthropy', *The Age*, 16 February 2011, accessed 16 February 2011, <http://www.theage.com.au/ opinion/society-and-culture/>.

17   C. Wilson, 'Girl at centre of St Kilda photo scandal alleges affair with Nixon', *The Age*, 18 February 2011, accessed 19 February 2011, <http://www.theage. com.au/afl/afl-news/>.

18   K. Kissane, M. Beck, & M. Gleeson, 'Nixon video: teen arrested', *The Age*, 22 February 2011, accessed 22 February 2011, <http://www.theage.com.au/afl/ afl-news/>.

19   P. Munro, 'It's payback time, says teen', *Sydney Morning Herald*, 20 February 2011, accessed 20 February 2011, <http://www.smh.com.au/afl/afl-news/>.

20   P. Munro, 'Nixon faces sex scandal inquiry', *The Age*, 20 February 2011, accessed 20 February 2011, <http://www.theage.com.au/afl/afl-news/>.

21   Kissane, Beck & Gleeson, 'Nixon video: teen arrested'.

22   A. Carey, 'Police will question Nixon', *The Age*, 23 February 2011, accessed 23 February 2011, <http://www.theage.com.au/afl/afl-news/>.

23   Munro, 'Nixon faces sex scandal inquiry'.

24   Carey, 'Police will question Nixon'.

25   C. Wilson, 'Nixon should be kicked out, not handballed', *The Age*, 25 February 2011, accessed 25 February 2011, <http://www.theage.com.au/afl/afl-news/>.

26   C. Wilson, 'Brown out of Nixon stable', *The Age*, 26 February 2011, accessed 26 February 2011, <http://www.theage.com.au/afl/afl-news/>.

27   P. Munro, 'Nixon could end up in supreme court', *The Age*, 27 February 2011, accessed 27 February 2011, <http://www.theage.com.au/afl/afl-news/>.

28   M. Beck & A. Khokhar, 'St Kilda teen lied she was pregnant', *The Age*, 7 March 2011, accessed 8 March 2011, <http://www.theage.com.au/afl/afl-news/>.

29 M. Beck, 'Nixon admits to substance problem', *The Age*, 8 March 2011, accessed 8 March 2011, <http://www.theage.com.au/afl/afl-news/>.

30 C. Wilson, 'Rehab won't save Nixon's business', *The Age*, 9 March 2011, accessed 26 March 2011, <http://www.theage.com.au/afl/afl-news/>.

31 *60 Minutes*, 'Kim Duthie interviewed', television broadcast, Australia, 6 March 2011.

32 M. Levy, 'AFL chief knew pregnancy claim was lie', *The Age*, 7 March 2011, accessed 8 March 2011, <http://www.theage.com.au/afl/afl-news/>.

33 M. Cooper, 'AFL players strip Nixon of agent accreditation', *The Age*, 24 March 2011, accessed 24 March 2011, <http://www.theage.com.au/afl/afl-news/>.

34 J. Pierik & A. Khokhar, 'No Appeal, Nixon gets out of football', *The Age*, 8 April 2011, accessed 8 April 2011, <http://www.theage.com.au/afl/afl-news/>.

35 The Age, 'Teen's family say they received death threats', *The Age*, 11 April 2011, accessed 11 April 2011, <http://www.theage.com.au/victoria/>.

36 The Age, 'Teen's family say they received death threats'.

37 P. Millar & A. Khokhar, 'Nixon takes out court order on teen', *The Age*, 15 April 2011, accessed 15 April 2011, <http://www.theage.com.au/afl/afl-news/>.

38 J. Niall, 'Nixon: the documentary', *The Age*, 20 April 2011, accessed 21 April 2011, <http://www.theage.com.au/afl/afl-news/>.

39 The Age, 'Nixon admits threatening to kill girl', *The Age*, 30 April 2011, accessed 30 April 2011, <http://www.theage.com.au/afl/afl-news/>.

40 R. Williams, 'Nixon walkout over sex and drugs', *The Age*, 1 May 2011, accessed 1 May 2011, <http://www.theage.com.au/victoria/>.

41 M. Levy, 'Nixon, teen had sex: report', *The Age*, 5 May 2011, accessed 5 May 2011, <http://www.theage.com.au/victoria/>.

42 B. Preiss, '"Joking about lying about lying": teen caught in her own web of deceit', *The Age*, 10 June 2011, accessed 16 August 2011, <http://www.theage.com.au/afl/>.

43 Preiss, '"Joking about lying about lying"'.

44 The Age, 'I assaulted Tegan, admits Nixon', *The Age*, 25 March 2013, accessed 25 March 2013, <http://www.theage.com.au/victoria/>.

45 J. Holroyd, 'Police drop teen sex case against Ricky Nixon', *The Age*, 1 August 2011, accessed 16 August 2011, <http://www.theage.com.au/victoria/>.

46 AFL, *Respect & Responsibility Policy Implementation Plan*, 2009, accessed 5 December 2010, <http://www.afl.com.au/portals/0/afl_docs/afl_hq/policies/r_r_policy.pdf>.

47 M. de Certeau, *The Practice of Everyday Life*, trans. S. F. Rendall, University of California Press, Berkeley, California, 1984, p. xix.

48 M. Dery, 'Culture jamming: hacking, slashing and sniping in the empire of signs', 1993, accessed 12 December 2013, <http://web.nwe.ufl.edu/~mlaffey/cultjam.html>.

49 R. Cover, 'Audience inter/active: interactive media, narrative control & reconceiving audience history', *New Media & Society,* vol. 8, no. 1, 2006, p. 144.

50 G. Meikle, *Future Active: Media Activism and the Internet*, Routledge, London & New York, 2002, p. 5.

51 Kissane, Beck & Gleeson, 'Nixon video: teen arrested'.

52 Levy, 'AFL chief knew pregnancy claim was lie'.

53 M. Levy, 'Teenager has received death threats', *The Age*, 24 December 2010, accessed 24 December 2010, <http://www.theage.com.au/victoria/>.

54 S. McMillan & M. Morrison, 'Coming of age with the internet: a qualitative exploration of how the internet has become an integral part of young people's lives', *New Media & Society*, vol. 8, no. 1, 2006, pp. 73–95.

55 D. Crystal, *Language and the Internet*, Second Edition, Cambridge University Press, Cambridge, 2006, pp. 31–35.

56 J. Burgess & J. Green, *YouTube: Online Video and Participatory Culture*, Polity, Cambridge, 2009, p. 24.

57 S. Livingstone, 'Taking risky opportunities in youthful content creation: teenagers' use of social networking sites for intimacy, privacy and self-expression', *New Media & Society,* vol. 10, no. 3, 2008, pp. 393–411; B. Alexander & A. Levine, 'Web 2.0 storytelling: emergence of a new genre', *Educause Review*, vol. 43, no. 6, 2008, p. 3.

58 N. Philadelphoff-Puren, 'The right language for rape', *Hecate,* vol. 29, no. 1, 2003, p. 52.

59 *60 Minutes,* 'Kim Duthie Interviewed'.

60 Millar & Sexton, 'Naked saints go viral'.

61 M. Levy, 'Nude-pic teen in AFL video rant', *The Age*, 22 December 2010, accessed 23 December 2010, <http://www.theage.com.au/afl/afl-news/>.

62 M. Levy, 'Details emerge of girl at centre of AFL nude pic scandal', *The Age*, 21 December 2010, accessed 21 December 2010, <http://www.theage.com.au/afl/afl-news/>.

63 S. Singh, 'Twitter reveals unsettling truths about "DikiLeaks"', *The Age*, 28 December 2010, accessed 11 January 2011, <http://www.theage.com.au/opinion/society-and-culture/>.

64 I. Tyler, 'Against abjection', *Feminist Theory,* vol. 10, no. 1, 2009, p. 90.

65 J. Butler, *Gender Trouble: Feminism and the Subversion of Identity,* Routledge, London & New York, 1990, p. 116.

66 S. Hall, 'Daubing the drudges of fury: men, violence and the piety of the "hegemonic masculinity" thesis', *Theoretical Criminology,* vol. 6, no. 1, 2002, pp. 36–37.

67 J. Bignell, *Media Semiotics: An Introduction*, Manchester University Press, Manchester, 1997, p. 57.

68 S. Ferguson, 'Code of silence', *Four Corners,* television broadcast, 11 May 2009.

69 A. Dowsley, & A. Harris, 'Adelaide players on teen's list', *Herald Sun*, 24 December 2010, accessed 24 December 2010, <http://www.adelaidenow.com.au/>.

70 Prestipino, 'Saints schoolgirl silenced by Facebook'.

71 P. Munro, 'Saints' teen: track star who took a wrong turn', *The Age*, 26 December 2010, accessed 1 January 2011, <http://www.theage.com.au/afl/afl-news/>.

72   W. M. Craig, K. Henderson, & J. G. Murphy, 'Prospective teachers' attitudes toward bullying and victimization', *School Psychology International,* vol. 21, no. 1, 2000, p. 7.

73   S. Lane, 'AFL boys' club', *The Age,* 7 March 2011, accessed 8 March 2011, <http://www.theage.com.au/afl/afl-news/>.

74   J. Baxter & K. Wallace, 'Outside in-group and out-group identities? Constructing male solidarity and female exclusion in UK builders' talk', *Discourse & Society,* vol. 20, no. 4, 2009, p. 423.

75   B. Heere & J. D. James, 'Sports teams and their communities: examining the influence of external group identities on team identity', *Journal of Sport Management,* vol. 21, no. 3, 2007, p. 326.

76   Munro, 'Saint's teen'.

77   C. Webb & M. Levy, 'Photo-scandal teen tackles Saints at new HQ', *The Age,* 11 January 2011, accessed 26 March 2011, <http://www.theage.com.au/afl/afl-news/>.

78   M. Levy, 'St Kilda nude-pic teen to demand apology at mediation session', *The Age,* 21 January 2011, accessed 26 March 2011, <http://www.theage.com.au/afl/afl-news/>.

79   Lane, 'AFL boys' club'.

80   H. Benedict, *Virgin or Vamp: How the Press Covers Sex Crimes,* Oxford University Press, New York, 1992; E. Madriz, 'Images of criminals and victims: a study on women's fear and social control', *Gender & Society,* vol. 11, no. 3, 1997, pp. 342–356; M. Meyers, *News Coverage of Violence Against Women: Engendering Blame,* Sage, Newbury Park, Calif., 1997.

81   Gamson, 'Jessica Hahn, media whore', p. 158.

82   Lane, 'AFL boys' club'.

83   Wilson & Lane, 'Saints players in the clear'.

84   Wilson & Lane, 'Saints players in the clear'.

85   Prestipino, 'Saints schoolgirl silenced by Facebook'.

86   Brodie, 'Naked photos pierce the "bubble"'.

87   A. Lowe & R. Sexton, 'Teen in nude pics scandal maintains rage online', *Sydney Morning Herald,* 24 December 2010, accessed 24 December 2010, <http://www.smh.com.au/afl/afl-news>.

88   A. Demetriou, 'It's not just footy, AFL is concerned for a young girl's welfare', *The Age,* 25 February 2011, accessed 25 February 2011, <http://www.theage.com.au/opinion/>.

89   J. Niall, 'The Man in the middle', *The Age,* 26 February 2011, accessed 26 February 2011, <http://www.theage.com.au/afl/afl-news/>.

90   *60 Minutes,* 'Kim Duthie interviewed'.

91   Pierik & Gannon, 'Nude-pic teenager strikes deal with Saints'.

92   Ferguson, 'Code of silence'.

93   C. Wilson, 'Signs of Ricky Nixon's unravelling apparent for years', *The Age,* 20 February 2011, accessed 20 February 2011, <http://www.theage.com.au/afl/afl-news/>.

94   Wilson, 'Signs of Rick Nixon's unravelling'.

95   Kissane, Beck & Gleeson, 'Nixon video: teen arrested'.

96   Munro, 'Nixon faces sex scandal inquiry'.

97   Niall, 'The man in the middle'.

98   Levy, 'Teenager has received death threats'.

99   Levy, 'Teenager has received death threats'.

100 Lowe & Sexton, 'Teen in nude pics scandal'.

101 Waterhouse-Watson, *Athletes, Sexual Assault*.

102 Lane, 'AFL boys' club'.

103 M. Foucault, *The Birth of Biopolitics: Lectures at the Collège de France, 1978–79*, trans. G. Burchell, ed. M. Senellart, Palgrave Macmillan, Hampshire, 2008, pp. 143–144.

104 M. Beck & J. Pierik, 'Nixon quizzed, Fevola lapses', *The Age*, 11 March 2011, accessed 11 March 2011, <http://www.theage.com.au/afl/afl-news/>.

105 J. Derrida, 'The rhetoric of drugs', trans. M. Israel, in E. Weber (ed), *Points... Interviews, 1974–1994*, Stanford University press, Stanford, Calif. 1995.

106 Beck, 'Nixon admits to substance problem'.

107 G. Slattery, 'Behind *The Challenge*', *Australian Football League*, 2011, accessed 27 March 2011, <http://www/afl.com.au/news/>.

108 D. Silkstone, 'Saints ban four for six weeks', *The Age*, 1 February 2011, accessed 1 February 2011, <http://www.theage.com.au/afl/afl-news/>.

109 D. Buchbinder, *Masculinities and Identities*, Melbourne University Press, Melbourne, 1994, p. 1.

110 L. Disch, 'Judith Butler and the politics of the performative', *Political Theory*, vol. 27, no. 4, 1999, p. 557.

111 J. Butler, *Excitable Speech: A Politics of the Performative*, Routledge, New York & London, 1997, p. 141.

112 T. Lovell, 'Resisting with authority: historical specificity, agency and the performative self', *Theory, Culture & Society*, vol. 20, no. 1, 2003, p. 7.

113 Disch, 'Judith Butler and the politics of the performative', p. 556.

114 M. Lloyd, 'Radical democratic activism and the politics of resignification', *Constellations*, vol. 14, no. 1, 2007, pp. 133–134.

115 M. Clarke, 'Rosa Parks' performativity, habitus, and ability to play the game', *Philosophy Today*, vol. 44, 2000, pp. 160–168.

116 Lovell, 'Resisting with authority', p. 7.

117 Lovell, 'Resisting with authority', p. 10.

118 Lane, 'AFL boys' club'.

Notes to Chapter 2: Situating Scandal

1   S. Lane, 'AFL boys' club', *The Age*, 7 March 2011, accessed 8 March 2011, <http://www.theage.com.au/afl/afl-news/>.

2   J. Butler, *The Psychic Life of Power: Theories in Subjection*, Stanford University Press, Stanford, Calif., 1997, p. 27.

3 J. Butler, *Gender Trouble: Feminism and the Subversion of Identity,* Routledge, London & New York, 1990, p. 140.

4 B. Wheaton, '"New lads"?: masculinities and the "new sport" participant', *Men and Masculinities,* vol. 2, no. 4, 2000, p. 438.

5 J. H. Frey, & D. S. Etizen, 'Sport and society', *Annual Review of Sociology,* no. 17, 1991, p. 516.

6 D. Nylund, 'When in Rome: heterosexism, homophobia, and sports talk radio', *Journal of Sport and Social Issues,* vol. 28, no. 2, 2004, p. 139.

7 B. Stewart & A. C. T. Smith, 'Drug use in sport: implications for public policy', *Journal of Sport & Social Issues,* vol. 32, no. 3, 2008, p. 287.

8 N. K. Davis & M. Duncan, 'Sports knowledge is power: reinforcing masculine privilege through fantasy sport league participation', *Journal of Sport and Social Issues,* vol. 30, no. 3, 2006, p. 245.

9 Wheaton, '"New Lads"?', p. 436.

10 Nylund, 'When in Rome', p. 136.

11 B. Heere & J. D. James, 'Sports teams and their communities: examining the influence of external group identities on team identity', *Journal of Sport Management,* vol. 21, no. 3, 2007, p. 326; R. Pringle, 'Masculinities, sport, and power: a critical comparison of Gramscian and Foucauldian inspired theoretical tools', *Journal of Sport and Social Issues,* vol. 29, no. 3, 2005, p. 264; S. M. Filiault & M. J. N. Drummond, 'The hegemonic aesthetic', *Gay & Lesbian Issues and Psychology Review,* vol. 3, no. 3, 2007, p. 177; K. Toffoletti, 'How is gender-based violence covered in the sporting news? An account of the Australian Rules Football League sex scandal', *Women's Studies International Forum,* vol. 30, no. 5, 2007, p. 433; K. E. Miller, M. J. Melnick, M. P. Farrell, D. F. Sabo, & G. M. Barnes, 'Jocks, gender, binge drinking, and adolescent violence', *Journal of Interpersonal Violence,* vol. 21, no. 1, 2006, p. 114.

12 R. W. Connell, *Gender and Power,* Polity, Cambridge, 1987; R. W. Connell, *Masculinities,* Polity, Cambridge, 1995.

13 Connell, *Masculinities,* p. 54.

14 Connell, *Masculinities,* p. 77.

15 C. Beasley, 'Rethinking hegemonic masculinity in a globalizing world', *Men and Masculinities,* vol. 11, no. 1, 2008, p. 88.

16 Filiault & Drummond, 'The hegemonic aesthetic', p. 182.

17 A. Stafford, Andrew. 'Lions investigates allegations', *The Age,* 6 September 2013, accessed 6 September 2013, <http:// www.theage.com.au/afl/afl-news/>.

18 M. Gleeson, 'Fiery dwarf jape AFL's latest sorry episode', *The Age,* 4 September 2013, accessed 6 September 2013, <http://www.theage.com.au/afl/afl-news/>.

19 Beasley, 'Rethinking hegemonic masculinity', p. 86.

20 Beasley, 'Rethinking hegemonic masculinity', p. 88.

21 Beasley, 'Rethinking hegemonic masculinity', p. 89.

22 Beasley, 'Rethinking hegemonic masculinity', p. 90.

23 Beasley, 'Rethinking hegemonic masculinity', p. 97.

24   R. Howson, 'A brief response to Christine Beasley's "Rethinking hegemonic masculinity in a globalizing world"', *Men and Masculinities,* vol. 11, no. 1, 2008, pp. 109–113.

25   A. Gramsci, *Selections from the Prison Notebooks,* trans. Q. Hoare and G N. Smith, International Publishers, New York, 1971, p. 258.

26   A. Milner, *Cultural Materialism,* Melbourne University Press, Melbourne, 1993, pp. 54–55.

27   F. Inglis, *Media Theory: An Introduction,* Blackwell, Oxford & Cambridge, Mass., 1990, p. 71.

28   R. Johnson, 'Three problematics: elements of a theory of working-class culture', in J. Clarke, C. Critcher & R. Johnson (eds), *Working Class Culture: Studies in history and theory,* Hutchinson, London, 1979, p. 233.

29   A. Milner, *Class,* Sage, London, 1999, p. 50.

30   S. Hall, 'The toad in the garden: Thatcherism among the theorists', in C. Nelson & L. Grossberg (eds), *Marxism and the Interpretation of Culture,* University of Illinois Press, Urbana and Chicago, 1988, p. 53.

31   R. Radhakrishnan, *Diasporic Mediations: Between Home and Location,* University of Minnesota Press, Minneapolis, 1996, p. 46.

32   Pringle, 'Masculinities, sport and power', p. 258.

33   M. Foucault, *Security, Territory, Population: Lectures at the Collège de France, 1977–78,* trans. G. Burchell, ed. M. Senellart, Palgrave Macmillan, Hampshire, 2007, p. 4.

34   D. Buchbinder, *Performance Anxieties: Re-producing Masculinity,* Allen & Unwin, St Leonards, NSW, 1997, pp. 30, 46.

35   D. Buchbinder, *Masculinities and Identities,* Melbourne University Press, Melbourne, 1994, p. 2.

36   Buchbinder, *Masculinities,* pp. 21–25.

37   M. Flood, 'Men, sex, and homosociality: how bonds between men shape their sexual relations with women', *Men and Masculinities,* vol. 10, no. 3, 2007, p. 11.

38   M. Simpson, 'Meet the metrosexual', *Salon,* 22 July 2002, accessed 22 January 2008, <http://www.salon.com>.

39   F. Jameson, 'Postmodernism and consumer society,' in H. Foster (ed), *Postmodern Culture,* Pluto Press, London, 1985.

40   P. Costello, 'Hard to be charitable about sports stars' philanthropy', *The Age,* 16 February 2011, accessed 16 February 2011, <http://www.theage.com.au/opinion/society-and-culture/>.

41   J. W. Messerschmidt, 'And now, the rest of the story: a commentary on Christine Beasley's "Rethinking hegemonic masculinity in a globalizing world"', *Men and Masculinities,* vol. 11, no. 1, 2008, p. 106; Beasley, 'Rethinking hegemonic masculinity', p. 86.

42   R. Mohr, *Gay Ideas: Outing and Other Controversies,* Beacon Press, Boston, 1992, pp. 163–164.

43   J. Clarkson, '"Everyday Joe" versus "pissy, bitchy queens": gay masculinity on straightacting.com', *The Journal of Men's Studies,* vol. 14, no 2, 2006, p. 187.

44 R. Cover, 'Bodies, movements and desires: lesbian/gay subjectivity and the stereotype', *Continuum: Journal of Media & Cultural Studies*, vol. 18, no. 1, 2004, p. 87.

45 A. M. Lunny, 'Provocation and "homosexual" advance: masculinized subjects as threat, masculinized subjects under threat', *Social & Legal Studies*, vol. 12, no. 3, 2003, p. 316.

46 R. Williams, *Keywords*, Fontana, Glasgow, 1976, pp. 80–81.

47 R. Williams, *Culture,* Fontana, Glasgow, 1981, p. 10.

48 R. Williams, *Marxism and Literature*, Oxford University Press, Oxford, 1977, p. 124.

49 L. Duggan, 'The new homonormativity: the sexual politics of neoliberalism', in R. Castronovo & D. Nelson (eds), *Materializing Democracy: Toward a Revitalized Cultural Politics*, Duke University Press, Durham, NC, 2002.

50 Williams, *Marxism and Literature,* p. 122.

51 S. Hall, 'Cultural studies: two paradigms', *Media, Culture, & Society,* vol. 2, 1980, p. 61.

52 S. C. Darnell & B. Wilson, 'Macho media: unapologetic hypermasculinity in Vancouver's "Talk Radio for Guys"', *Journal of Broadcasting & Electronic Media*, vol. 50, no. 3, 2006, pp. 444–466.

53 Fox Sports, 'Brawling Brendan flying home', *Fox Sports*, 1 November 2006, accessed 18 June 2011, <http://www.foxsports.com.au/afl/brawling-brendan-flying-home/>.

54 Brisbane Times, 'Bingle "clears the decks" on Fevola affair', *Brisbane Times*, 2 September 2007, accessed 21 June 2011, <http://www.brisbanetimes.com.au/articles/>.

55 The Age, 'Bingle sues Fevola over nude photo', *The Age*, 2 March 2010, accessed 21 June 2011, <http://www.theage.com.au/breaking-news-national/>.

56 P. Millar, ' Police will not charge Fevola over Brownlow antics', *The Age*, 9 September 2010, accessed 9 September 2010, <http://www.theage.com.au/afl/afl-news/>.

57 R. Connolly, 'Fevola's antics show he's a dinosaur from another era', *The Age*, 9 September 2010, accessed 9 September 2010, <http://www.theage.com.au/afl/afl-news/>.

58 J. Butler, *Bodies That Matter: On The Discursive Limits of 'Sex'*, Routledge, London & New York, 1993, p. 116.

59 Butler, *Gender Trouble*, pp. 31–32; Butler, *Psychic Life*, p. 27.

60 Beasley, 'Rethinking hegemonic masculinity', p. 86.

61 Pringle, 'Masculinities, sport, and power', p. 265.

62 J. Pierik & M. Beck, 'I hit rock bottom: Fevola bares his soul', *The Age*, 11 March 2011, accessed 11 March 2011, <http://www.theage.com.au/afl/afl-news/>.

63 C. Gilmour & D. Rowe, 'When Becks came to Sydney: multiple readings of a sport celebrity', *Soccer & Society,* vol. 11, no. 3, 2010, pp. 230, 237.

64 Filiault & Drummond, 'The hegemonic aesthetic', p. 180.

65 Wheaton, '"New Lads"?', p. 445.

66 G. Whannel, 'Television and the transformation of sport', *The Annals of the American Academy of Political and Social Science,* vol. 625, September, 2009, p. 205.

67 T. Ward, 'Marketing sports nationalism 1975–1985', *Soccer & Society,* vol. 10, no. 5, 2009, p. 662.

68 G. Linnell, *Football Ltd: The Inside Story of the AFL,* Ironbark, Sydney, 1995.

69 Independent Weekly, 'AFL wants SANFL name change', *Independent Weekly,* 27 June 2008, accessed 3 January 2009, <http://independentweekly.com.au>.

70 Frey & Etizen, 'Sport and Society', p. 509.

71 C. Rojek, 'Sports celebrity and the civilizing process', *Sport in Society,* vol. 9, no. 4, 2006, pp. 683–684.

72 B. Anderson, *Imagined Communities: Reflections on the Origins and Spread of Nationalism,* Verso, London, 1983, p. 7.

73 Anderson, *Imagined Communities,* p. 9.

74 Anderson, *Imagined Communities,* p. 36.

75 J. Izod, 'Television sport and the sacrificial hero', *Journal of Sport and Social Issues,* vol. 20, no. 2, 1996, p. 176.

76 Ward, 'Marketing sports nationalism', p. 669.

77 M. Rosello, *Declining the Stereotype: Ethnicity and Representation in French Cultures,* University Press of New England, Hanover, NH, 1998.

78 M. Straw, 'Traumatized masculinity and American national identity in Hollywood's Gulf War', *New Cinemas: Journal of Contemporary Film,* vol. 6, no. 2, 2008, p. 130.

79 M. Cronin, 'Sam Maguire: forgotten hero and national icon', *Sport in History,* vol. 25, no. 2, 2005, p. 195.

80 E. Probyn, 'Sporting bodies: dynamics of shame and pride', *Body & Society,* vol. 6, no. 1, 2000, p. 15.

81 T. O'Regan, 'Introducing critical multiculturalism', *Continuum: Journal of Media & Cultural Studies,* vol. 8, no. 2, 1994, pp. 7–19.

82 K. Jaworski, '"Elegantly wasted": The celebrity deaths of Michael Hutchence and Paula Yates', *Continuum: Journal of Media & Cultural Studies,* vol. 22, no. 6, 2008, p. 784.

83 B. S. Turner & J. Edmunds, 'The distaste of taste: Bourdieu, cultural capital and the Australian postwar elite', *Journal of Consumer Culture,* vol. 2, no. 2, 2002, p. 235.

84 Connolly, 'Fevola's antics'.

85 F. Furedi, 'Celebrity culture', *Society,* vol. 47, no. 6, 2010, p. 493.

86 G. Debord, *Society of the Spectacle,* Black & Red, Detroit, 1967, p. 60.

87 Furedi, 'Celebrity culture', p. 493.

88 Furedi, 'Celebrity culture', pp. 494–495.

89 C. Kurzman, C. Anderson, C. Key, Y. O. Lee, M. Moloney, A. Silver, M. W. van Ryn, 'Celebrity status', *Sociological Theory,* vol. 25, no. 4, 2007, p. 352.

90 A. Nalapat & A. Parker, 'Sport, celebrity and popular culture: Sachin Tendulkar, cricket and Indian nationalisms', *International Review for the Sociology of Sport,* vol. 40, no. 4, 2005, p. 434.

91   Rojek, 'Sports celebrity', pp. 682–683.

92   Frey & Etizen, 'Sport and society', p. 503.

93   Frey & Etizen, 'Sport and society', p. 508.

94   G. Clanton, 'The sport star: modern sport and the cultural economy of sporting celebrity', *Contemporary Sociology: A Journal of Reviews,* vol. 36, no. 1, 2007, p. 49.

95   Frey & Etizen, 'Sport and society', p. 503.

96   M. Foucault, *Society Must Be Defended: Lectures at the Collège de France, 1975–76,* ed. M. Bertani & A. Fontana, trans. David Macey, Penguin, London, 2004, p. 250.

97   S. J. Collier, 'Topologies of power: Foucault's analysis of political government beyond "governmentality"', *Theory, Culture & Society,* vol. 26, no. 6, 2009, pp. 86–87.

98   Foucault, *Society Must Be Defended*, p. 246.

99   Foucault, *Security, Territory, Population*, p. 4.

100   Foucault, *Security, Territory, Population*, p. 4.

101   L. McNay, 'Self as enterprise: dilemmas of control and resistance in Foucault's *The Birth of Biopolitics*', *Theory, Culture & Society,* vol. 26, no. 6, 2009, p. 65.

102   M. Foucault, *The Birth of Biopolitics: Lectures at the Collège de France, 1978–79,* trans. G. Burchell, ed. M. Senellart, Palgrave Macmillan, Hampshire, 2008, p. 276.

103   T. Terranova, 'Another life: The nature of political economy in Foucault's genealogy of biopolitics', *Theory, Culture & Society,* vol. 26, no. 6, 2009, p. 243.

104   Whannel, 'Television and the transformation of sport', p. 213.

105   Rojek, 'Sports celebrity', p. 685.

106   Whannel, 'Television and the transformation of sport', p. 213.

107   Furedi, 'Celebrity culture', p. 494.

108   D. Archard, 'Privacy, the public interest and a prurient public', in M. Kieran (ed), *Media Ethics*, Routledge, London & New York, 1998, p. 90.

109   M. Kieran (ed), *Media Ethics*, Routledge, London & New York, 1998, p. xiii.

110   C. C. Gauthier, 'Privacy invasion by the news media: three ethical models', *Journal of Mass Media Ethics,* vol. 17, no. 1, 2002, pp. 26–27, 32.

111   C. Wilson, 'Brisbane to sack Fevola', *The Age*, 19 February 2011, accessed 19 February 2011, <http://www.theage.com.au/afl/afl-news/>.

Notes to Chapter 3: Bad bonds

1   K. Andersson, 'Constructing young masculinity: a case study of heroic discourse on violence', *Discourse & Society,* vol. 19, no. 2, 2008, pp. 139–161; J. W. Messerschmidt, 'Making bodies matter: adolescent masculinities, the body and varieties of violence', *Theoretical Criminology,* vol. 3, no. 2, 1999, pp. 197–220.

2   K. Lyon & J. Berry, 'Saints close ranks on rape probe', *The Age,* 18 March 2004, accessed 11 December 2013, <http://www.theage.com.au/articles/2004/03/17/>.

3   A. Lowe, 'Court suppresses rape-accused photo', *The Age,* 30 October 2009, accessed 11 December 2013, <http://www.theage.com.au/national/>.

4 J. Niall, 'Player's worst outcome may be club's best result', *The Age,* 9 September 2010, accessed 9 September 2010, <http://www.theage.com.au/afl/afl-news/>; C. Wilson, 'Bingle is not fair game, AFL must show better leadership', *The Age*, 14 March 2010, accessed 5 August 2011, <http://www.theage.com.au/afl/afl-news/>; D. Baynes 'Rugby League sex scandals concern sponsors, Prime Minister Rudd', 15 May 2009, accessed 6 December 2010, <http://www.bloomberg.com/apps/news/>.

5 M. Foucault, *The Hermeneutics of the Subject: Lectures at the Collège de France, 1981–82,* ed. F. Gros, trans. G. Burchell, Picador, New York, 2005, p. 428.

6 R. Dobson, 'Should you shake ya booties before a match?' *Sunday Times,* 17 June 2006, accessed 10 March 2011, <http://www.timesonline.co.uk/tol/life_and_style/health/features/>.

7 L. E. Porter & L J. Alison, 'Examining group rape: a descriptive analysis of offender and victim behaviour', *European Journal of Criminology*, vol. 3, no. 3, 2006, p. 359.

8 Porter & Alison, 'Examining group rape'.

9 Brisbane Times, 'Police horrified by high school dance gang rape', *Brisbane Times*, 27 October 2009, accessed 28 October 2009, <http://www.brisbanetimes.com.au/world/>.

10 L. Rickard, 'Boys, 11 and 12, on sex charges', *WA Today*, 24 March 2011, accessed 24 March 2011, <http://www.watoday.com.au/wa-news/>.

11 M. Calligeros, 'Schoolies' dirty sex secret', *Brisbane Times*, 20 November 2009, accessed 18 August 2010, <http://www.brisbanetimes.com.au/queensland/>.

12 A. Lowe, 'Charges dropped in pack rape case', *The Age*, 8 July 2010, accessed 8 July 2010, <http://www.theage.com.au/national/>.

13 K. Plummer, *Telling Sexual Stories: Power, Change and Social Worlds,* Routledge, London & New York, 1995, pp. 3–4.

14 Calligeros, 'Schoolies' dirty sex secret'.

15 The Full Wiki, *List of Australian Rules Football Incidents: Wikis,* accessed 9 December 2013, <http://www.thefullwiki.org/ List_of_Australian_rules_football_incidents>.

16 The Full Wiki, *List of off-field incidents involving rugby league players: Wikis,* accessed 9 December 2013, <http://www.thefullwiki.org/List_of_off-field_incidents_involving_rugby_league_players>.

17 L. Beaumont, 'Feminist wary over rugby role', *The Age,* 7 March 2004, accessed 9 December 2013, <http://www.theage.com.au/articles/2004/03/06/>.

18 Waterhouse-Watson, Deb (2011). '(Un)reasonable doubt: a "narrative immunity" for footballers against sexual assault allegations', *M/C Journal*, vol. 14, no. 1, 2011, accessed 3 January 2012, <http://journal.media-culture.org.au>.

19 J. Magnay, 'Ex-Shark denies any role in scandal', *Brisbane Times*, 16 May 2009, accessed 11 December 2013, <http://www.brisbanetimes.com.au/sport/league/>.

20 The Age, 'Group sex incident degrading: minister', *The Age*, 15 May 2009, accessed 17 May 2009, <http://www.theage.com.au/articles/>.

21 J. Chandler, 'Trying to see beyond murk of sport sex debate', *The Age*, 16 May 2009, accessed 17 May 2009, <http://www.theage.com.au/articles/>.

22 D. Sygall, 'Why Johns may not be off the scene for too long', *Sydney Morning Herald*, 17 May 2009, accessed 17 May 2009, <http://www.smh.com.au/news/lhqnews/>.

23 Magnay, 'Ex-Shark denies any role in scandal'.

24 S. Ferguson, 'Code of silence', *Four Corners,* Australian Broadcasting Corporation, television broadcast, 11 May 2009.

25 T. Fullerton, 'Fair game?' *Four Corners,* Australian Broadcasting Corporation, television broadcast, 3 May 2004.

26 Fullerton, 'Fair game?'.

27 P. R. Sanday, *Fraternity Gang Rape: Sex, Brotherhood, and Privilege on Campus*, second edition, New York University Press, New York & London, 2007, p. 145.

28 S. E. Ullman, 'A comparison of gang and individual rape incidents', *Violence and Victims*, vol. 14, no. 2, 1999, pp. 130–131.

29 R. Hinds & J. Halloran, 'St Kilda name players involved in sex allegations', *Sydney Morning Herald,* 17 March 2004, accessed 13 August 2011, <http://www.smh.com.au/articles/>.

30 S. Butcher & S. Shtargot, 'Saints in the clear over rape allegations', *The Age*, 7 May 2004, accessed 13 August 2011, <http://www.theage.com.au/articles/>.

31 Sydney Morning Herald, 'AFL pair won't face rape charges', *Sydney Morning Herald*, 7 May 2004, accessed 12 August 2011, <http://www.smh.com.au/articles/>.

32 Sydney Morning Herald, 'Saints case may be reopened', *Sydney Morning Herald*, 22 June 2010, accessed 13 August 2011, <http://news.smh.com.au/breaking-news-national/>.

33 Sydney Morning Herald, 'Saints case may be reopened'.

34 A. Langmaid & R. Vaughan, 'Mick Malthouse hit with $7500 fine for sledging Stephen Milne', *Perth Now*, 11 April 2010, accessed 14 August 2011, <http://www.perthnow.com.au/sport/>.

35 E. Hunt, 'Stephen Milne case should have gone on – Ex-Cop', *Herald Sun*, 21 June 2010, accessed 14 August 2011, <http://www.adelaidenow.com.au/sport/afl/>.

36 C. Wilson, 'Milne faces four charges of rape', *The Age*, 18 June 2013, accessed 18 June 2013, <http://www.theage.com.au/afl/afl-news/>.

37 C. Wilson, 'Saints at odds over Milne', *The Age*, 20 June 2013, accessed 20 June 2013, <http://www.theage.com.au/afl/afl-news/>.

38 Wilson, 'Saints at odds over Milne'.

39 E. Quayle, 'Milne back in Saints team', *The Age*, 11 July 2013, accessed 12 July 2013, <http://www.theage.com.au/afl/afl-news/>.

40 The Age, 'Police charge Lovett with rape', *The Age*, 15 February 2010, accessed 15 February 2010, <http://www.theage.com.au/afl/afl-news/>.

41 S. Lane, '"Bullied" Lovett in $2m bid', *The Age*, 17 February 2010, accessed 18 February 2010, <http://www.theage.com.au/afl/afl-news/>.

42   A. Lowe, 'Lovett charged with second count of rape', *The Age*, 7 May 2010, accessed 7 May 2010, <http://www.theage.com.au/afl/afl-news/>.

43   A. Lowe, 'Former St Kilda player Lovett raped woman while she slept, court hears', *The Age*, 11 August 2010, accessed 12 August 2010, <http://www.theage.com.au/victoria/>.

44   A. Lowe, 'Accuser's "help" pleas', *The Age*, 12 August 2010, accessed 12 August 2010, <http://www.theage.com.au/victoria/>.

45   Lowe, 'Accuser's "help" pleas'.

46   A. Lowe, '"How could you bring the club down like this?"', *The Age*, 29 July 2011, accessed 20 July 2011, <http://www.theage.com.au/victoria/>.

47   Lowe, 'Lovett charged with second count'.

48   A. Lowe, 'Jury finds Lovett not guilty of rape charges', *The Age*, 22 July 2011, accessed 23 July 2011, <http://www.theage.com.au/victoria/>.

49   A. Lowe, 'Rape trial told Lovett felt entitled', *The Age*, 21 July 2011, accessed 21 July 2011, <http://www.theage.com.au/victoria/>.

50   M. Beck, 'New sex assault probe on Lovett', *The Age*, 10 August 2011, accessed 10 August 2011, <http://www.theage.com.au/victoria/>.

51   N. Philadelphoff-Puren, 'Dereliction: women, rape and football', *Australian Feminist Law Journal,* vol. 21, no. 2, 2004, p. 42.

52   K. Toffoletti, 'How is gender-based violence covered in the sporting news? An account of the Australian Rules Football League sex scandal', *Women's Studies International Forum,* vol. 30, no. 5, 2007, p. 432.

53   L. Chalip, 'Toward a distinctive sport management discipline', *Journal of Sport Management,* vol. 20, no. 1, 2006, p. 5.

54   Toffoletti, 'How is gender-based violence covered', p. 433.

55   S. R. Bird, 'Welcome to the men's club: homosociality and the maintenance of hegemonic masculinity', *Gender and Society,* vol. 10, no. 2, 1996, p. 121.

56   W. E. Connolly, *Identity/difference: Democratic Negotiations of Political Paradox,* Cornell University Press, Ithaca & London, 1991, p. 73.

57   Toffoletti, 'How is gender-based violence covered', p. 433.

58   Toffoletti, 'How is gender-based violence covered', p. 434.

59   Philadelphoff-Puren, 'Dereliction', p. 48.

60   D. Silkstone, 'Saints ban four for six weeks', *The Age*, 1 February 2011, accessed 1 February 2011, <http://www.theage.com.au/afl/afl-news/>.

61   S. Hall, 'Daubing the drudges of fury: men, violence and the piety of the "hegemonic masculinity" thesis', *Theoretical Criminology,* vol. 6, no. 1, 2002, pp. 36–37.

62   K. D. Magnus, 'The unaccountable subject: Judith Butler and the social conditions of intersubjective agency', *Hypatia*, vol. 21, no. 2, 2006, p. 94.

63   C. Houston, 'Saints in Milne legal fund row', *The Age*, 1 December 2013, accessed 1 December 2013, <http://www.theage.com.au/afl/afl-news/>.

64   M. Flood, 'Men, sex, and homosociality: how bonds between men shape their sexual relations with women', *Men and Masculinities,* vol. 10, no. 3, 2007, p. 342.

65   Bird, 'Welcome to the men's club', p. 121.

66   E. K. Sedgwick, *Between Men: English Literature and Male Homosocial Desire*, Columbia University Press, New York, 1985, p. 20.

67   Flood, 'Men, sex, and homosociality', p. 342.

68   K. Franklin, 'Enacting masculinity: antigay violence and group rape as participatory theater', *Sexuality Research & Social Policy: Journal of the National Sexuality Resource Center,* vol. 1, no. 2, 2004, p. 36.

69   M. L. Knowles & W. L. Gardner, 'Benefits of membership: the activation and amplification of group identities in response to social rejection', *Personality and Social Psychology Bulletin,* vol. 34, no. 9, 2008, p. 1201.

70   Franklin, 'Enacting masculinity', p. 30.

71   T. Horeck, *Public Rape: Representing Violation in Fiction and Film*, Routledge, London & New York, 2004, p. 27.

72   L. A. 't Hart-Kerkhoffs, R. R. J. M. Vermeiren, L. M. C. Jansen & T. A. H. Doreleijers, 'Juvenile Group Sex Offenders: A Comparison of Group Leaders and Followers', *Journal of Interpersonal Violence*, vol. 26, no. 1, 2011, pp. 5, 15.

73   Franklin, 'Enacting masculinity', p. 28.

74   Sanday, *Fraternity Gang Rape*, pp. 198–199.

75   J. K. Ehrhart & B. R. Sandler, *Campus Gang Rape: Party Games?,* Association of American Colleges, Washington, DC, 1985.

76   Sanday, *Fraternity Gang Rape*, p. 124.

77   Sanday, *Fraternity Gang Rape*, p. 2.

78   Sanday, *Fraternity Gang Rape*, p. 148.

79   P. Y. Martin & R. A. Hummer, 'Fraternities and rape on campus', *Gender and Society,* vol. 3, no. 4, 1989, p. 459.

80   Martin & Hummer, 'Fraternities and rape on campus', pp. 463–466.

81   Philadelphoff-Puren, 'Dereliction', p. 45.

82   Martin & Hummer, 'Fraternities and rape on campus', pp. 463–466.

83   J. Butler, *Gender Trouble: Feminism and the Subversion of Identity,* Routledge, London & New York, 1990, p. 143.

84   V. Bell, 'Performativity and belonging: an introduction', *Theory, Culture & Society,* vol. 16, no. 2, 1999, p. 3.

85   J. Butler, *Bodies That Matter: On The Discursive Limits of 'Sex',* Routledge, London & New York, 1993, p. 12.

86   Butler, *Gender Trouble*, pp. 31–32; J. Butler, *The Psychic Life of Power: Theories in Subjection*, Stanford University Press, Stanford, Calif., 1997, p. 27.

87   Butler, *Gender Trouble*, p. 33.

88   R. W. Connell, *Gender and Power,* Polity, Cambridge, 1987; R. W. Connell, *Masculinities*, Polity, Cambridge, 1995.

89   T. Jefferson, 'Subordinating hegemonic masculinity', *Theoretical Criminology,* vol. 6, no. 1, 2002, pp. 63–88; Hall, 'Daubing the drudges of fury'.

90   Philadelphoff-Puren, 'Dereliction', p. 48.

91   J. Butler, *Giving an account of Oneself,* Fordham University Press, New York, 2005, p. 42.

92   Franklin, 'Enacting masculinity', p. 29.

93 Magnus, 'The unaccountable subject', p. 96.

94 Butler, *Bodies That Matter*, p. 116.

95 Butler, *Bodies That Matter*, p. 2.

96 D. Fuss, *Identification Papers*, Routledge, New York & London, 1995, p. 49.

97 Franklin, 'Enacting masculinity', p. 35.

98 Bell, 'Performativity and belonging', p. 3.

99 Magnus, 'The unaccountable subject', p. 96.

100 J. Butler, *Frames of War: When is Life Grievable?*, Verso, London & New York, 2009, pp. 23–24.

101 Butler, *Frames of War*, p. 49.

102 H. Tajfel, *Differentiation Between Social Groups: Studies in the Social Psychology of Inter-group Relations*, Academic Press, London, 1978.

103 J. Baxter & K. Wallace, 'Outside in-group and out-group identities? Constructing male solidarity and female exclusion in UK builders' talk', *Discourse & Society*, vol. 20, no. 4, 2009, pp. 413–414.

104 R. M. Chow, B. S. Lowery & E. D. Knowles, 'The two faces of dominance: the differential effect of ingroup superiority and outgroup inferiority on dominant-group identity and group esteem', *Journal of Experimental Social Psychology*, vol. 44, no. 4, 2007, p. 1073.

105 M. M. Patterson, R. S. Bigler & W. B. Swann Jr., 'When personal identities confirm versus conflict with group identities: evidence from an inter-group paradigm', *European Journal of Social Psychology*, vol. 40, no. 4, 2010, pp. 654–655.

106 T. Postmes, R. Spears, A. T. Lee & R. J. Novak, 'Individuality and social influence in groups: inductive and deductive routes to group identity', *Journal of Personality and Social Psychology*, vol. 89, no. 5, 2005, p. 748.

107 cited, K. J. Corn & G. A. Dunn, 'Let the Bon Temps roll: sacrifice, scapegoats, and good times', in G. A. Dunn & R. Housel (eds), *True Blood and Philosophy: We Wanna Think Bad Things with You*, John Wiley & Sons, Hoboken, NJ, 2010, p. 143.

108 Martin & Hummer, 'Fraternities and rape on campus', p. 464.

109 Franklin, 'Enacting masculinity', p. 26.

110 Flood, 'Men, sex, and homosociality', p. 342.

111 Chow, Lowery & Knowles, 'The two faces of dominance'; B. Heere & J. D. James, 'Sports teams and their communities: examining the influence of external group identities on team identity', *Journal of Sport Management*, vol. 21, no. 3, 2007, pp. 319–337; Knowles & Gardner, 'Benefits of membership'; E. Goffman, *The Presentation of the Self in Everyday Life*, Penguin, London, 1969.

112 Chalip, 'Toward a distinctive sport management.'

113 J. Butler, *Precarious Life*, Verso, London, 2004, p. 31.

114 Butler, *Precarious Life*, pp. 42–43.

115 Ferguson, 'Code of silence'.

116 Butler, *Precarious Life*, p. 44.

117 Butler, *Giving an Account of Oneself*, p. 29.

118   Butler, *Frames of War*, pp. 77–78.

119   Sanday, *Fraternity Gang Rape*, p. 5.

120   Magnus, 'The unaccountable subject', p. 97.

121   Waterhouse-Watson, 'Unreasonable doubt'.

122   Martin & Hummer, 'Fraternities and rape on campus', p. 470.

123   R. Cover, 'Object(ives) of desire: romantic coupledom versus promiscuity, sub-jectivity and sexual identity', *Continuum: Journal of Media & Cultural Studies*, vol. 24, no. 2, 2010, pp. 251–263.

124   Chandler, 'Trying to see beyond murk of sport sex debate'.

125   Butler, *Giving an Account of Oneself*, p. 25.

126   Butler, *Giving an Account of Oneself*, p. 28.

127   E. Probyn, 'Sporting bodies: dynamics of shame and pride', *Body & Society*, vol. 6, no. 1, 2000, p. 22; S. Munt, *Queer Attachments: The Cultural Politics of Shame*, Ashgate, 2007, p. 80.

128   D. Buchbinder, *Masculinities and Identities*, Melbourne University Press, Melbourne, 1994, p. 1.

Notes to Chapter 4: Bodies, Pleasures and Compulsions

1   M. Levy, 'Teens should watch Cousins doco with parents', *The Age,* 23 August 2010, accessed 23 August 2010, <http://www.theage.com.au/entertainment/tv-and-radio/>.

2   A. Hamilton, 'Brendan Fevola of the Brisbane Lions admits gambling addiction', *Herald Sun*, 15 April 2010, accessed 19 July 2011, <http://www.heraldsun.com.au/sport/afl/>.

3   D. Buckingham, 'Introducing identity', in D. Buckingham (ed), *Youth, Identity, and Digital Media,* MIT Press, Cambridge, Mass., 2008, p. 10; F. Furedi, 'Celebrity culture', *Society,* vol. 47, no. 6, 2010, p. 494.

4   S. Munt, 'Framing intelligibility, identity, and selfhood: a reconsideration of spatio–temporal models. *Reconstruction,* vol. 2, no. 3, 2002, p. 19, accessed 5 January 2003, <www.reconstruction.ws/023/munt.htm>.

5   Sydney Morning Herald, 'Fevola sent home from Ireland in disgrace', *Sydney Morning Herald,* 31 October 2006, accessed 24 July 2011, <http://www.smh.com.au/news/afl/>.

6   The Age, 'AFL player probed for urinating on bar', *The Age,* 11 April 2011, accessed 11 April 2011, <http://www.theage.com.au/victoria/>.

7   T. Hunter, 'Bulldogs stars caught harassing motorists during Hong Kong trip', *The Age,* 7 February 2011, accessed 7 February 2011, <http://www.theage.com.au/afl/afl-news>.

8   P. Carlyon, 'Wayne Carey, the little boy who never grew up', *Herald Sun*, 23 October 2009, accessed 12 December 2013, <http:// www.heraldsun.com.au/news/victoria/>.

9   A. Krien, 'Out of bounds: sex and the AFL', *The Monthly,* April, p. 40.

10   Carlyon, 'Wayne Carey'.

11   Krien, 'Out of bounds', p. 40.

12 A. Denton, 'Wayne Carey interview', *Enough Rope,* Australian Broadcasting Corporation, television broadcast, 31 March, episode 161, transcript accessed 12 December 2013, <http://www.abc.net.au/tv/enoughrope/transcripts/s2201719.htm>.

13 Denton, 'Wayne Carey interview'.

14 Denton, 'Wayne Carey interview'.

15 R. Willingham, 'Sex, death and binge drinking', *The Age,* 21 November 2008, accessed 22 November 2008, <http://www.theage.com.au/national/>.

16 L. Dubecki, 'Locking out modern life is not the answer', *The Age,* 2 June 2008, accessed 3 June 2008, <http://www.theage.com.au/opinion/>.

17 M. Fyfe, 'Alcopop tax fails to curb teenage drinkers', *The Age,* 26 September 2010, accessed 26 September 2010, <http://www.theage.com.au/victoria/>.

18 M. Bachelard, 'Hitting the drink', *The Age,* 15 June 2008, accessed 15 June 2008, <http://www.theage.com.au/national/>.

19 J. Stark, 'Time for a happy ending, say booze experts', *The Age,* 24 July 2011, accessed 24 July 2011, <http://www.theage.com.au/victoria/>.

20 K. Kubacki, D. Siemieniako & S. Rundle-Thiele, 'College binge drinking: a new approach', *Journal of Consumer Marketing,* vol. 28, no. 3, 2011, p. 225.

21 D. Black, J. Lawson & S. Fleishman, 'Excessive alcohol use by non-elite sportsmen', *Drug and Alcohol Review,* vol. 18, no. 2, 1999, p. 202.

22 J. S. Lawson & A. R. Evans, 'Prodigious alcohol consumption by Australian Rugby League footballers', *Drug and Alcohol Review,* vol. 11, no. 2, 1992, pp. 193–194.

23 R. Rennie & A. Lowe, 'Didak, Shaw out for season', *The Age,* 5 August 2008, accessed 22 July 2011, <http://www.theage.com.au/national/>.

24 T. Clarke, 'Cousins banned after drinking binge', *The Age,* 12 April 2010, accessed 13 April 2010, <http://www.theage.com.au/afl/afl-news/>.

25 Clarke, 'Cousins banned after drinking binge'.

26 Rennie & Lowe, 'Didak, Shaw out for season'.

27 D. Barrett, 'AFL captains join forces to tackle Melbourne CBD violence', *Herald Sun,* 28 August 2009, accessed 24 July 2011, <http://www.heraldsun.com.au/news/victoria/>.

28 P. Schwab, 'Personal reflections on Australian Rules football and alcohol consumption', *Stand4 Drug and Alcohol Education Unit,* accessed 24 July 2011, <http://www.concernaustralia.org.au/.

29 E. Dunning & I. Waddington, 'Sport as a drug and drugs in sport: some exploratory comments', *International Review for the Sociology of Sport,* vol. 38, no. 3, 2003, p. 356.

30 Dunning & Waddington, 'Sport as a drug and drugs in sport', p. 356.

31 J. Brenner & K. Swanik, 'High-risk drinking characteristics in collegiate athletes', *Journal of American College Health,* vol. 56, no. 3, 2007, p. 267.

32 Dunning & Waddington, 'Sport as a drug and drugs in sport', p. 355.

33 C. Rojek, 'Sports celebrity and the civilizing process', *Sport in Society,* vol. 9, no. 4, 2006, p. 685.

34   B. Stewart & A. C. T. Smith, 'Drug use in sport: implications for public policy', *Journal of Sport & Social Issues,* vol. 32, no. 3, 2008, p. 287.

35   D. Silkstone, 'Saints ban four for six weeks', *The Age,* 1 February 2011, accessed 11 February 2011, <http://www.theage.com.au/afl/afl-news/>.

36   S. Spits & W. Brodie, 'Six AFL players tested positive to illicit drugs in the past year', *The Age,* 22 June 2011, accessed 22 June 2011, <http://www.theage.com.au/afl/afl-news/>.

37   Denton, 'Wayne Carey interview'.

38   M. Robinson, 'West Coast Eagles warned of Ben Cousins' ways in 2001', *The Advertiser,* 19 October 2007, accessed 18 July 2011, <http://www.adelaidenow.com.au/sport/afl/>.

39   L. Johnson, 'Kerr caught on police drug tapes', *Brisbane Times,* 23 March 2007, accessed 23 July 2011, <http://www.brisbanetimes.com.au/news/national/>.

40   J. Fiske, *Media Matters: Everyday Culture and Political Change,* University of Minnesota Press, Minneapolis, 1996, p. 32.

41   P. Atkinson, *The Ethnographic Imagination: Textual Constructions of Reality,* Routledge, London & New York, 1990, pp. 170–171.

42   A. Joinson, 'Causes and implications of disinhibited behavior on the internet', in J. Gackenbach (ed), *Psychology and the Internet: Intrapersonal, Interpersonal, and Transpersonal Implications,* Academic Press, San Diego, p. 49.

43   R. C. Schehr, 'Conventional risk discourse and the proliferation of fear', *Criminal Justice Policy Review,* vol. 16, no. 1, 2005, p. 48.

44   P. Mayock, '"Scripting" risk: young people and the construction of drug journeys', *Drugs: Education, Prevention and Policy,* vol. 12, no. 5, 2005, pp. 349–368.

45   P. Hudson, '$12m campaign targets teen party drug scene', *The Age,* 17 April 2005, accessed 17 April 2005, <http://www.theage.com.au/news/National/.

46   J. Hartley, '"When your child grows up too fast": juvenation and the boundaries of the social in the news media', *Continuum,* vol. 12, no. 1, 1998, p. 14.

47   J. Zylinska, 'Guns n' rappers: moral panics and the ethics of cultural studies', *Culture Machine,* vol. 6, accessed 12 December 2013, <http://www.culturemachine.net/index.php/cm/article/viewArticle/7/6>.

48   W. J. Brown & M. A. C. de Matviuk, 'Sports celebrities and public health: Diego Maradona's influence on drug use prevention', *Journal of Health Communication,* vol. 15, no. 4, 2010, p. 359.

49   P. Hellard, 'Mainwaring's death may be trigger for Ben Cousins', *Herald Sun,* 19 October 2007, accessed 22 July 2011, <http://www.heraldsun.com.au/news/national/>.

50   P. Strelan & R. J. Boeckmann, 'Why drug testing in elite sport does not work: perceptual deterrence theory and the role of Personal moral beliefs', *Journal of Applied Social Psychology,* vol. 36, no. 12, 2006, p. 2923.

51   G. Clanton, 'The sport star: modern sport and the cultural economy of sporting celebrity', *Contemporary Sociology: A Journal of Reviews,* vol. 36, no. 1, 2007, p. 49.

52   D. V. Hanstad & I. Waddington, 'Sport, health and drugs: a critical re-examination of some key issues and problems', *Perspectives in Public Health*, vol. 129, no. 4, 2009, p. 174.

53   Strelan & Boeckmann, 'Why drug testing in elite sport does not work', p. 2910.

54   AFL, *Anti-Doping Code*, 1 January 2010. accessed 12 December 2013, <http://www.aflcommunityclub.com.au/fileadmin/user_upload/Play_AFL/AFLAnti-DopingCode2010ASADA.pdf>.

55   AFL Players Association, 'Illicit Drug Policy', August 2008, accessed 13 December 2013, <http://www.aflpa.com.au/behind_the_scenes/ rules_and_regulations/>.

56   The Age, 'Dr Ziggy Switkowski's full report', *The Age*, 6 May 2013, accessed 7 May 2013, <http://www.theage.com.au/afl/afl-news/>.

57   J. Pierik, 'ASADA report has landed', *The Age*, 2 August 2013, accessed 12 December 2013, <http://www.theage.com.au/afl/afl-news/>.

58   C. Wilson, 'Hird and his club pay highest of prices', *The Age*, 28 August 2013, accessed 28 August 2013, <http://www.theage.com.au/afl/afl-news/>.

59   M. Hawthorne, 'Emergency Essendon meeting planned as players' health fears grow', *The Age*, 16 August 2013, accessed 16 August 2013, <http://www.theage.com.au/afl/essendon-bombers/>.

60   J. Derrida, 'The rhetoric of drugs', trans. M. Israel, in E. Weber (ed), P. Kamuf et al. (trans), *Points … Interviews, 1974–1994*, Stanford University Press, Stanford, Calif., 1995, pp. 229–230.

61   N. McKeganey, J. Neale, S. Parkin & C. Mills, 'Communities and drugs: beyond the rhetoric of community action', *Probation Journal*, vol. 51, no. 4, 2004, p. 345.

62   F. Measham & K. Brain, '"Binge" drinking, British alcohol policy and the new culture of intoxication', *Crime, Media, Culture*, vol. 1, no. 3, 2005, pp. 265–266.

63   Measham & Brain, '"Binge" drinking", p. 266.

64   H. Wechsler & A. E. Davenport, 'Binge drinking, tobacco, and illicit drug use and involvement in college athletics', *Journal of American College Health*, vol. 45, no. 5, 1997, pp. 195–200.

65   I. McDonald, 'Situating the sport documentary', *Journal of Sport & Social Issues*, vol. 31, no. 3, 2007, p. 210.

66   Furedi, 'Celebrity culture', p. 494.

67   Levy, 'Teens should watch Cousins doco with parents'.

68   K. Quinn, 'Cousins documentary silent on the "why" behind his downfall', *The Age*, 26 August 2010, accessed 26 August 2010, <http://www.theage.com.au/opinion/blogs/the-vulture/>.

69   J. Hogan, 'Cousins shaved down to beat drug test', *The Age*, 27 August 2010, accessed 27 August 2010, <http://www.theage.com.au/afl/afl-news>.

70   C. Gilmour & D. Rowe, 'When Becks came to Sydney: multiple readings of a sport celebrity', *Soccer & Society*, vol. 11, no. 3, 2010, p. 236.

71   M. Blake, 'Don't show drugs, Cousins urged', *The Age*, 12 August 2010, accessed 23 August 2010, <http://www.theage.com.au/afl/afl-news/>.

72   Levy, 'Teens should watch Cousins doco with parents'.

73   Quinn, 'Cousins documentary silent on the "why" behind his downfall'.

74   J. Schembri, 'Brutal portrayal of star's addiction', *The Age*, 26 August 2010, accessed 26 August 2010, <http://www.theage.com.au/entertainment/tv-and-radio/>.

75   Quinn, 'Cousins documentary silent on the "why" behind his downfall'.

76   S. Robbins, 'Will Cousins' final confession lead to redemption?' *The Age*, 5 August 2010, accessed 18 July 2011, <http://www.theage.com.au/sport/blogs/sally-stands-up/>.

77   P. Toohey, 'Behind the documentary: Ben wanted money and revenge', *Perth Now*, 20 July 2010, accessed 18 July 2011, <http://www.perthnow.com.au/entertainment/perth-confidential/>.

78   G. Baum, 'A story of opportunities squandered', *Real Footy*, 18 October 2007, accessed 23 October 2007, <http://realfooty.com.au/news/news/>.

79   Baum, 'A story of opportunities squandered'.

80   Baum, 'A story of opportunities squandered'.

81   Stewart & Smith, 'Drug use in sport', p. 278.

82   T. Jones, 'Jury split on drugs documentary', *NineMSN, Wide World of Sports*, 27 August 2010, accessed 19 July 2011, <http://www.ninemsn.com.au/article.aspx?id=7951972>.

83   Stewart & Smith, 'Drug use in sport', p. 278.

84   McKeganey et al., 'Communities and drugs', p. 354.

85   G. Baum, 'Integrity of the game at stake', *The Age*, 16 July 2011, accessed 17 July 2011, <http://www.theage.com.au/afl/afl-news/>.

86   Quinn, 'Cousins documentary silent on the "why" behind his downfall'.

87   Baum, 'A story of opportunities squandered'.

88   T. Hutchison, 'Cousins deserves his club's support', *The Age*, 20 October 2007, accessed 23 October 2007, <http://www.theage.com.au/news/opinion/>.

89   Toohey, 'Behind the documentary'.

90   J. Pierik, & S. Lane, 'Players united in pay dispute', *The Age*, 30 June 2011, accessed 30 June 2011, <http://www.theage.com.au/afl/afl-news/>.

91   D. Petrie, 'A champion of a far more important cause', *The Age*, 25 August 2010, accessed 25 August 2010, <http://www.theage.com.au/afl/afl-news/>.

92   Toohey, 'Behind the documentary'.

93   Toohey, 'Behind the documentary'.

94   Stewart & Smith, 'Drug use in sport', p. 286.

95   M. Gard, & R. Meyenn, 'Boys, bodies, pleasure and pain: interrogating contact sports in schools', *Sport, Education and Society*, vol. 5, no. 1, 2000, p. 24.

96   AFL, *Junior Development for Football Clubs*. Australian Football League, Melbourne, 2004, p. 14.

97   M. Foucault, *Ethics, Subjectivity and Truth*, ed. P. Rabinow, trans. R. Hurley et. al., New York University Press, New York, 1994, pp. 165–166.

98   M. Foucault, *Language, Counter-Memory, Practice: Selected Essays and Interviews*. ed. D. F. Bouchard, trans. D. F. Bouchard & S. Simon, Cornell University Press, Ithaca, NY, 1977, p. 226.

99   J. Lechte, 'Art, love, and melancholy in the work of Julia Kristeva', in J. Fletcher
      & A. Benjamin (eds), *Abjection, Melancholia, and Love: The Work of Julia Kristeva*,
      Routledge, London & New York, 1990, p. 32.

100   Derrida, 'The rhetoric of drugs', pp. 229–230.

101   Derrida, 'The rhetoric of drugs', pp. 235–236.

102   E. Probyn, *Blush: Faces of Shame*, University of Minnesota Press, Minneapolis,
      2005, p. 78.

103   Derrida, 'The rhetoric of drugs', p. 235.

104   Derrida, 'The rhetoric of drugs', p. 240.

105   Derrida, 'The rhetoric of drugs', p. 236.

106   Derrida, 'The rhetoric of drugs', pp. 243–244.

107   B. Guthrie, 'Football's big gamble', *The Age*, 5 June 2011, accessed 5 June 2011,
      <http://www.theage.com.au/opinion/>.

108   M. Boulton, 'Network in place to nab offenders', *The Age*, 16 July 2011, accessed
      17 July 2011, <http://www.theage.com.au/afl/afl-news/>.

109   K. Murphy, M. Boulton & P. Bartley, 'All bets off: clamp on footy odds', *The Age*,
      28 May 2011, accessed 28 May 2011, <http://www.theage.com.au/national/>.

110   P. Bibby & J. Swan, 'Gillard moves to ban live odds, restrict gambling ads
      during games', *The Age*, 26 May 2013, accessed 26 May 2013, <http://www.
      theage.com.au/opinion/political-news/>.

111   C. Wilson, 'Heath Shaw suspended for betting on football', *The Age*, 15 July
      2011, accessed 15 July 2011, <http://www.theage.com.au/afl/afl-news/>.

112   C. Wilson, 'I thought it was minor, a little bet: Shaw', *The Age*, 16 July 2011,
      accessed 16 July 2011, <http://www.theage.com.au/afl/afl-news/>.

113   M. Gleeson, 'One stupid moment', *The Age*, 16 July 2011, accessed 17 July 2011,
      <http://www.theage.com.au/afl/afl-news/>.

114   C. Saltau, 'Inside info: players warned', *The Age*, 16 July 2011, accessed 17 July
      2011, <http://www.theage.com.au/afl/afl-news/>.

115   Baum, 'Integrity of the game at stake'.

116   Baum, 'Integrity of the game at stake'.

117   The Age, 'Fallen idol', *The Age*, 1 August 2013, accessed 12 December 2013,
      <http://www.theage.com.au/afl/afl-news/>.

118   Hamilton, 'Brendan Fevola of the Brisbane Lions admits gambling'.

119   Hamilton, 'Brendan Fevola of the Brisbane Lions admits gambling'.

120   L. Ham, 'Footy show axes Fevola after Brownlow antics', *The Age*, 23 Septem-
      ber 2009, accessed 19 July 2011, <http://www.theage.com.au/afl/afl-news/>.

121   J. Niall, 'Fevola close to joining Brisbane', *The Age*, 7 October 2009, accessed
      21 July 2011, <http://www.theage.com.au/articles/>.

122   P. Lutton & W. Brodie, 'Don't prejudge me: Fev protests innocence', *The Age*,
      8 September 2010, accessed 8 September 2010, <http://www.theage.com.au/afl/
      afl-news/>.

123   R. Devlin & T. Sheahan, 'Brendan Fevola sacked by Brisbane Lions for
      "multiple" contract breaches', *Perth Now*, 21 February 2011, accessed 21 July 2011,
      <http://www.perthnow.com.au/sport/>.

124 M. Robinson & M. Stevens, 'Two alcohol–related incidents in China revealed as causes for Brendan Fevola's sacking', *Herald Sun,* 22 February 2011, accessed 21 July 2011, <http://www.foxsports.com.au/afl/>.

125 C. Vickery, 'Fevola's confession draws huge audience to *Footy Show*', *Herald Sun,* 11 March 2011, accessed 19 July 2011, <http://www.heraldsun.com.au/entertainment/tv-radio/>.

126 M. Warner, 'Brendan Fevola tells *The Footy Show* he gambled nearly $1 million, attempted suicide', *Perth Now,* 11 March 2011, accessed 22 July 2011, <http://www.perthnow.com.au/news/>.

127 Derrida, 'The rhetoric of drugs', pp. 240–241.

128 C. K. Erickson, 'Is pathological gambling an "addiction"?' *Addiction Professional,* vol. 5, no. 3, 2007, p. 12.

129 Erickson, 'Is pathological gambling an "addiction"?', p. 12.

130 Herald Sun, 'Alex Fevola blames AFL culture for "creating a monster"', *Herald Sun,* 2 May 2011, accessed 3 May 2011, <http://www.heraldsun.com.au/entertainment/tv-radio/>.

131 Herald Sun, 'Alex Fevola blames AFL culture'.

132 C. Trenwith, 'Cousins in hospital with head injury after fall', *WA Today,* 10 January 2012, accessed 11 January 2012, <http://watoday.com.au/wa-news/>.

133 R. King, 'Ben Cousins charged with drug possession', *The Age,* 28 March 2012, accessed 28 March 2012, <http://www.theage.com.au/wa-news/>.

134 A. Orr, 'Ben Cousins in Perth park "fight"', *WA Today,* 5 August 2013, accessed 5 August 2013, <http://www.watoday.com.au/wa-news/>.

Notes to Chapter 5: Undoing exclusions

1 Throughout this chapter, I use the term 'queer' to mean gay men, lesbians, bisexual persons and transgendered persons (LGBT) as well as others who do not identify or practice sexual behaviours as wholly heterosexual or 'straight'. The term queer was reclaimed in LGBT community in the early 1990s, partly as a radical distancing from 1980s lesbian/gay norms, partly as a term adopted to describe younger persons in LGBT community, and partly through what came to be known as 'queer theory' – the academic study of sexualities and gender from a cultural studies and poststructuralist theory perspective. All of these meanings apply in using the term queer in this chapter, while acknowledging that it can be – and has been – used as a term of abuse or harassment in football culture in both on-field and off-field contexts.

2 The Age, '"Don't ask, don't tell" belongs in the past', *The Age,* 26 May 2010, accessed 29 May 2010, <http://www.theage.com.au/opinion/blogs/>; D. Kakmi, 'Akermanis merely highlights what we've long suspected', *The Age,* 25 May 2010, accessed 25 March 2011, <http://www.theage.com.au/opinion/>.

3 J. Pierik, 'End may be nigh for Aka', *The Age,* 30 May 2010, accessed 30 May 2010, <http://www.theage.com.au/afl/afl-news>.

4   T. Hunter, 'Akermanis "gay" storm: activist demands apology', *Brisbane Times,* 21 May 2010, accessed 29 May 2010, <http://www.brisbanetimes.com.au/afl/afl-news>.

5   S. Zeeland, *The Masculine Marine: Homoeroticism in The U.S. Marine Corps,* Harrington Park Press, New York & London, 1996.

6   M. Peacock, 'Ian Thorpe's coming out – why did it take so long and what does it say about us?', *7.30,* Australian Broadcasting Corporation, television broadcast, 14 July 2014.

7   E. Anderson, *Trailblazing: America's First Openly Gay High School Coach,* Alyson Press, Hollywood, Calif., 2000; E. Anderson, 'Openly gay athletes: contesting hegemonic masculinity in a homophobic environment', *Gender & Society,* vol. 16, no. 6, 2002, pp. 860–77; G. Hekma, '"As long as they don't make an issue of it…": gay men and lesbians in organized sports in the Netherlands', *Journal of Homosexuality,* vol. 35, no. 1, 1998, pp. 1–23; M. Messner, *Power at Play: Sports and the Problem of Masculinity,* Beacon, Boston, Mass., 1992.

8   E. Anderson, 'Updating the outcome: gay athletes, straight teams, and coming out in educationally based sport teams', *Gender & Society,* vol. 25, no. 2, 2011, pp. 250–268.

9   R. Cover, 'First contact: queer theory, sexual identity, and 'mainstream' film', *International Journal of Gender and Sexuality,* vol. 5, no. 1, 2000, pp. 71–89.

10   A. Langmaid & R. Vaughan, 'Mick Malthouse hit with $7500 fine for sledging Stephen Milne', *Perth Now,* 11 April 2010, accessed 14 August 2011, <http://www.perthnow.com.au/sport>.

11   S. Bradley, 'Stars of the AFL come out in support of gays', *The Age,* 11 April 2010, accessed 6 May 2011, <http://www.theage.com.au/afl/afl-news>.

12   M. Shmith, 'Come out to play, they say, but how safe is the full light of gay?' *The Age,* 22 May 2010, accessed 22 May 2010, <http://www.theage.com.au/opinion/society-and-culture>.

13   Bradley, 'Stars of the AFL come out in support of gays'.

14   Bradley, 'Stars of the AFL come out in support of gays'.

15   C. Symons, M. Sbaraglia, L. Hillier & A. Mitchell, *Come Out to Play: The Sports Experience of Lesbian, Gay, Bisexual and Transgender (LGBT) People in Victoria,* Institute of Sport, Exercise and Active Living (ISEAL) and the School of Sport and Exercise at Victoria University, Melbourne, 2010, p. 6.

16   Symons et al., *Come Out to Play,* p. 10.

17   Coming out – that is, revealing that one is not heterosexual – is not, of course, as clear-cut as a simple announcement but often involves grey areas of hints, knowledge shared with some but not others, and various codes of passing. That is, the closet is not a simple in/out dichotomy. See R. Cover, 'Queer Youth, Risk and the Passing/Coming Out Dichotomy', in D. R. Cooley & K. Harrison (eds), *Identity and Passing: Critical Essays,* Ashgate, London, 2012, pp. 105–137.

18   J. Akermanis, 'Stay in the closet, Jason Akermanis tells homosexuals', *Herald Sun,* 20 May 2010, accessed 29 May 2010, <http://www.heraldsun.com.au/sport>.

19 Hunter, 'Akermanis "gay" storm'.

20 Bradley, 'Stars of the AFL come out in support of gays'.

21 K. Martindale, 'What makes lesbianism thinkable?: theorizing lesbianism from Adrienne Rich to Queer Theory', in N. Mandell (ed), *Feminist Issues: Race, Class and Sexuality,* Prentice Hall, Scarborough, Ontario, 1995, p. 68.

22 J. Butler, 'Imitation and gender insubordination', in D. Fuss (ed) *Inside/Out: Lesbian Theories, Gay Theories,* Routledge, London, p. 15.

23 U. Vaid, *Virtual Equality: The Mainstreaming of Gay and Lesbian Liberation,* Anchor, New York, 1995, p. 296.

24 G. Walton, 'H-Cubed: A primer on bullying and sexuality diversity for educators', *Professional Development Perspectives,* vol. 6, no. 2, 2006, p. 14.

25 Walton, 'H-Cubed', p. 14.

26 E. McDermott, K. Roen & J. Scourfield, 'Avoiding shame: young LGBT people, homophobia and self-destructive behaviours', *Culture, Health & Sexuality,* vol. 10, no. 8, 2008, p. 827.

27 D. Eribon, *Insult and the Gay Self,* trans. M. Lucey, Duke University Press, Durham & London, 2004.

28 D. L. Espelage, & S. M. Swearer, 'Addressing research gaps in the intersection between homophobia and bullying', *School Psychology Review,* vol. 37, no. 2, 2008, pp. 155–159.

29 D. Altman, *Homosexual Oppression and Liberation,* New York University Press, New York, 1971.

30 E. K. Sedgwick, *Between Men: English Literature and Male Homosocial Desire,* Columbia University Press, New York, 1985, pp. 3–4.

31 D. Altman, *The Homosexualization of America, The Americanization of the Homosexual,* St. Martin's Press, New York, 1982, p. 22.

32 M. Warner, 'Pleasures and dangers of shame', in D. M. Halperin & V. Traub (eds), *Gay Shame,* The University of Chicago Press, Chicago & London, 2009, p. 291.

33 M. Foucault, *Society Must Be Defended: Lectures at the Collège de France, 1975–76,* ed. M. Bertani & A. Fontana, trans. D. Macey, Penguin, London, 2004, pp. 242–243, 246.

34 Foucault, *Society Must Be Defended,* p. 253.

35 M. Foucault, *Security, Territory, Population: Lectures at the Collège de France, 1977–78,* trans. G. Burchell, ed. M. Senellart, Palgrave Macmillan, Hampshire, 2007, p. 63.

36 Akermanis, 'Stay in the Closet'.

37 Sydney Morning Herald, 'Gay Olympic swimmer angered by Aker', *Sydney Morning Herald,* 20 May 2010, accessed 29 May 2010, <http://www.smh.com.au/afl/afl-news>.

38 M. Gard & R. Meyenn, 'Boys, bodies, pleasure and pain: interrogating contact sports in schools', *Sport, Education and Society,* vol. 5, no. 1, 2000, p. 20.

39 M. Simpson, *Male Impersonators: Men Performing Masculinity,* Cassell, London, 1994, p. 84.

40 N. Oswin, 'Critical geographies and the uses of sexuality: deconstructing queer space', *Progress in Human Geography,* vol. 32, no. 1, 2008, p. 90.

41 E. Probyn, 'Sporting bodies: dynamics of shame and pride', *Body & Society,* vol. 6, no. 1, 2000, p. 20.

42 R. Cover, 'The naked subject: nudity, context and sexualisation in contemporary culture', *Body & Society,* vol. 9, no. 3, 2003, p. 56.

43 Cover, 'The naked subject', p. 54.

44 A. Caldwell, 'Men's nude bonding no flash in the pan', *Courier Mail,* 26 September 2009, accessed 23 October 2010, <http://www.couriermail.com.au/news/queensland>.

45 Caldwell, 'Men's nude bonding no flash in the pan'.

46 T. Bennett, 'Texts, readers, reading formations', *Literature and History,* vol. 9, no. 2, 1983, p. 218.

47 P. Turton-Turner, 'The role of ridicule in naked charity calendars', *Continuum: Journal of Media & Cultural Studies,* vol. 21, no. 3, 2007, pp. 419–432.

48 M. Bakhtin, *Rabelais and his World,* trans. H. Iswolsky, Indiana University Press, Bloomington: Indiana, 1984.

49 R. Parker, 'The carnivalization of the world', in R. N. Lancaster & M. Di Leonardo (eds), *The Gender/Sexuality Reader: Culture, History, Political Economy,* Routledge, New York and London, p. 367.

50 W. H. Blanchard, 'The group process in gang rape', *Journal of Social Psychology,* vol. 49, no. 2, 1959, p. 259.

51 Blanchard, 'The group process in gang rape', p. 263.

52 P. R. Sanday, *Fraternity Gang Rape: Sex, Brotherhood, and Privilege on Campus,* Second Ed., New York University Press, New York & London, 2007, p. 42.

53 K. Franklin, 'Enacting masculinity: antigay violence and group rape as participatory theater', *Sexuality Research & Social Policy: Journal of the National Sexuality Resource Center,* vol. 1, no. 2, 2004, p. 35.

54 M. Flood, 'Men, sex, and homosociality: how bonds between men shape their sexual relations with women', *Men and Masculinities,* vol. 10, no. 3, 2007, p. 341.

55 Symons et al., *Come Out to Play,* p. 7.

56 Flood, 'Men, sex, and homosociality', p. 354.

57 E. K. Sedgwick, *Epistemology of the Closet,* Penguin, London, 1990, p. 35.

58 R. Hennessy, 'Queer theory, left politics', *Rethinking Marxism,* vol. 7, no. 3, 1994, pp. 86–87.

59 Sedgwick, *Epistemology,* p. 35.

60 E. Grosz, *Volatile Bodies: Toward a Corporeal Feminism.* Allen & Unwin, St. Leonards, NSW, 1994, p. 139.

61 D. Buchbinder, *Masculinities and Identities,* Melbourne University Press, Melbourne, 1994, p. 1.

62 E. Anderson, A. Adams & I. Rivers, '"I kiss them because I love them": the emergence of heterosexual men kissing in British institutes of education', *Archives of Sexual Behavior,* vol. 41, no. 2, 2012, pp. 421–430.

63 Symons et al., *Come Out to Play,* p. 43.

64   J. Stark, 'Dear AFL: can't you save us from all our problems?' *The Age*, 16 September 2012, accessed 16 September 2012, <http://www.theage.com.au/afl/afl-news>.

65   J. Stark, 'Slurs and innuendo fuel culture of homophobia', *The Age*, 16 September 2012, accessed 14 December 2013, <http://www.theage.com.au/afl/afl-news>.

66   A. Stephens, 'There's no dragging the heels on this march', *The Age*, 4 February 2013, accessed 4 February 2013, <http://www.theage.com.au/victoria>.

67   J. Stark, 'No joy for gay pride as AFL rules out themed match', *The Age*, 19 May 2013, accessed 14 December 2013, <http://www.theage.com.au/afl/afl-news>.

68   J. Stark, 'AFL stars come out against gay slurs', *The Age*, 5 May 2013, accessed 5 May 2013, <http://www.theage.com.au/afl/afl-news>.

Notes to Chapter 6: Vulnerable Bodies

1   Brisbane Times, 'Bingle 'clears the decks' on Fevola affair', *Brisbane Times*, 2 September 2007, accessed 21 June 2011, <http://www.brisbanetimes.com.au/articles>.

2   J. Medew & M. Levy, 'Bingle lying, says Brereton', *The Age*, 13 March 2010, accessed 4 August 2011, <http://www.theage.com.au/national>.

3   A. Sharpe, 'Inside the life of Lara Bingle', *Perth Now*, 5 March 2010, accessed 4 August 2011, <http://www.perthnow.com.au/entertainment/perth-confidential>.

4   A. Petrie, 'AFL to quiz Brendan Fevola over Lara Bingle photo', *The Age*, 3 March 2010, accessed 4 August 2011, <http://www.theage.com.au/afl/afl-news>.

5   Sharpe, 'Inside the life of Lara Bingle'.

6   Petrie, 'AFL to quiz Brendan Fevola'.

7   P. Hudson & F. Byrne, 'Lara Bingle to take legal action against Brendan Fevola over nude photo as Deputy PM Julia Gillard slams "compromising" pictures', *Herald Sun,* 2 March 2010, accessed 4 August 2011, <http://www.heraldsun.com.au/entertainment/confidential>.

8   Petrie, 'AFL to quiz Brendan Fevola'.

9   J. Chadwick, 'AFL lashes out at Bingle's legal team', *The Age*, 12 March 2010, accessed 4 August 2011, <http://news.theage.com.au/breaking-news-sport>.

10   P. FitzSimons, 'Interview with a bad boy, fireworks assured', *The Age*, 1 May 2011, accessed 4 August 2011, <http://www.theage.com.au/afl/afl-news>.

11   Chadwick, 'AFL lashes out at Bingle's legal team'.

12   J. Pierik & C. Marcus, 'AFL in Bingle blue as Clarke to depart', *The Age*, 14 March 2010, accessed 5 August 2011, <http://www.theage.com.au/national>.

13   Pierik & Marcus, 'AFL in Bingle blue as Clarke to depart'.

14   B. Wilson, 'Footy must stop violence on and off the field', *The Age*, 11 July 2010, accessed 11 July 2010, <http://www.theage.com.au/opinion/society-and-culture>.

15   C. Wilson, 'Bingle is not fair game, AFL must show better leadership', *The Age*, 14 March 2010, accessed 5 August 2011, <http://www.theage.com.au/afl/afl-news>.

16   J. Butler, *Precarious Life*, Verso, London, 2004.

17 J. Butler, *Frames of War: When is Life Grievable?* Verso, London & New York, 2009.

18 J. Butler, 'Reply from Judith Butler to Mills and Jenkins', *Differences: A Journal of Feminist Cultural Studies,* vol. 18, no. 2, 2007, p. 187.

19 Butler, 'Reply from Judith Butler to Mills and Jenkins', p. 181.

20 A. Lingis, *The Community of Those who have Nothing in Common*, Indiana University Press, Bloomington & Indianapolis, 1994, p. 31.

21 Lingis, *Community of Those who have Nothing in Common*, p. 157.

22 Butler, 'Reply from Judith Butler to Mills and Jenkins', p. 194.

23 B. Plant, 'Welcoming dogs: Levinas and "the animal" question', *Philosophy and Social Criticism,* vol. 27, no. 1, 2011, p. 60.

24 J. Derrida, *Adieu to Emmanuel Levinas*, trans. P. Brault & M. Naas, Stanford University Press, Stanford, Calif., 1999, pp. 72–83.

25 J. Pugliese, 'The Incommensurability of law to justice: refugees and Australia's Temporary Protection Visa', *Law and Literature*, vol. 16, no. 3, 2004, p. 291.

26 Butler, *Frames of War*, p. 75.

27 AFL *Respect & Responsibility: Creating a Safe and Inclusive Environment for Women at all Levels of Australian Football*, 2005, accessed 12 January 2011, <http://www.afl.com.au/portals/0/afl_docs/afl_hq/Policies/Respect%20&%20Responsibility%20Policy.pdf>.

28 S. Lash & M. Featherstone, 'Recognition and difference: politics, identity, multiculture', *Theory, Culture & Society*, vol. 18, no. 2–3, 2001, pp. 3–4.

29 N. Fraser, 'Recognition without ethics?' *Theory, Culture & Society*, vol. 18, no. 2–3, 2001, p. 27.

30 J. Butler, 'Longing for recognition', *Studies in Gender and Sexuality,* vol. 1, no. 3, 2000, pp. 271–90.

31 Butler, 'Longing for recognition', p. 272.

32 E. Ferrarese, 'Judith Butler's "not particularly postmodern insight" of recognition', *Philosophy & Social Criticism*, vol. 37, no. 7, 2011, pp. 759–773.

33 F. Jenkins, 'Judith Butler: disturbance, provocation and the ethics of non-violence', *Humanities Research,* vol. 16, no. 2, 2010, p. 113.

34 Ferrarese, 'Judith Butler's "not particularly postmodern insight"', p. 769.

35 Ferrarese, 'Judith Butler's "not particularly postmodern insight"', p. 769.

36 Butler, *Frames of War*, p. 2.

37 Butler, *Frames of War*, pp. 2, 50.

38 Butler, *Frames of War*, p. 5.

39 Butler, *Frames of War*, p. 50.

40 Butler, *Frames of War*, p. 6.

41 Butler, *Frames of War*, pp. 3–4.

42 Butler, *Frames of War*, pp. 6–7.

43 Butler, *Frames of War*, p. 75.

44 Butler, *Frames of War*, pp. 77–78.

45 Butler, *Frames of War*, p. 141.

46 Butler, *Frames of War*, pp. 23–24.

47   Butler, *Frames of War*, p. 143.

48   E. Gilson, 'Vulnerability, ignorance, and oppression', *Hypatia*, vol. 26, no. 2, 2011, p. 309.

49   Butler, *Frames of War*, p. 12.

50   Butler, *Frames of War*, pp. 34–35.

51   Butler, *Frames of War*, pp. 30–31.

52   J. Butler, *Bodies That Matter: On The Discursive Limits of 'Sex'*, Routledge, London & New York, 1993.

53   J. Butler, 'Violence, mourning, politics', *Studies in Gender and Sexuality*, vol. 4, no. 1, 2003, p. 15.

54   Butler, *Frames of War*, pp. 2–3.

55   Butler, *Frames of War*, p. 34.

56   B. J. Gabbe, C. F. Finch, & P. A. Cameron, 'Priorities for reducing the burden of injuries in sport: the example of Australian football', *Journal of Science and Medicine in Sport*, vol. 10, no. 5, 2007, p. 274.

57   Sydney Morning Herald, 'Aussie Rules "most injury-prone sport"', *Sydney Morning Herald,* 7 July 2006, accessed 10 July 2011, <http://www.smh.com.au/news/Sport>.

58   Gabbe, Finch & Cameron, 'Priorities for reducing the burden of injuries', p. 273.

59   Gabbe, Finch & Cameron, 'Priorities for reducing the burden of injuries', pp. 273–274.

60   C. Wilson, 'AFL is tougher than Rugby League, says Hunt', *Brisbane Times*, 28 May 2011, accessed 28 May 2011, <http://www.brisbanetimes.com.au/afl//afl-news>.

61   Gabbe, Finch & Cameron, 'Priorities for reducing the burden of injuries', pp. 274–275.

62   A. Cooper, 'Clean up junior footy violence: Roos', *The Age*, 23 May 2011, accessed 23 May 2011, <http://www.theage.com.au/afl/afl-news>.

63   G. McGee, 'Retired Demons star Daniel Bell seeking brain damage compensation', *Herald Sun*, 31 March 2011, accessed 8 April 2011, <http://www.heraldsun.com.au/sport/afl>.

64   McGee, 'Retired Demons star Daniel Bell'; J. Anderson, 'David Parkin backs AFL concussion rules', *Herald Sun*, 31 March 2011, accessed 8 April 2011, <http://www.heraldsun.com.au/sport/afl>.

65   J. Pierik, 'Concern at brain damage denials', *The Age*, 3 March 2013, accessed 3 March 2013, <http://www.theage.com.au/afl/afl-news>.

66   M. Boulton, 'Our game is brutal: AFL chief', *The Age*, 14 May 2011, accessed 14 May 2011, <http://www.theage.com.au/afl/afl-news>.

67   S. Lane, 'Coach welfare concern', *The Age*, 23 April 2011, accessed 23 April 2011, <http://www.theage.com.au/afl/afl-news>.

68   A. Styles & S. White, 'Swans player's life hangs in the balance', *WA Today*, 3 May 2011, accessed 3 May 2011, <http://www.watoday.com.au/wa-news>.

69   M. Gard & R. Meyenn, 'Boys, bodies, pleasure and pain: interrogating contact sports in schools', *Sport, Education and Society,* vol. 5, no. 1, 2000, p. 19.

70 Gard & Meyenn, 'Boys, bodies, pleasure and pain', p. 24.

71 A. Turner, J. Barlow & B. Ilbery, 'Play hurt, live hurt: living with and managing osteoarthritis from the perspective of ex-professional footballers', *Journal of Health Psychology,* vol. 7, no. 3, 2002, pp. 285. 297.

72 J. Jansz, 'Masculine identity and restrictive emotionality', in A. H. Fischer (ed), *Gender and Emotion: Social Psychological Perspectives,* Cambridge University Press, Cambridge, 2000, pp. 166–186.

73 T. Lane, 'Sport leaves no stone unturned', *The Age,* 10 July 2011, accessed 10 July 2011, <http://www.theage.com.au/afl/afl-news>.

74 G. Hand & M. O'Keefe, 'Retired Demons star Daniel Bell seeking brain damage compensation', *Perth Now,* 31 March 2011, accessed 8 April 2011, <http://www.perthnow.com.au/sport/afl>.

75 R. Braham, C. Finch, A. McIntosh & P. McCrory, 'Community level Australian football: a profile of injuries', *Journal of Science and Medicine in Sport,* vol. 7, no. 1, 2004, p. 102.

76 Gilson, 'Vulnerability, ignorance, and oppression', p. 312.

77 Jenkins, 'Judith Butler', p. 109.

78 P. Costello, 'Hard to be charitable about sports stars' philanthropy', *The Age,* 16 February 2011, accessed 16 February 2011, <http://www.theage.com.au/opinion/society-and-culture>.

BIBLIOGRAPHY

60 Minutes, 'Kim Duthie interviewed', television broadcast, Australia, 6 March 2011.

AFL, *Junior Development for Football Clubs,* Australian Football League, Melbourne, 2004.

——, *Respect & Responsibility: Creating a Safe and Inclusive Environment for Women at all Levels of Australian Football*, 2005, accessed 12 January 2011, <http://www.afl.com.au/staticfile/AFL%20Tenant/AFL/Files/Respect_&_Responsibility_Policy.pdf>.

——, *Respect & Responsibility Policy Implementation Plan,* accessed 5 December 2010, <http://www.docstoc.com/docs/32920125/Implementation-Plan-for-the-Respect-and-Responsibility-Policy>.

——, *Anti-Doping Code*, 1 January 2010, accessed 12 December 2013, <http://www.aflcommunityclub.com.au/fileadmin/user_upload/Play_AFL/AFLAnti-DopingCode2010ASADA.pdf>.

AFL Players Association, 'Illicit Drug Policy', August 2008, accessed 13 December 2013, <http://www.aflplayers.com.au/illicit-drugs-policy/>.

Akermanis, J., 'Stay in the closet, Jason Akermanis tells homosexuals', *Herald Sun*, 20 May 2010, accessed 29 May 2010, <http://www.heraldsun.com.au/sport>.

Albergo, L., 'Gambling investigation', *Australian Football Association of North America*, 18 February 2007, accessed 29 August 2011, <http://www.afana.com/drupal5/news/2007/02/18/gambling_investigation-377>.

Alexander, B. & Levine, A., 'Web 2.0 storytelling: emergence of a new genre', *Educause Review*, vol. 43, no. 6, 2008, pp. 1-8.

Altman, D., *Homosexual Oppression and Liberation*, New York University Press, New York, 1971.

——, *The Homosexualization of America, The Americanization of the Homosexual*, St. Martin's Press, New York, 1982.

Anderson, B., *Imagined Communities: Reflections on the Origins and Spread of Nationalism*, Verso, London, 1982.

Anderson, E., *Trailblazing: America's First Openly Gay High School Coach*, Alyson Press, Hollywood, Calif., 2000.

——, 'Openly gay athletes: contesting hegemonic masculinity in a homophobic environment', *Gender & Society*, vol. 16, no. 6, 2002, pp. 860–77.

——, 'Updating the outcome: gay athletes, straight teams, and coming out in educationally based sport teams', *Gender & Society*, vol. 25, no. 2, 2011, pp. 250–268.

Anderson, E., Adams, A. & Rivers, I., '"I kiss them because I love them": the emergence of heterosexual men kissing in British institutes of education', *Archives of Sexual Behavior*, vol. 41, no. 2, 2012, pp. 421–430.

Anderson, J., 'David Parkin backs AFL concussion rules', *Herald Sun*, 31 March 2011, accessed 8 April 2011, <http://www.heraldsun.com.au/sport/afl>.

Andersson, K., 'Constructing young masculinity: a case study of heroic discourse on violence', *Discourse & Society*, vol. 19, no. 2, 2008, pp. 139–161.

Archard, D., 'Privacy, the public interest and a prurient public', in M. Kieran (ed), *Media Ethics*, Routledge, London & New York, 1998, pp. 82–96.

Atkinson, P., *The Ethnographic Imagination: Textual Constructions of Reality*, Routledge, London & New York, 1992.

Attwood, F., 'Sexed up: theorizing the sexualization of culture', *Sexualities*, vol. 9, no. 1, 2006, pp. 77–94.

Bachelard, M., 'Hitting the drink', *The Age*, 15 June 2008, accessed 15 June 2008, <http://www.theage.com.au/national>.

Bakhtin, M., *Rabelais and his World*, trans. H. Iswolsky, Indiana University Press, Bloomington, Indiana, 1984.

Barrett, D., 'AFL captains join forces to tackle Melbourne CBD violence', *Herald Sun*, 28 August 2009, accessed 24 July 2011, <http://www.heraldsun.com.au/news/victoria>.

Baum, G., 'A story of opportunities squandered', *Real Footy*, 18 October 2007, accessed 23 October 2007, <http://realfooty.com.au/news/news>.

——, 'Integrity of the game at stake', *The Age*, 16 July 2011, accessed 17 July 2011, <http://www.theage.com.au/afl/afl-news>.

Baxter, J. & Wallace, K., 'Outside in-group and out-group identities? Constructing male solidarity and female exclusion in UK builders' talk', *Discourse & Society,* vol. 20, no. 4, 2009, pp. 411–429.

Baynes, D., 'Rugby League sex scandals concern sponsors, Prime Minister Rudd', May 15 2009, accessed 6 December 2010, <http://www. bloomberg.com/apps/news?pid=newsarchive&sid=ahyDXkncDg_0>.

Beasley, C., 'Rethinking hegemonic masculinity in a globalizing world', *Men and Masculinities,* vol. 11, no. 1, 2008, pp. 86–103.

Beaumont, L., 'Feminist wary over rugby role', *The Age,* 7 March 2004, accessed 9 December 2013, <http://www.theage.com.au/articles/2004/ 03/06/>.

Beck, M., 'Nixon admits to substance problem', *The Age*, 8 March 2011, accessed 8 March 2011, <http://www.theage.com.au/afl/afl-news>.

——, 'New sex assault probe on Lovett', *The Age*, 10 August 2011, accessed 10 August 2011, <http://www.theage.com.au/victoria>.

Beck, M. & Khokhar, A., 'St Kilda teen lied she was pregnant', *The Age*, 7 March 2011, accessed 8 March 2011, <http://www.theage.com.au/ afl/afl-news>.

Beck, M. & Pierik, J., 'Nixon quizzed, Fevola lapses', *The Age*, 11 March 2011, accessed 11 March 2011, <http://www.theage.com.au/afl/afl-news>.

Bell, V., 'Performativity and belonging: an introduction', *Theory, Culture & Society,* vol. 16, no. 2, 1999, pp. 1–10.

Benedict, H., *Virgin or Vamp: How the Press Covers Sex Crimes*, Oxford University Press, New York, 1992.

Bennett, T., 'Texts, readers, reading formations', *Literature and History,* vol. 9, no. 2, 1983, pp. 214–227.

Bibby, P. & Swan, J., 'Gillard moves to ban live odds, restrict gambling ads during games', *The Age*, 26 May 2013, accessed 26 May 2013, <http:// www.theage.com.au/opinion/political-news>.

Bignell, J., *Media Semiotics: An Introduction*, Manchester University Press, Manchester, 1997.

Bird, S. R., 'Welcome to the men's club: homosociality and the maintenance of hegemonic masculinity', *Gender and Society,* vol. 10, no. 2, 1996, pp. 120–132.

Black, D., Lawson, J. & Fleishman, S., 'Excessive alcohol use by non-elite sportsmen', *Drug and Alcohol Review,* vol. 18, no. 2, 1999, pp. 201–205.

Blake, M., 'Don't show drugs, Cousins urged', *The Age*, 12 August 2010, accessed 23 August 2010, <http://www.theage.com.au/afl/afl-news>.

Blanchard, W. H., 'The group process in gang rape', *Journal of Social Psychology*, vol. 49, no. 2, 1959, pp. 259–266.

Boulton, M., 'Network in place to nab offenders', *The Age*, 16 July 2011, accessed 17 July 2011, <http://www.theage.com.au/afl/afl-news>.

——, 'Our game is brutal: AFL chief', *The Age*, 14 May 2011, accessed 14 May 2011, <http://www.theage.com.au/afl/afl-news>.

Boxill, J., *Sports Ethics: An Anthology*, Blackwell, Oxford and Melbourne, 2003.

Bradley, S., 'Stars of the AFL come out in support of gays', *The Age*, 11 April 2010, accessed 6 May 2011, <http://www.theage.com.au/afl/afl-news>.

Braham, R., Finch, C., McIntosh, A. & McCrory, P., 'Community level Australian football: a profile of injuries', *Journal of Science and Medicine in Sport*, vol. 7, no. 1, 2004, pp. 96–105.

Brenner, J. & Swanik, K. 'High-risk drinking characteristics in collegiate athletes', *Journal of American College Health*, vol. 56, no. 3, 2007, pp. 267–272.

Brisbane Times, 'Bingle 'clears the decks' on Fevola affair', *Brisbane Times*, 2 September 2007, accessed 21 June 2011, <http://www.brisbanetimes.com.au/articles>.

——, 'Police horrified by high school dance gang rape', *Brisbane Times*, 27 October 2009, accessed 28 October 2009, <http://www.brisbanetimes.com.au/world>.

Brodie, W. 'Naked photos pierce the "bubble"', *The Age*, 21 December 2010, accessed 21 December 2010, <http://www.theage.com.au/afl/afl-news>.

Brown, W. J. & de Matviuk, M. A. C., 'Sports celebrities and public health: Diego Maradona's influence on drug use prevention', *Journal of Health Communication*, vol. 15, no. 4, 2010, pp.358–373.

Buchbinder, D., *Masculinities and Identities*, Melbourne University Press, Melbourne, 1994.

——, *Performance Anxieties: Re-producing Masculinity*, Allen & Unwin, St Leonards, NSW, 1997.

Buckingham, D., 'Introducing identity', in D. Buckingham (ed), *Youth, Identity, and Digital Media*, MIT Press, Cambridge, Mass., 2008, pp. 1–24.

Burgess, J. & Green, J., *YouTube: Online Video and Participatory Culture*, Polity, Cambridge, 2009.

Butcher, S. & Shtargot, S., 'Saints in the clear over rape allegations', *The Age*, 7 May 2008, accessed 13 August 2011, <http://www.theage.com.au/articles>.

Butler, B. & Callinan, R., 'Fevola faces bankruptcy over debt', *The Age*, 4 September 2013, accessed 4 September 2013, <http://www.theage.com.au/afl/afl-news>.

Butler, B. & Millar, P., 'Teen denies asking $20,000 for photo', *The Age*, 22 December 2010, accessed 22 December 2010, <http://www.theage.com.au/afl/afl-news>.

Butler, J., *Gender Trouble: Feminism and the Subversion of Identity*, Routledge, London & New York, 1990.

——, 'Imitation and gender insubordination', in Diana Fuss (ed), *Inside/Out: Lesbian Theories, Gay Theories*. London: Routledge, pp. 13–31.

——, *Bodies That Matter: On The Discursive Limits of 'Sex'*, Routledge, London & New York, 1993.

——, *Excitable Speech: A Politics of the Performative*, Routledge, New York & London, 1997.

——, *The Psychic Life of Power: Theories in Subjection*, Stanford University Press, Stanford, Calif., 1997.

——, 'Longing for recognition', *Studies in Gender and Sexuality*, vol. 1, no. 3, 2000, pp. 271–90.

——, 'Violence, mourning, politics', *Studies in Gender and Sexuality*, vol. 4, no. 1, 2003, pp. 9–37.

——, *Precarious Life*, Verso, London, 2004.

——, *Giving an Account of Oneself*, Fordham University Press, New York, 2005.

——, 'Reply from Judith Butler to Mills and Jenkins', *Differences: A Journal of Feminist Cultural Studies*, vol. 18, no. 2, 2007, pp. 180–195.

——, *Frames of War: When is Life Grievable?* Verso, London & New York, 2009.

Caldwell, A., 'Men's nude bonding no flash in the pan', *Courier Mail*, 26 September 2009, accessed 23 October 2010, <http://www.couriermail.com.au/news/queensland>.

Calligeros, M., 'Schoolies' dirty sex secret', *Brisbane Times*, 20 November 2009, accessed 18 August 2010, <http://www.brisbanetimes.com.au/queensland>.

Carey, A., 'Police will question Nixon', *The Age*, 23 February 2011, accessed 23 February 2011, <http://www.theage.com.au/afl/afl-news>.

Carlyon, P., 'Wayne Carey, the little boy who never grew up', *Herald Sun*, 23 October 2009, accessed 12 December 2013, <http://www.heraldsun.com.au/news/victoria>.

Chadwick, J., 'AFL lashes out at Bingle's legal team', *The Age*, 12 March 2010, accessed 4 August 2011, <http://news.theage.com.au/breaking -news-sport>.

Chalip, L., 'Toward a distinctive sport management discipline', *Journal of Sport Management*, vol. 20, no. 1, 2006, pp. 1–21.

Chandler, J., 'Trying to see beyond murk of sport sex debate', *The Age*, 16 May 2009, accessed 17 May 2009, <http://www.theage.com.au/ articles>.

Chow, R. M., Lowery, B. S. & Knowles, E. D., 'The two faces of dominance: the differential effect of ingroup superiority and outgroup inferiority on dominant–group identity and group esteem', *Journal of Experimental Social Psychology*, vol. 44, no. 4, 2007, pp. 1073–1081.

Clanton, G., 'The sport star: modern sport and the cultural economy of sporting celebrity', *Contemporary Sociology: A Journal of Reviews*, vol. 36, no. 1, 2007, pp. 48–49.

Clarke, M., 'Rosa Parks' performativity, habitus, and ability to play the game', *Philosophy Today*, 44, suppl., 2000, pp. 160–168.

Clarke, T., 'Cousins banned after drinking binge', *The Age*, 12 April 2010, accessed 13 April 2010, <http://www.theage.com.au/afl/afl-news>.

Clarkson, J., '"Everyday Joe" versus "pissy, bitchy queens": gay masculinity on straightacting.com', *The Journal of Men's Studies*, vol. 14, no 2, 2006, pp. 191–207.

Coakley, J., Hallinan, C., Jackson, S. & Mewett, P., *Sports in Society: Issues and Controversies in Australia and New Zealand*. McGraw–Hill Australia, New South Wales, 2009.

Collier, S. J., 'Topologies of power: Foucault's analysis of political government beyond "governmentality"', *Theory, Culture & Society*, vol. 26, no. 6, 2009, pp. 78–108.

Connell, R. W., *Gender and Power*, Polity, Cambridge, 1987.

——, *Masculinities*, Polity, Cambridge, 1995.

Connolly, R., 'Fevola's antics show he's a dinosaur from another era', *The Age*, 9 September 2010, accessed 9 September 2010, <http://www.theage. com.au/afl/afl-news>.

Connolly, W. E., *Identity/Difference: Democratic Negotiations of Political Paradox*, Cornell University Press, Ithaca & London, 1991.

Connor, J. M. & Mazanov, J., 'The inevitability of scandal: lessons for sponsors and administrators', *International Journal of Sports Marketing & Sponsorship*, vol. 11, no. 3, 2010, pp. 212–220.

Cooper, A., 'Clean up junior footy violence: Roos', *The Age*, 23 May 2011, accessed 23 May 2011, <http://www.theage.com.au/afl/afl-news>.

Cooper, M., 'AFL players strip Nixon of agent accreditation', *The Age*, 24 March 2011, accessed 24 March 2011, <http://www.theage.com.au/afl/afl-news>.

Corn, K. J. & Dunn, G. A., 'Let the Bon Temps roll: sacrifice, scapegoats, and good times', in G. A. Dunn & R. Housel (eds), *True Blood and Philosophy: We Wanna Think Bad Things with You,* John Wiley & Sons, Hoboken, NJ, 2010, pp. 139–155.

Costello, P., 'Hard to be charitable about sports stars' philanthropy', *The Age*, 16 February 2011, accessed 16 February 2011, <http://www.theage.com.au/opinion/society-and-culture>.

Cover, R., 'First contact: queer theory, sexual identity, and "mainstream" film', *International Journal of Gender and Sexuality*, vol. 5, no. 1, 2000, pp. 71–89.

——, 'The naked subject: nudity, context and sexualisation in contemporary culture', *Body & Society,* vol. 9, no. 3, 2003, pp. 53–72.

——, 'Bodies, movements and desires: lesbian/gay subjectivity and the stereotype', *Continuum: Journal of Media & Cultural Studies*, vol. 18, no. 1, 2004, pp. 81–98.

——, 'Audience inter/active: Interactive media, narrative control & reconceiving audience history', *New Media & Society,* vol. 8, no. 1, 2006, pp. 213–232.

——, 'Object(ives) of desire: romantic coupledom versus promiscuity, subjectivity and sexual identity', *Continuum: Journal of Media & Cultural Studies*, vol. 24, no. 2, 2010, pp. 251–263.

——, 'Queer Youth, Risk and the Passing/Coming Out Dichotomy', in D. R. Cooley & K. Harrison (eds), *Identity and Passing: Critical Essays*, Ashgate, London, 2012, pp. 105–137.

Craig, W. M., Henderson, K. & Murphy, J. G., 'Prospective teachers' attitudes toward bullying and victimization', *School Psychology International*, vol. 21, no. 1, 2000, pp. 5–21.

Cronin, M., 'Sam Maguire: forgotten hero and national icon', *Sport in History*, vol. 25, no. 2, 2005, pp. 189–205.

Crystal, D., *Language and the Internet*, Second Edition, Cambridge University Press, Cambridge, 2006.

Darnell, S. C. & Wilson, B., 'Macho media: unapologetic hypermasculinity in Vancouver's "Talk Radio for Guys"', *Journal of Broadcasting & Electronic Media*, vol. 50, no. 3, 2006, pp. 444–466.

Davis, N. W. & Duncan, M. C., 'Sports knowledge is power: reinforcing masculine privilege through fantasy sport league participation', *Journal of Sport and Social Issues,* vol. 30, no. 3, 2006, pp. 244–264.

de Certeau, M., *The Practice of Everyday Life*, trans. S. F. Rendall, University of California Press, Berkeley, Calif, 1984.

Debord, G., *Society of the Spectacle*, Black & Red, Detroit, Mich., 1967.

Demetriou, A., 'It's not just footy, AFL is concerned for a young girl's welfare', *The Age*, 25 February 2011, accessed 25 February 2011, <http://www.theage.com.au/opinion>.

Denton, A., 'Wayne Carey interview', *Enough Rope,* Australian Broadcasting Corporation, television broadcast, 31 March, episode 161, transcript accessed 12 December 2013, <http://www.abc.net.au/tv/enoughrope/transcripts/s2201719.htm>.

Derrida, J., 'The rhetoric of drugs', trans. M. Israel, in E. Weber (ed), P. Kamuf et al. (trans), *Points . . . Interviews, 1974–1994*, Stanford University Press, Stanford, Calif., 1995, pp. 228–254.

——, *Adieu to Emmanuel Levinas*, trans. P. Brault & M. Naas, Stanford University Press, Stanford, Calif., 1999.

Dery, M., 'Culture jamming: hacking, slashing and sniping in the empire of signs', 1983, accessed 12 December 2003, <http://web.nwe.ufl.edu/~mlaffey/cultjam.html>.

Devlin, R. & Sheahan, T., 'Brendan Fevola sacked by Brisbane Lions for "multiple" contract breaches', *Perth Now*, 21 February 2011, accessed 21 July 2011, <http://www.perthnow.com.au/sport>.

Disch, L., 'Judith Butler and the politics of the performative', *Political Theory*, vol. 27, no. 4, 1999, pp. 545–559.

Dobson, R., 'Should you shake ya booties before a match?' *Sunday Times*, 17 June 2006, accessed 10 March 2011, <http://www.timesonline.co.uk/tol/life_and_style/health/features/>.

Dowsley, A. & Harris, A., 'Adelaide players on teen's list', *Herald Sun*, 24 December 2010, accessed 24 December 2010, <http://www.adelaidenow.com.au>.

Dubecki, L., 'Locking out modern life is not the answer', *The Age*, 2 June 2008, accessed 3 June 2008, <http://www.theage.com.au/opinion>.

Duggan, L., 'The new homonormativity: the sexual politics of neoliberalism', in R. Castronovo and D. Nelson (eds), *Materializing Democracy: Toward a Revitalized Cultural Politics*, Duke University Press, Durham, NC, 2002, pp. 175–194.

Dunning, E. & Waddington, I., 'Sport as a drug and drugs in sport: some exploratory comments', *International Review for the Sociology of Sport*, vol. 38, no. 3, 2003, pp. 351–368.

Ehrhart, J. K. & Sandler, B. R., *Campus Gang Rape: Party Games?* Association of American Colleges, Washington, DC, 1985.

Eribon, D., *Insult and the Gay Self*, trans. M. Lucey, Duke University Press, Durham & London, 2004.

Erickson, C. K., 'Is pathological gambling an "addiction"?' *Addiction Professional*, vol. 5, no. 3, 2007, pp. 12.

Espelage, D. L. & Swearer, S. M., 'Addressing research gaps in the intersection between homophobia and bullying', *School Psychology Review*, vol. 37, no. 2, 2008, pp. 155–159.

Ferguson, S., 'Code of silence', *Four Corners*, Australian Broadcasting Corporation, television broadcast, 11 May 2009.

Ferrarese, E., 'Judith Butler's "not particularly postmodern insight" of recognition', *Philosophy & Social Criticism*, vol. 37, no. 7, 2011, pp. 759–773.

Filiault, S. M. & Drummond, M. J. N., 'The hegemonic aesthetic', *Gay & Lesbian Issues and Psychology Review*, vol. 3, no. 3, 2007, pp. 175–184.

Fiske, J., *Media Matters: Everyday Culture and Political Change*, University of Minnesota Press, Minneapolis, 1996.

FitzSimons, P., 'Interview with a bad boy, fireworks assured', *The Age*, 1 May 2011, accessed 4 August 2011, <http://www.theage.com.au/afl/afl-news>.

Flood, M., 'Men, sex, and homosociality: how bonds between men shape their sexual relations with women', *Men and Masculinities*, vol. 10, no. 3, 2007, pp. 339–359.

Foucault, M., *Language, Counter-Memory, Practice: Selected Essays and Interviews*. ed. D. F. Bouchard, trans. D. F. Bouchard & S. Simon, Cornell University Press, Ithaca, NY, 1977.

——, *Ethics, Subjectivity and Truth*, ed. P. Rabinow, trans. R. Hurley et. al., New York University Press, New York, 1994.

——, *Society Must Be Defended: Lectures at the Collège de France, 1975–76*, ed. M. Bertani & A. Fontana, trans. D. Macey, Penguin, London, 2004.

——, *The Hermeneutics of the Subject: Lectures at the Collège de France, 1981–82*, ed. F. Gros, trans. G. Burchell, Picador, New York, 2005.

——, *Security, Territory, Population: Lectures at the Collège de France, 1977–78*, trans. G. Burchell, ed. M. Senellart, Palgrave Macmillan, Hampshire, 2007.

——, *The Birth of Biopolitics: Lectures at the Collège de France, 1978–79*. trans. G. Burchell, ed. M. Senellart, Palgrave Macmillan, Hampshire, 2008.

Fox Sports, 'Brawling Brendan flying home', *Fox Sports*, 1 November 2006, accessed 18 July 2011, <http://www.foxsports.com.au/afl/brawling-brendan-flying-home>.

Franklin, K., 'Enacting masculinity: antigay violence and group rape as participatory theater', *Sexuality Research & Social Policy: Journal of the National Sexuality Resource Center*, vol. 1, no. 2, 2004, pp. 25–40.

Fraser, N., 'Recognition without ethics?' *Theory, Culture & Society*, vol. 18, no. 2–3, 2001, pp. 21–42.

Frey, J. H. & Eitzen, D. S., 'Sport and society', *Annual Review of Sociology*, no. 17, 1991, pp. 503–22.

Fullerton, T., 'Fair game?' *Four Corners*, Australian Broadcasting Corporation, television broadcast, 3 May 2004.

Furedi, F., 'Celebrity culture', *Society*, vol. 47, no. 6, 2010, pp. 493–497.

Fuss, D., *Identification Papers*, Routledge, New York & London, 1995.

Fyfe, M., 'Alcopop tax fails to curb teenage drinkers', *The Age*, 26 September 2010, accessed 26 September 2010, <http://www.theage.com.au/victoria>.

Gabbe, B. J., Finch, C. F. & Cameron, P. A., 'Priorities for reducing the burden of injuries in sport: the example of Australian football', *Journal of Science and Medicine in Sport*, vol. 10, no. 5, 2007, pp. 273–276.

Gamson, J., 'Jessica Hahn, media whore: sex scandals and female publicity', *Critical Studies in Media Communication*, vol. 18, no. 2, 2001, pp. 157–173.

Gard, M. & Meyenn, R., 'Boys, bodies, pleasure and pain: interrogating contact sports in schools', *Sport, Education and Society*, vol. 5, no. 1, 2000, pp. 19–34.

Gauthier, C. C., 'Privacy invasion by the news media: three ethical models', *Journal of Mass Media Ethics*, vol. 17, no. 1, 2002, pp. 20–34.

Gilmour, C. & Rowe, D., 'When Becks came to Sydney: multiple readings of a sport celebrity', *Soccer & Society*, vol. 11, no. 3, 2010, pp. 229–241.

Gilson, E., 'Vulnerability, ignorance, and oppression', *Hypatia*, vol. 26, no. 2, 2011, pp. 308–332.

Gleeson, M., 'One stupid moment', *The Age*, 16 July 2011, accessed 17 July 2011, <http://www.theage.com.au/afl/afl-news>.

——, 'Fiery dwarf jape AFL's latest sorry episode', *The Age*, 4 September 2013, accessed 6 September 2013, <http://www.theage.com.au/afl/afl-news>.

Goffman, E., *The Presentation of the Self in Everyday Life*, Penguin, London, 1969.

Gramsci, A., *Selections from the Prison Notebooks,* trans. Q. Hoare & G. N. Smith, International Publishers, New York, 1971.

Green, M. & Houlihan, B., 'Governmentality, modernization, and the "disciplining" of national sporting organizations: athletics in Australia and the United Kingdom', *Sociology of Sport Journal*, vol. 23, no. 1, 2006, pp. 47–71.

Grosz, E., *Volatile Bodies: Toward a Corporeal Feminism,* Allen & Unwin, St Leonards, NSW, 1994.

Guthrie, B., 'Footy needs to clean up its act off the field', *The Age,* 21 August 2011, accessed 23 August 2011, Avail.at: http://www.theage.com.au/opinion/politics>.

——, 'Football's big gamble', *The Age*, 5 June 2011, accessed 5 June 2011, <http://www.theage.com.au/opinion>.

Hall, Steve, 'Daubing the drudges of fury: men, violence and the piety of the "hegemonic masculinity" thesis', *Theoretical Criminology,* vol. 6, no. 1, 2002, pp. 35–61.

Hall, Stuart, 'Cultural studies: two paradigms', *Media, Culture, & Society,* vol. 2, 1980, pp. 57–72.

——, 'The toad in the garden: Thatcherism among the theorists', in C. Nelson & L. Grossberg (eds), *Marxism and the Interpretation of Culture*, University of Illinois Press, Urbana & Chicago, 1988, pp. 35–73.

Ham, L., 'Footy show axes Fevola after Brownlow antics', *The Age,* 23 September 2009, accessed 19 July 2011, <http://www.theage.com.au/afl/afl-news>.

Hamilton, A., 'Brendan Fevola of the Brisbane Lions admits gambling addiction', *Herald Sun,* 15 April 2010, accessed 19 July 2011, <http://www.heraldsun.com.au/sport/afl>.

Hand, G. & O'Keefe, M., 'Retired Demons star Daniel Bell seeking brain damage compensation', *Perth Now,* 31 March 2011, accessed 8 April 2011, <http://www.perthnow.com.au/sport/afl>.

Hanlon, P., 'Dogs on notice over Hong Kong prank', *The Age*, 8 February 2011, accessed 8 February 2011, <http://www.theage.com.au/afl/afl-news>.

Hanstad, D. V. & Waddington, I., 'Sport, health and drugs: a critical re-examination of some key issues and problems', *Perspectives in Public Health,* vol. 129, no. 4, 2009, p. 174–182.

Hartley, J., '"When your child grows up too fast": juvenation and the boundaries of the social in the news media', *Continuum,* vol. 12, no. 1, 1998, pp. 9–30.

Hawthorne, M., 'Players emailed "Saints girl" pic', *The Age*, 29 May 2010, accessed 29 May 2010, <http://www.theage.com.au/victoria>.

——, 'Emergency Essendon meeting planned as players' health fears grow', *The Age*, 16 August 2013, accessed 16 August 2013. <http://www.theage.com.au/afl/essendon-bombers>.

Heere, B. & James, J. D., 'Sports teams and their communities: examining the influence of external group identities on team identity', *Journal of Sport Management,* vol. 21, no. 3, 2007, pp. 319–337.

Hekma, G., '"As long as they don't make an issue of it ...": gay men and lesbians in organized sports in the Netherlands', *Journal of Homosexuality,* vol. 35, no. 1, 1998, pp. 1–23.

Hellard, P., 'Mainwaring's death may be trigger for Ben Cousins', *Herald Sun*, 19 October 2007, accessed 22 July 2011, <http://www.heraldsun.com.au/news/national>.

Hennessy, R., 'Queer theory, left politics', *Rethinking Marxism,* vol. 7, no. 3, 1994, pp. 85–111.

Herald Sun, 'Alex Fevola blames AFL culture for "creating a monster"', *Herald Sun*, 2 May 2011, accessed 3 May 2011, <http://www.heraldsun.com.au/entertainment/tv-radio>.

Hickey, C. & Kelly, P., 'Preparing to *not* be a footballer: higher education and professional sport', *Sport, Education and Society,* vol. 13, no. 4, 2008, pp. 477–494.

Hinds, R. & Halloran, J., 'St Kilda name players involved in sex allegations', *Sydney Morning Herald,* 17 March 2004, accessed 13 August 2011, <http://www.smh.com.au/articles>.

Hogan, J., 'Cousins shaved down to beat drug test', *The Age*, 27 August 2010, accessed 27 August 2010, <http://www.theage.com.au/afl/afl-news>.

Holroyd, J., 'Police drop teen sex case against Ricky Nixon', *The Age*, 1 August 2011, accessed 16 August 2011, <http://www.theage.com.au/victoria>.

Horeck, T., *Public Rape: Representing Violation in Fiction and Film,* Routledge, London & New York, 2004.

Houston, C., 'Saints in Milne legal fund row', *The Age*, 1 December 2013, accessed 1 December 2013, <http://www.theage.com.au/afl/afl-news>.

Howson, R., 'A brief response to Christine Beasley's "Rethinking hegemonic masculinity in a globalizing world"', *Men and Masculinities,* vol. 11, no. 1, 2008, pp. 109–113.

Hudson, P., '$12m campaign targets teen party drug scene', *The Age*, 17 April 2005, accessed 17 April 2005, <http://www.theage.com.au/news/National>.

Hudson, P. & Byrne, F., 'Lara Bingle to take legal action against Brendan Fevola over nude photo as Deputy PM Julia Gillard slams "compromising" pictures', *Herald Sun,* 2 March 2010, accessed 4 August 2011, <http://www.heraldsun.com.au/entertainment/confidential>.

Hunt, E., 'Stephen Milne case should have gone on – Ex-Cop', *Herald Sun,* 21 June 2010, accessed 14 August 2011, <http://www.adelaidenow.com.au/sport/afl>.

Hunter, T., 'Akermanis "gay" storm: activist demands apology', *Brisbane Times,* 21 May 2010, accessed 29 May 2010, <http://www.brisbanetimes.com.au/afl/afl-news>.

——, 'Bulldogs stars caught harassing motorists during Hong Kong trip', *The Age,* 7 February 2011, accessed 7 February 2011, <http://www.theage.com.au/afl/afl-news>.

Hutchison, T., 'Cousins deserves his club's support', *The Age,* 20 October 2007, accessed 23 October 2007, <http://www.theage.com.au/news/opinion>.

Independent Weekly, 'AFL wants SANFL name change', *Independent Weekly,* 27 June 2008, accessed 3 January 2009, <http://independentweekly.com.au>.

Inglis, F., *Media Theory: An Introduction.,* Blackwell, Oxford & Cambridge, Mass., 1990.

Izod, J., 'Television sport and the sacrificial hero', *Journal of Sport and Social Issues,* vol. 20, no. 2, 1996, pp. 173–193.

Jameson, F., 'Postmodernism and consumer society', in H. Foster (ed), *Postmodern Culture,* Pluto Press, London, 1985, pp. 111–125.

Jansz, J., 'Masculine identity and restrictive emotionality', in A. H. Fischer (ed), *Gender and Emotion: Social Psychological Perspectives*, Cambridge University Press, Cambridge, 2000, pp. 166–186.

Jaworski, K., '"Elegantly wasted": The celebrity deaths of Michael Hutchence and Paula Yates', *Continuum: Journal of Media & Cultural Studies,* vol. 22, no. 6, 2008, pp. 777–791.

Jefferson, T., 'Subordinating hegemonic masculinity', *Theoretical Criminology,* vol. 6, no. 1, 2002, pp. 63–88.

Jenkins, F., 'Judith Butler: disturbance, provocation and the ethics of non-violence', *Humanities Research,* vol. 16, no. 2, 2010, pp. 93–115.

Johnson, L., 'Kerr caught on police drug tapes', *Brisbane Times,* 23 March 2007, accessed 23 July 2011, <http://www.brisbanetimes.com.au/news/national>.

Johnson, R., 'Three problematics: elements of a theory of working-class culture', in J. Clarke, C. Critcher & R. Johnson (eds), *Working Class Culture: Studies in History and Theory,* Hutchinson, London, 1979, pp. 201–237.

Joinson, A., 'Causes and implications of disinhibited behavior on the internet', in J. Gackenbach (ed), *Psychology and the Internet: Intrapersonal, Interpersonal, and Transpersonal Implications*, Academic Press, San Diego, Calif., 1998, pp. 43–60.

Jones, T., 'Jury split on drugs documentary', *NineMSN, Wide World of Sports*, 27 August 2010, accessed 19 July 2011, <http://www.ninemsn.com.au/article.aspx?id=7951972>.

Kakmi, D., 'Akermanis merely highlights what we've long suspected', *The Age*, 25 May 2010, accessed 25 March 2011, <http://www.theage.com.au/opinion>.

Kieran, M., *Media Ethics,* Routledge, London & New York, 1998.

King, R., 'Ben Cousins charged with drug possession', *The Age*, 28 March 2012, accessed 28 March 2012, <http://www.theage.com.au/wa-news>.

Kissane, K., Beck, M. & Gleeson, M., 'Nixon video: teen arrested', *The Age*, 22 February 2011, accessed 22 February 2011, <http://www.theage.com.au/afl/afl-news>.

Knowles, M. L. & Gardner, W. L., 'Benefits of membership: the activation and amplification of group identities in response to social rejection', *Personality and Social Psychology Bulletin,* vol. 34, no. 9, 2008, pp. 1200–1213.

Krien, A., 'Out of bounds: sex and the AFL', *The Monthly,* April, 2011, pp. 36–43.

Kubacki, K., Siemieniako, D. & Rundle-Thiele, S., 'College binge drinking: a new approach', *Journal of Consumer Marketing,* vol. 28, no. 3, 2011, pp. 225–233.

Kurzman, C., Anderson, C., Key, C., Lee, Y. O., Moloney, M., Silver, A. & van Ryn, M. W., 'Celebrity status', *Sociological Theory,* vol. 25, no. 4, 2007, pp. 347–367.

Lane, S., '"Bullied" Lovett in $2m bid', *The Age*, 17 February 2010, accessed 18 February 2010, <http://www.theage.com.au/afl/afl-news>.

——, 'AFL boys' club', *The Age*, 7 March 2011, accessed 8 March 2011, <http://www.theage.com.au/afl/afl-news>.

——, 'Coach welfare concern', *The Age*, 23 April 2011, accessed 23 April 2011, <http://www.theage.com.au/afl/afl-news>. Accessed 23 April 2011.

Lane, T., 'Sport leaves no stone unturned', *The Age*, 10 July 2011, accessed 10 July 2011, <http://www.theage.com.au/afl/afl-news>.

Langmaid, A. & Vaughan, R., 'Mick Malthouse hit with $7500 fine for sledging Stephen Milne', *Perth Now*, 11 April 2010, accessed 14 August 2011, <http://www.perthnow.com.au/sport>.

Lash, S. & Featherstone, M., 'Recognition and difference: politics, identity, multiculture', *Theory, Culture & Society*, vol. 18, no. 2–3, 2001, pp. 1–19.

Lawson, J. S. & Evans, A. R., 'Prodigious alcohol consumption by Australian Rugby League footballers', *Drug and Alcohol Review,* vol. 11, no. 2, 1992, pp. 193–195.

Lechte, J., 'Art, love, and melancholy in the work of Julia Kristeva', in J. Fletcher & A. Benjamin (eds.), *Abjection, Melancholia, and Love: The Work of Julia Kristeva*, Routledge, London & New York, 1990, pp. 24–41.

Levy, M., 'Demetriou blasts St Kilda Schoolgirl email forwarders', *The Age*, 4 June 2010, accessed 4 June 2010, <http://www.theage.com.au/afl/afl-news>.

——, 'Details emerge of girl at centre of AFL nude pic scandal', *The Age*, 21 December 2010, accessed 21 December 2010, <http://www.theage.com.au/afl/afl-news>.

——, 'Nude-pic teen in AFL video rant', *The Age*, 22 December 2010, accessed 23 December 2010, <http://www.theage.com.au/afl/afl-news>.

——, 'Teenager has received death threats', *The Age*, 24 December 2010, accessed 24 December 2010, <http://www.theage.com.au/victoria>.

——, 'Teens should watch Cousins doco with parents', *The Age,* 23 August 2010, accessed 23 August 2010, <http://www.theage.com.au/entertainment/tv-and-radio>.

——, 'St Kilda nude-pic teen to demand apology at mediation session', *The Age*, 21 January 2011, accessed 26 March 2011, <http://www.theage.com.au/afl/afl-news>.

——, 'AFL chief knew pregnancy claim was lie', *The Age*, 7 March 2011, accessed 8 March 2011, <http://www.theage.com.au/afl/afl-news>.

——, 'Nixon, teen had sex: report', *The Age*, 5 May 2011, accessed 5 May 2011, <http://www.theage.com.au/victoria>.

Lingis, A., *The Community of Those who have Nothing in Common*, Indiana University Press, Bloomington & Indianapolis, 1994.

Linnell, G., *Football Ltd: The Inside Story of the AFL*, Ironbark, Sydney, 1995.

Livingstone, S., 'Taking risky opportunities in youthful content creation: teenagers' use of social networking sites for intimacy, privacy and self-expression', *New Media & Society,* vol. 10, no. 3, 2008, pp. 393–411.

Lloyd, M., 'Radical democratic activism and the politics of resignification', *Constellations,* vol. 14, no. 1, 2007, pp. 129–146.

Lovell, T., 'Resisting with authority: historical specificity, agency and the performative self', *Theory, Culture & Society,* vol. 20, no. 1, 2003, pp. 1–17.

Lowe, A., 'Court suppresses rape–accused photo', *The Age,* 30 October 2009, accessed 11 December 2013, <http://www.theage.com.au/national/>.

——, 'Lovett charged with second count of rape', *The Age,* 7 May 2010, accessed 7 May 2010, <http://www.theage.com.au/afl/afl-news>.

——, 'Charges dropped in pack rape case', *The Age,* 8 July 2010, accessed 8 July 2010, <http://www.theage.com.au/national>.

——, 'Former St Kilda player Lovett raped woman while she slept, court hears', *The Age,* 11 August 2010, accessed 12 August 2010, <http://www.theage.com.au/victoria>.

——, 'Accuser's "help" pleas', *The Age,* 12 August 2010, accessed 12 August 2010, <http://www.theage.com.au/victoria>.

——, '"How could you bring the club down like this?"', *The Age,* 29 July 2011, accessed 29 July 2011, <http://www.theage.com.au/victoria>.

——, 'Rape trial told Lovett felt entitled', *The Age,* 21 July 2011, accessed 21 July 2011, <http://www.theage.com.au/victoria>.

——, 'Jury finds Lovett not guilty of rape charges', *The Age,* 22 July 2011, accessed 23 July 2011, <http://www.theage.com.au/victoria>.

Lowe, A. & Sexton, R., 'Teen in nude pics scandal maintains rage online', *Sydney Morning Herald,* 24 December 2010, accessed 24 December 2010, <http://www.smh.com.au/afl/afl-news>.

Lunny, A. M. ' Provocation and 'homosexual' advance: masculinized subjects as threat, masculinized subjects under threat', *Social & Legal Studies,* vol. 12, no. 3, 2003, pp. 311–333.

Lutton, P. & Brodie, W., 'Don't prejudge me: Fev protests innocence', *The Age,* 8 September 2010, accessed 8 September 2010, <http://www.theage.com.au/afl/afl-news>.

Lyon, K. & Berry, J., 'Saints close ranks on rape probe', *The Age,* 18 March 2004, accessed 11 December 2013, <http://www.theage.com.au/articles/2004/03/17>.

Madriz, E., 'Images of criminals and victims: a study on women's fear and social control', *Gender & Society,* vol. 11, no. 3, 1997, pp. 342–356.

Magnay, J., 'Ex-Shark denies any role in scandal', *Brisbane Times*, 16 May 2009, accessed 11 December 2013, <http://www.brisbanetimes.com.au/sport/league/>.

Magnus, K. D., 'The unaccountable subject: Judith Butler and the social conditions of intersubjective agency', *Hypatia*, vol. 21, no. 2, 2006, pp. 81–103.

Martin, P. Y. & Hummer, R. A., 'Fraternities and rape on campus', *Gender and Society*, vol. 3, no. 4, 1989, pp. 457–473.

Martindale, K., 'What makes lesbianism thinkable?: theorizing lesbianism from Adrienne Rich to Queer Theory', in N. Mandell (ed), *Feminist Issues: Race, Class and Sexuality*, Prentice Hall, Scarborough, Ontario, 1995, pp. 67–94.

Mawson, L. M., 'Sportswomanship: the cultural acceptance of sport for women versus the accommodation of cultured women in sport', in L. K. Fuller (ed), *Sport, Rhetoric and Gender: Historical Perspectives and Media Representations*, Palgrave Macmillan, New York, 2006, pp. 19–30.

Mayock, P., '"Scripting" risk: young people and the construction of drug journeys', *Drugs: Education, Prevention and Policy*, vol. 12, no. 5, 2005, pp. 349–368.

McDermott, E., Roen, K. & Scourfield, J., 'Avoiding shame: young LGBT people, homophobia and self-destructive behaviours', *Culture, Health & Sexuality*, vol. 10, no. 8, 2008, pp. 815–829.

McDonald, I., 'Situating the sport documentary', *Journal of Sport & Social Issues*, vol. 31, no. 3, 2007, pp. 208–225.

McGee, G., 'Retired Demons star Daniel Bell seeking brain damage compensation', *Herald Sun*, 31 March 2011, accessed 8 April 2011, <http://www.heraldsun.com.au/sport/afl>.

McKeganey, N., Neale, J., Parkin, S. & Mills, C., 'Communities and drugs: beyond the rhetoric of community action', *Probation Journal*, vol. 51, no. 4, 2004, pp. 343–361.

McMillan, S. & Morrison, M., 'Coming of age with the internet: a qualitative exploration of how the internet has become an integral part of young people's lives', *New Media & Society*, vol. 8, no. 1, 2006, pp. 73–95.

McNay, L., 'Self as enterprise: dilemmas of control and resistance in Foucault's *The Birth of Biopolitics*', *Theory, Culture & Society*, vol. 26, no. 6, 2009, pp. 55–77.

Measham, F. & Brain, K., '"Binge" drinking, British alcohol policy and the new culture of intoxication', *Crime, Media, Culture*, vol. 1, no. 3, 2005, pp. 262–283.

Medew, J. & Levy, M., 'Bingle lying, says Brereton', *The Age*, 13 March 2010, accessed 4 August 2011, <http://www.theage.com.au/national>.

Meikle, G., *Future Active: Media Activism and the Internet*, Routledge, London & New York, 2002.

Messerschmidt, J. W., 'Making bodies matter: adolescent masculinities, the body and varieties of violence', *Theoretical Criminology*, vol. 3, no. 2, 1999, pp. 197–220.

——, 'And now, the rest of the story: a commentary on Christine Beasley's "Rethinking hegemonic masculinity in a globalizing world"', *Men and Masculinities*, vol. 11, no. 1, 2008, pp. 104–108.

Messner, M., *Power at Play: Sports and the Problem of Masculinity*, Beacon, Boston, Mass., 1992.

Meyers, M., *News Coverage of Violence Against Women: Engendering Blame*, Sage, Newbury Park, Calif., 1997.

Millar, P., 'Police will not charge Fevola over Brownlow antics', *The Age*, 9 September 2010, accessed 9 September 2010, <http://www.theage.com.au/afl/afl-news>.

Millar, P. & Khokhar, A., 'Nixon takes out court order on teen', *The Age*, 15 April 2011, accessed 15 April 2011, <http://www.theage.com.au/afl/afl-news>.

Millar, P. & Sexton, R., 'Naked Saints go viral', *The Age*, 21 December 2010, accessed 21 December 2010, <http://www.theage.com.au/afl/afl-news>.

Miller, K. E., Melnick, M. J., Farrell, M. P., Sabo, D. F. & Barnes, G. M., 'Jocks, gender, binge drinking, and adolescent violence', *Journal of Interpersonal Violence*, vol. 21, no. 1, 2006, pp. 105–120.

Milner, A., *Cultural Materialism*, Melbourne University Press, Melbourne, 1993.

——, *Class*, Sage, London, 1999.

Mohr, R., *Gay Ideas: Outing and Other Controversies*, Beacon Press, Boston, Mass., 1992.

Munro, P., 'Saints' teen: track star who took a wrong turn', *The Age*, 26 December 2010, accessed 1 January 2011, <http://www.theage.com.au/afl/afl-news>.

——, 'It's payback time, says teen', *Sydney Morning Herald*, 20 February 2011, accessed 20 February 2011, <http://www.smh.com.au/afl/afl-news>.

——, 'Nixon faces sex scandal inquiry', *The Age*, 20 February 2011, accessed 20 February 2011, <http://www.theage.com.au/afl/afl-news>.

——, 'Nixon could end up in Supreme Court', *The Age*, 27 February 2011, accessed 27 February 2011, <http://www.theage.com.au/afl/afl-news>.

Munt, S., 'Framing intelligibility, identity, and selfhood: a reconsideration of spatio–temporal models', *Reconstruction,* vol. 2, no. 3, 2002, accessed 5 January 2003, <www.reconstruction.ws/023/munt.htm>.

——, *Queer Attachments: The Cultural Politics of Shame'*, Ashgate, Aldershot, 2007.

Murphy, K., Boulton, M. & Bartley, P., 'All bets off: clamp on footy odds', *The Age*, 28 May 2011, accessed 28 May 2011, <http://www.theage.com.au/national>.

Nalapat, A. & Parker, A., 'Sport, celebrity and popular culture: Sachin Tendulkar, cricket and Indian nationalisms', *International Review for the Sociology of Sport,* vol. 40, no. 4, 2005, pp. 433–446.

Niall, J., 'Fevola close to joining Brisbane', *The Age,* 7 October 2009, accessed 21 July 2011, <http://www.theage.com.au/articles>.

——, 'Player's worst outcome may be club's best result', *The Age,* 9 September 2010, accessed 9 September 2010, <http://www.theage.com.au/afl/afl-news>.

——, 'The man in the middle', *The Age*, 26 February 2011, accessed 26 February 2011, <http://www.theage.com.au/afl/afl-news>.

——, 'Nixon: the documentary', *The Age*, 20 April 2011, accessed 21 April 2011, <http://www.theage.com.au/afl/afl-news>.

Nylund, D., 'When in Rome: heterosexism, homophobia, and sports talk radio', *Journal of Sport and Social Issues*, vol. 28, no. 2, 2004, pp. 136–168.

O'Regan, T., 'Introducing critical multiculturalism', *Continuum: Journal of Media & Cultural Studies*, vol. 8, no. 2, 1994, pp. 7–19.

Orr, A., 'Ben Cousins in Perth park "fight"', *WA Today*, 5 August 2013, accessed 5 August 2013, <http://www.watoday.com.au/wa-news>.

Oswin, N., 'Critical geographies and the uses of sexuality: deconstructing queer space', *Progress in Human Geography,* vol. 32, no. 1, 2008, pp. 89–103.

Parker, R., 'The carnivalization of the world', in R. N. Lancaster & M. Di Leonardo (eds), *The Gender/Sexuality Reader: Culture, History, Political Economy,* Routledge, New York and London, 1997, pp. 361–377.

Paterson, J. J., 'Disciplining athletes for off-field indiscretions: a comparative review of the Australian Football League and the National Football League's personal conduct policies', *Australian and New Zealand Sports Law Journal*, vol. 4, no. 1, 2009, pp. 105–144.

Patterson, M. M., Bigler, R. S. & Swann Jr., W. B., 'When personal identities confirm versus conflict with group identities: evidence from an intergroup paradigm', *European Journal of Social Psychology,* vol. 40, no. 4, 2010, pp. 652–670.

Peacock, M., 'Ian Thorpe's coming out – why did it take so long and what does it say about us?', *7.30,* Australian Broadcasting Corporation, television broadcast, 14 July 2014.

Petrie, A., 'AFL to quiz Brendan Fevola over Lara Bingle photo', *The Age,* 3 March 2010, accessed 4 August 2011, <http://www.theage.com.au/afl/afl-news>.

Petrie, D., 'A champion of a far more important cause', *The Age,* 25 August 2010, accessed 25 August 2010, <http://www.theage.com.au/afl/afl-news>.

Philadelphoff-Puren, N., 'The right language for rape', *Hecate,* vol. 29, no. 1, 2003, pp. 47–58.

——, 'Dereliction: women, rape and football', *Australian Feminist Law Journal,* vol. 21, no. 2, 2004, pp. 35–51.

Pierik, J., 'End may be nigh for Aka', *The Age,* 30 May 2010, accessed 30 May 2010, <http://www.theage.com.au/afl/afl-news>.

——, 'Partying claims dog Suns' Ablett', *The Age,* 18 April 2011, accessed 18 April 2011, <http://www.theage.com.au/afl/afl-news>.

——, 'Concern at brain damage denials', *The Age,* 3 March 2013, accessed 3 March 2013, <http://www.theage.com.au/afl/afl-news>.

——, 'ASADA report has landed', *The Age,* 2 August 2013, accessed 12 December 2013, <http://www.theage.com.au/afl/afl-news>.

Pierik, J. & Beck, M., 'I hit rock bottom: Fevola bares his soul', *The Age,* 11 March 2011, accessed 11 March 2011, <http://www.theage.com.au/afl/afl-news>.

Pierik, J. & Gannon, G., 'Nude-pic teenager strikes deal with Saints', *The Age,* 22 January 2011, <http://www.theage.com.au/afl/afl-news>.

Pierik, J. & Khokhar, A., 'No appeal, Nixon gets out of football', *The Age,* 8 April 2011, accessed 8 April 2011, <http://www.theage.com.au/afl/afl-news>.

Pierik, J. & Lane, S., 'Players united in pay dispute', *The Age,* 30 June 2011, accessed 30 June 2011, <http://www.theage.com.au/afl/afl-news>.

Pierik, J. & Marcus, C., 'AFL in Bingle blue as Clarke to depart', *The Age,* 14 March 2010, accessed 5 August 2011, <http://www.theage.com.au/national>.

316

Plant, B., 'Welcoming dogs: Levinas and "the animal" question', *Philosophy and Social Criticism,* vol. 27, no. 1, 2011, pp. 49–71.

Plummer, K., *Telling Sexual Stories: Power, Change and Social Worlds*, Routledge, London & New York, 1995.

Porter, L. E. & Alison, L. J., 'Examining group rape: a descriptive analysis of offender and victim behaviour', *European Journal of Criminology*, vol. 3, no. 3, 2006, pp. 357–381.

Postmes, T., Spears, R., Lee, A. T. & Novak, R. J., 'Individuality and social influence in groups: inductive and deductive routes to group identity', *Journal of Personality and Social Psychology,* vol. 89, no. 5, 2005, pp. 747–763.

Preiss, B., '"Joking about lying about lying": teen caught in her own web of deceit', *The Age*, 10 June 2011, accessed 16 August 2011, <http://www.theage.com.au/afl>.

Prestipino, D., 'Saints schoolgirl silenced by Facebook over nude photos', *Perth Now*, 21 December 2010, accessed 21 December 2010, http://www.perthnow.com.au/news>.

Pringle, R., 'Masculinities, sport, and power: a critical comparison of Gramscian and Foucauldian inspired theoretical tools', *Journal of Sport and Social Issues*, vol. 29, no. 3, 2005, pp. 256–278.

Probyn, E., 'Sporting bodies: dynamics of shame and pride', *Body & Society,* vol. 6, no. 1, 2000, pp. 13–28.

——, *Blush: Faces of Shame.* University of Minnesota Press, Minneapolis, 2005.

Pugliese, J., 'The Incommensurability of law to justice: refugees and Australia's Temporary Protection Visa', *Law and Literature*, vol. 16, no. 3, 2004, pp. 285–311.

Quayle, E., 'Milne back in Saints team', *The Age*, 11 July 2013, accessed 12 July 2013, <http://www.theage.com.au/afl/afl-news>.

Quinn, K., 'Cousins documentary silent on the "why" behind his downfall', *The Age*, 26 August 2010, accessed 26 August 2010, <http://www.theage.com.au/opinion/blogs/the-vulture>.

Radhakrishnan, R., *Diasporic Mediations: Between Home and Location*, University of Minnesota Press, Minneapolis, 1996.

Rennie, R. & Lowe, A., 'Didak, Shaw out for season', *The Age*, 5 August 2008, accessed 22 July 2011, <http://www.theage.com.au/national>.

Rickard, L., 'West Coast player fined, suspended for disparaging remarks over Demon player's mother', *The Age*, 16 August 2011, accessed 16 August 2011, <http://www.theage.com.au/afl/afl-news>.

——, 'Boys, 11 and 12, on sex charges', *WA Today*, 24 March 2011, accessed 24 March 2011, <http://www.watoday.com.au/wa-news>.

Robbins, S., 'Will Cousins' final confession lead to redemption?' *The Age*, 5 August 2010, accessed 18 July 2011, <http://www.theage.com.au/sport/blogs/sally-stands-up>.

Robinson, M., ' West Coast Eagles warned of Ben Cousins' ways in 2001', *The Advertiser*, 19 October 2007, accessed 18 July 2011, <http://www.adelaidenow.com.au/sport/afl>.

Robinson, M. & Stevens, M., 'Two alcohol–related incidents in China revealed as causes for Brendan Fevola's sacking', *Herald Sun,* 22 February 2011, accessed 21 July 2011, <http://www.foxsports.com.au/afl>.

Rojek, C., 'Sports celebrity and the civilizing process', *Sport in Society*, vol. 9, no. 4, 2006, pp. 674–690.

Rosello, M., *Declining the Stereotype: Ethnicity and Representation in French Cultures,* University Press of New England, Hanover, NH, 1998.

Saltau, C., 'Inside info: players warned', *The Age,* 16 July 2011, accessed 17 July 2011, <http://www.theage.com.au/afl/afl-news>.

Sanday, P. R., *Fraternity Gang Rape: Sex, Brotherhood, and Privilege on Campus*, second edition, New York University Press, New York & London, 2007.

Schehr, R. C., 'Conventional risk discourse and the proliferation of fear', *Criminal Justice Policy Review,* vol. 16, no. 1 2005, pp. 38–58.

Schembri, J., 'Brutal portrayal of star's addiction', *The Age*, 26 August 2010, accessed 26 August 2010, <http://www.theage.com.au/entertainment/tv-and-radio>.

Schwab, P., 'Personal reflections on Australian Rules football and alcohol consumption', *Stand4 Drug and Alcohol Education Unit*, 2008, accessed 24 July 2011, <http://www.concernaustralia.org.au>.

Sedgwick, E. K., *Between Men: English Literature and Male Homosocial Desire,* Columbia University Press, New York, 1985.

——, *Epistemology of the Closet*, Penguin, London, 1990.

Sharpe, A., 'Inside the life of Lara Bingle', *Perth Now*, 5 March 2010, accessed 4 August 2011, <http://www.perthnow.com.au/entertainment/perth-confidential>.

Shmith, M., 'Come out to play, they say, but how safe is the full light of gay?' *The Age*, 22 May 2010, accessed 22 May 2010, <http://www.theage.com.au/opinion/society-and-culture>.

Silkstone, D., 'Saints ban four for six weeks', *The Age*, 1 February 2011, accessed 1 February 2011, <http://www.theage.com.au/afl/afl-news>.

Simpson, M., *Male Impersonators: Men Performing Masculinity*, Cassell, London, 1994.

——, 'Meet the metrosexual', *Salon,* 22 July 2002, accessed 22 January 2008, <salon.com>.

Singh, S., 'Twitter reveals unsettling truths about "DikiLeaks"', *The Age*, 28 December 2010, accessed 11 January 2011, <http://www.theage.com.au/opinion/society-and-culture>.

Slattery, G., 'Behind *The Challenge*', *Australian Football League*, 2011, accessed 27 March 2011, <http://www/afl.com.au/news>.

Spits, S., 'Nixon demands apology over St Kilda schoolgirl sex claim', *The Age,* 27 May 2010, accessed 29 May 2010, <http://www.theage.com.au/afl/afl-news>.

——, 'Saints take action over explicit photograph', *The Age*, 20 December 2010, accessed 20 December 2010, <http://www.theage.com.au/afl/afl-news>.

Spits, S. & Brodie, W., 'Six AFL players tested positive to illicit drugs in the past year', *The Age*, 22 June 2011, accessed 22 June 2011, <http://www.theage.com.au/afl/afl-news>.

Stafford, A., 'Lions investigates allegations', *The Age*, 6 September 2013, accessed 6 September 2013, <http://www.theage.com.au/afl/afl-news>.

Stark, J., 'Time for a happy ending, say booze experts', *The Age*, 24 July 2011, accessed 24 July 2011, <http://www.theage.com.au/victoria>.

——, 'Dear AFL: can't you save us from all our problems?' *The Age*, 16 September 2012, accessed 16 September 2012, <http://www.theage.com.au/afl/afl-news>.

——, 'Slurs and innuendo fuel culture of homophobia', *The Age*, 16 September 2012, accessed 14 December 2013, <http://www.theage.com.au/afl/afl-news>.

——, 'AFL stars come out against gay slurs', *The Age*, 5 May 2013, accessed 5 May 2013, <http://www.theage.com.au/afl/afl-news>.

——, 'No joy for gay pride as AFL rules out themed match', *The Age*, 19 May 2013, accessed 14 December 2013, <http://www.theage.com.au/afl/afl-news>.

Steele, J., 'Scandals great and small', *Hofstra Law Review,* vol. 36, no. 2, 2007, pp. 497–520.

Stephens, A., 'There's no dragging the heels on this march', *The Age*, 4 February 2013, accessed 4 February 2013, <http://www.theage.com.au/victoria>.

Stewart, B. & Smith, A. C. T., 'Drug use in sport: implications for public policy', *Journal of Sport & Social Issues,* vol. 32, no. 3, 2008, pp. 278–298.

Straw, M., 'Traumatized masculinity and American national identity in Hollywood's Gulf War', *New Cinemas: Journal of Contemporary Film,* vol. 6, no. 2, 2008, pp. 127–143.

Strelan, P. & Boeckmann, R. J., 'Why drug testing in elite sport does not work: perceptual deterrence theory and the role of Personal moral beliefs', *Journal of Applied Social Psychology,* vol. 36, no. 12, 2006, pp. 2909–2934.

Styles, A. & White, S., 'Swans player's life hangs in the balance', *WA Today,* 3 May 2011, accessed 3 May 2011, <http://www.watoday.com.au/wa-news>.

Sydney Morning Herald, 'AFL pair won't face rape charges', *Sydney Morning Herald,* 7 May 2004, accessed 12 August 2011, <http://www.smh.com.au/articles>.

——, 'Fevola sent home from Ireland in disgrace', *Sydney Morning Herald,* 31 October 2006, accessed 24 July 2011, <http://www.smh.com.au/news/afl>.

——, 'Aussie Rules "most injury-prone sport"', *Sydney Morning Herald,* 7 July 2006, accessed 10 July 2011, <http://www.smh.com.au/news/Sport>.

——, 'Saints case may be reopened', *Sydney Morning Herald,* 22 June 2010, accessed 13 August 2011, <http://news.smh.com.au/breaking-news-national>.

——, 'Gay Olympic swimmer angered by Aker', *Sydney Morning Herald,* 20 May 2010, accessed 29 May 2010, <http://www.smh.com.au/afl/afl-news>.

Sygall, D., 'Why Johns may not be off the scene for too long', *Sydney Morning Herald,* 17 May 2009, accessed 17 May 2009, <http://www.smh.com.au/news/lhqnews>.

Symons, C., Sbaraglia, M., Hillier, L. & Mitchell, A., *Come Out to Play: The Sports Experience of Lesbian, Gay, Bisexual and Transgender (LGBT) People in Victoria,* Institute of Sport, Exercise and Active Living (ISEAL) and the School of Sport and Exercise at Victoria University, Melbourne, 2010.

't Hart-Kerkoffs, L. A., Vermeiren, R. R. J. M., Jansen, L. M. C. & Doreleijers, T. A. H., 'Juvenile Group Sex Offenders: A Comparison of Group Leaders and Followers', *Journal of Interpersonal Violence,* vol. 26, no. 1, 2011, pp. 3–20.

Tajfel, H., *Differentiation Between Social Groups: Studies in the Social Psychology of Inter-group Relations,* Academic Press, London, 1978.

Terranova, T., 'Another life: The nature of political economy in Foucault's genealogy of biopolitics', *Theory, Culture & Society,* vol. 26, no. 6, 2009, pp. 234–262.

The Age, 'Group sex incident degrading: minister', *The Age,* 15 May 2009, accessed 17 May 2009, <http://www.theage.com.au/articles>.

——, 'Bingle sues Fevola over nude photo', *The Age,* 2 March 2010, accessed 21 June 2011, <http://www.theage.com.au/breaking-news-national>.

——, 'Police charge Lovett with rape', *The Age,* 15 February 2010, accessed 15 February 2010, <http://www.theage.com.au/afl/afl-news>.

——, '"Don't ask, don't tell" belongs in the past', *The Age,* 26 May 2010, accessed 29 May 2010, <http://www.theage.com.au/opinion/blogs>.

——, 'Teen's family say they received death threats', *The Age,* 11 April 2011, accessed 11 April 2011, <http://www.theage.com.au/victoria>.

——, 'Nixon admits threatening to kill girl', *The Age,* 30 April 2011, accessed 30 April 2011, <http://www.theage.com.au/afl/afl-news>.

——, 'AFL player probed for urinating on bar', *The Age,* 11 April 2011, accessed 11 April 2011, <http://www.theage.com.au/victoria>.

——, 'I assaulted Tegan, admits Nixon', *The Age,* 25 March 2013, accessed 25 March 2013, <http://www.theage.com.au/victoria>.

——, 'Dr. Ziggy Switskowski's full report', *The Age,* 6 May 2013, accessed 7 May 2013, <http://www.theage.com.au/afl/afl-news>.

——, 'Fallen idol', *The Age,* 1 August 2013, accessed 12 December 2013, <http://www.theage.com.au/afl/afl-news>.

The Full Wiki, *List of Australian Rules Football Incidents: Wikis,* accessed 9 December 2013, <http://www.thefullwiki.org/ List_of_Australian_rules_football_incidents>.

——, *List of off-field incidents involving rugby league players: Wikis,* accessed 9 December 2013, <http://www.thefullwiki.org/List_of_off-field_incidents_involving_rugby_league_players>.

Toffoletti, K., 'How is gender-based violence covered in the sporting news? An account of the Australian Rules Football League sex scandal', *Women's Studies International Forum,* vol. 30, no. 5, 2007, pp. 427–438.

Toohey, P., 'Behind the documentary: Ben wanted money and revenge', *Perth Now,* 20 July 2010, accessed 18 July 2011, <http://www.perthnow.com.au/entertainment/perth-confidential>.

Trenwith, C., 'Cousins in hospital with head injury after fall', *WA Today,* 10 January 2013, accessed 11 January 2012, <http://watoday.com.au/wa-news>.

Trosby, E., 'Public relations, football and the management of player transgressions in Australia', *Public Communication Review*, vol. 1, no. 2, 2010, pp. 49–66.

Turner, A., Barlow, J. & Ilbery, B., 'Play hurt, live hurt: living with and managing osteoarthritis from the perspective of ex-professional footballers', *Journal of Health Psychology*, vol. 7, no. 3, 2002, pp. 285–301.

Turner, B. S. & Edmunds, J., 'The distaste of taste: Bourdieu, cultural capital and the Australian postwar elite', *Journal of Consumer Culture*, vol. 2, no. 2, 2002, pp. 219–239.

Turton-Turner, P., 'The role of ridicule in naked charity calendars', *Continuum: Journal of Media & Cultural Studies*, vol. 21, no. 3, 2007, pp. 419–432.

Tyler, I., 'Against abjection', *Feminist Theory*, vol. 10, no. 1, 2009, pp. 77–98.

Ullman, S. E., 'A comparison of gang and individual rape incidents', *Violence and Victims*, vol. 14, no. 2, 1999, pp. 123–133.

Vaid, U., *Virtual Equality: The Mainstreaming of Gay and Lesbian Liberation*, Anchor, New York, 1995.

Vickery, C., 'Fevola's confession draws huge audience to *Footy Show*', *Herald Sun* 11 March 2011, accessed 19 July 2011, <http://www.heraldsun.com.au/entertainment/tv-radio>.

Walton, G., 'H-Cubed: A primer on bullying and sexuality diversity for educators', *Professional Development Perspectives*, vol. 6, no. 2, 2006, pp. 13–20.

Ward, T., 'Marketing sports nationalism 1975–1985', *Soccer & Society*, vol. 10, no. 5, 2009, pp. 662–675.

Warner, M., 'Pleasures and dangers of shame', in D. M. Halperin & C. Traub (eds), *Gay Shame*, The University of Chicago Press, Chicago & London, 2009, pp. 283–296.

Warner, M., 'Brendan Fevola tells *The Footy Show* he gambled nearly $1 million, attempted suicide', *Perth Now*, 11 March 2011, accessed 22 July 2011, <http://www.perthnow.com.au/news>.

Waterhouse-Watson, D., '(Un)reasonable doubt: a "narrative immunity" for footballers against sexual assault allegations', *M/C Journal*, vol. 14, no. 1, 2011, accessed 3 January 2012, <http://journal.media-culture.org.au>.

——, *Athletes, Sexual Assault, and 'Trials by Media'*, Routledge, London & New York, 2013.

Webb, C. & Levy, M., 'Photo-scandal teen tackles Saints at new HQ', *The Age*, 11 January 2011, accessed 26 March 2011, <http://www.theage.com.au/afl/afl-news>.

Wechsler, H. & Davenport, A. E., 'Binge drinking, tobacco, and illicit drug use and involvement in college athletics', *Journal of American College Health,* vol. 45, no. 5, 1997, pp. 195–200.

Whannel, G., 'Television and the transformation of sport', *The Annals of the American Academy of Political and Social Science,* vol. 625, September, 2009, pp. 205–218.

Wheaton, B., '"New lads"?: masculinities and the "new sport" participant', *Men and Masculinities,* vol. 2, no. 4, 2000, pp. 434–456.

Williams, R., *Keywords,* Fontana, Glasgow, 1976.

——, *Marxism and Literature,* Oxford University Press, Oxford, 1977.

——, *Culture,* Fontana, Glasgow, 1981.

Williams, R., 'Nixon walkout over sex and drugs', *The Age,* 1 May 2011, accessed 1 May 2011, <http://www.theage.com.au/victoria>.

Willingham, R., 'Sex, death and binge drinking', *The Age,* 21 November 2008, accessed 22 November 2008, <http://www.theage.com.au/national>.

Wilson, B., 'Footy must stop violence on and off the field', *The Age,* 11 July 2010, accessed 11 July 2010, <http://www.theage.com.au/opinion/society-and-culture>.

Wilson, C., 'Bingle is not fair game, AFL must show better leadership', *The Age,* 14 March 2010, accessed 5 August 2011, <http://www.theage.com.au/afl/afl-news>.

——, 'Girl at centre of St Kilda photo scandal alleges affair with Nixon', *The Age,* 18 February 2011, accessed 19 February 2011, <http://www.theage.com.au/afl/afl-news>.

——, 'Signs of Ricky Nixon's unravelling apparent for years', *The Age,* 20 February 2011, accessed 20 February 2011, <http://www.theage.com.au/afl/afl-news>.

——, 'Nixon should be kicked out, not handballed', *The Age,* 25 February 2011, accessed 25 February 2011, <http://www.theage.com.au/afl/afl-news>.

——, 'Brown out of Nixon stable', *The Age,* 26 February 2011, accessed 26 February 2011, <http://www.theage.com.au/afl/afl-news>.

——, 'Rehab won't save Nixon's business', *The Age,* 9 March 2011, accessed 26 March 2011, <http://www.theage.com.au/afl/afl-news>.

——, 'Brisbane to sack Fevola', *The Age,* 19 February 2011, accessed 19 February 2011, <http://www.theage.com.au/afl/afl-news>.

——, 'Health Shaw suspended for betting on football', *The Age,* 15 July 2011, accessed 15 July 2011, <http://www.theage.com.au/afl/afl-news>.

——, 'I thought it was minor, a little bet: Shaw', *The Age*, 16 July 2011, accessed 16 July 2011, <http://www.theage.com.au/afl/afl-news>.

——, 'AFL is tougher than Rugby League, says Hunt', *Brisbane Times*, 28 May 2011, accessed 28 May 2011, <http://www.brisbanetimes.com.au/afl//afl-news>.

——, 'Milne faces four charges of rape', *The Age*, 18 June 2013, accessed 18 June 2013, <http://www.theage.com.au/afl/afl-news>.

——, 'Saints at odds over Milne', *The Age*, 20 June 2013, accessed 20 June 2013, <http://www.theage.com.au/afl/afl-news>.

——, 'Hird and his club pay highest of prices', *The Age*, 28 August 2013, accessed 28 August 2013, <http://www.theage.com.au/afl/afl-news>.

Wilson, C. & Lane, S., 'Saints players in the clear after schoolgirl sex investigation', *The Age*, 27 May 2010, accessed 27 May 2010, <http://www.theage.com.au/afl/afl-news>.

Zakus, D. H., Skinner, J. & Edwards, A., 'Social capital in Australian sport', *Sport in Society*, vol. 12, no. 7, 2009, pp. 986–998.

Zeeland, S., *The Masculine Marine: Homoeroticism in The U.S. Marine Corps*, Harrington Park Press, New York & London, 1996.

Zylinska, J., 'Guns n' rappers: moral panics and the ethics of cultural studies', *Culture Machine*, vol. 6, 2004, accessed 12 December 2013, <http://www.culturemachine.net/index.php/cm/article/viewArticle/7/6>.

INDEX

INDEX